Then I Am Strong

Moving from
My Mother's Daughter
To God's Child

by
Meg Blaine Corrigan

1/31/11
Judy,
Thank you so much
for all your support
and encouragement
while this book was
being born!
Love & Blessings,
Meg

Cloud 9 Publishing
Minneapolis, Minnesota
www.cloud9publ.wordpress.com

ISBN 10: 1-886352-35-6
ISBN 13: 978-1-886352-35-3

For additional copies of this book, to inquire about quantity
discounts, or for more information about the author, go to
www.megcorrigan.com.

Cover photo and author photo by Debra Fisher Goldstein
Photography, www.goldfishcommunications.com

ACKNOWLEDGMENTS

I would like to extend my thanks to those who made this book a reality:

To my editor and friend, Connie Anderson, whose gifted efforts and relentless patience led me from the status of a novice writer to become a published author.

To my friends and colleagues from the Women of Words writers group, especially, Debra Fisher Goldstein for her amazing photography; Nadia Giordana for her wise council and technical savvy in getting my book into print; and Diane Keyes, and Gloria Van Demmeltraadt for proofreading my book.

To my early mentors, Jim Matison and Dianne Del Giorno, who helped me begin this project with their wise counsel and sage advice.

To the "small army" of people who read my manuscript and pronounced my work fit to print, encouraging me greatly along the way.

To all of the "saints" and "angels unaware" who stood by me while "A New Creature In Christ" was being born, and who taught me more about life and happiness than my own experiences could have rendered.

To my wonderful husband, Patrick, my soul mate, my best friend, for showing me by his example that sobriety is not just the absence of alcohol, but an attitude and a way of life.

To my God who has always been by my side, even when I thought He had gone away for good; for His affirmation of stepparents, one of whom He gave the incredible responsibility of raising His only Son, my Lord and Savior, Jesus Christ.

Dedication

In compassionate memory of my mother, Verel Rollins Blaine,
In memory of my father, Mayhue Delbert Blaine,
my aunt, Ethel "Sally" Blaine Millett,
and my mother-in-law, Ellie Corrigan
and a very special canine companion named Bayfield.

For all the children who have grown up in homes
ravaged by addiction, and for the strength that they
carry into adulthood.

INTRODUCTION

After my father's death, I was sorting through his belongings and came across a photograph that took my breath away. The photo was of my mother, in her turquoise satin pajamas, lying in a heap on the floor. It was obvious that she was drunk. Why did my father take the photo? To try to have her committed to be treated for her alcoholism? To assure himself that he was not the crazy one (a questionable premise, even then)? Certainly not to be cruel or sadistic.

The photograph prompted me to write this memoir. My intention was never to paint my family as being bad or wrong. This story is about one family, profoundly affected by alcoholism, and how that disease found its way into many other aspects of each of our lives. The disease shaped who we were and how we reacted to triumph and tragedy. A family disease, it left each of us changed in some way, and, in turn, influenced others we encountered along the way. But alcoholism did not have the last word in my own life. I discovered One Who could, and did, deliver me from the craziness that had been my childhood.

My parents' troubles and trials, successes and near misses, have clearly all gone into my emotional blender. Once (and only once) when my mother had achieved sobriety for a short period of time, she asked for my forgiveness for the things she had done. I told her that I would not be the person I am today if even one tiny detail of my life had been changed. If God takes our confessed sins and throws them into the deepest part of the ocean, never to be dredged up again, then surely I can forgive my mother for having an illness that has also caused others so much pain.

And so, armed with my father's letters and my mother's remembrances, I embarked on a long and cathartic journey into who we are, this family that was torn apart by the oppression of addiction, but held together by strands of love. I learned a lot during the process, about my parents, about myself, and most of all about my God.

This story cannot be told without acknowledging the profound grace and relentless love of our Lord and Savior Jesus Christ. I believe that, without Him, there can be no lasting peace, no perfect mercy, no true healing, no hope in the face of tragedy. God pursued me relentlessly, even when I tried my best to shut him out of my life.

It is my profound hope that my readers will find help and healing, humor and compassion in my story, and that my words will in some way assist others in their journey through life's beautiful, profound and intricate labyrinth.

So I will boast all the more gladly of my weaknesses, so that the power of Christ may dwell in me. Therefore, I am content with weaknesses, insults, hardships, persecution, and calamities for the sake of Christ; for whenever I am weak, then I am strong.

2 Corinthians 12:9 & 10

Over and over again in a hundred different ways, I learn in Alanon that I must let go. It will do nothing constructive for me if I retaliate for injuries I suffer because of the alcoholic. I am not empowered by God to even up scores and make others 'pay for what they did to me.' I will learn to relax my stubborn grip on all the details of my sufferings, and allow the solutions to unfold by themselves.

May 11th
One Day at a Time in Alanon

Verel and Ruth Rollins, 1913

Prologue
The Child That No One Wanted

No one can make you feel inferior without your permission.
Eleanor Roosevelt

The afternoon train wheeled slowly to a stop at the Kirksville depot. It was a comfortable means of transportation for Aunt Annie in 1927, especially since her husband had worked on the railroad and she got her passage for free. He was killed shortly after they were married, while uncoupling two freight cars, and the railroad company widow's pension left Annie well cared-for. She never remarried and had no children, but she loved to visit her relatives.

Verel always described Annie was an austere woman, with a large and disproportionate face nestled in a scratch of gray-brown hair that refused to follow instructions. Annie was what Annie wanted to be: overbearing, insolent, rude and quick to wear out her welcome anywhere she went. She was the oldest of the Day girls, and she wielded her position of superiority in a self-assured and intolerant manner.

Verel accompanied her mother Birdie May and her brother Aubrey to collect Annie from the train station. Annie rarely if ever announced her coming and she stayed as long as she felt like with no explanation, regardless of how much work Birdie May and her daughters had with the rooming house. But this time Annie had written beforehand. Birdie knew she had best drop what she was doing and meet her sister, or there would be hell to pay.

"Hello, Birdie!" Annie greeted her sister in her crackling voice, as she stepped from the train car. "Nice to see you! And Aubrey, you're looking mighty fine." She approached Verel and took her chin in her hand. "And here's Verel, the child that no one wanted!"

This was her standard greeting every time she saw Verel (even if she'd only seen her five minutes before in another room), and it seemed Verel lived in the shadow of Aunt Annie's prophesy all of her life. It seems all adults have it within their power to invoke either blessings or curses on children. Aunt Annie always chose the curse.

Verel's family was of English descent, aristocracy she believed. Birdie May and Walter Rollins had a scant eighth grade education. No one in the family was never too sure what Walter did for a living He would disappear for weeks on end and return with some half-baked scheme or another that he always thought would make him rich. He may have suffered from some type of mental illness, perhaps bipolar disorder or schizophrenia. His behavior, as Verel later described it, was erratic and impulsive, but he showed no remorse for the chaos and sorrow he brought into his wife's already meager existence. Verel's brothers had tried everything to help their mother extricate herself from her husband's mysterious hold, but Birdie remained loyal to Walter right up until her death.

Birdie must have been a strong woman, both physically and emotionally. She bore six sons and two daughters, Verel being the youngest. By the time Verel came along, Walter had been in and out of debt so many times, the whole family had given up on him. Verel remembered her oldest brother Stanley, twenty-five years her senior, not speaking a single word to her until she was well into her twenties. He was married and had a daughter of his own when Verel made her first appearance, making Verel an aunt before she was born. Though she and her niece, Dorothy, became closer than sisters, Stanley viewed his baby sister as his parents' last little indiscretion. He thought it was such a disgrace that she was ever conceived. He said his father had no right coming back home and impregnating his mother after so many years of strife. He visibly displayed disgust whenever Verel was in his presence, treatment which most likely did untold damage to her emotional development. Stanley also chose curses over blessings where Verel was concerned. The sins of the fathers were to be visited upon Verel's, though she obviously was not to blame for her own conception and birth.

She heard it said, over and over during her childhood: *Poor Verel, the child that no one wanted.*

But her mother had wanted her, and loved her, and believed in her. And so did her older sister, Ruth.

Part I

Me and My Horse, Lito, about 1960

Chapter 1
The Importance of Riding

Each day of our lives we make deposits in the memory banks of our children.

Charles R. Swindoll
The Strong Family

In 1960, my family lived in Colorado Springs, Colorado where my father, an Air Force Colonel and pilot, was stationed. I was thirteen years old then, and I didn't know anybody who had died. My mother never allowed me to go to funerals, and she avoided them herself at all costs. In our home nothing led me to believe death was even a reality. Of course, I knew that everyone has to die sometime, and that was certainly okay for other people to think about. Dying simply was not a family value that we embraced. Why go to someone's funeral when you know they certainly aren't coming to yours?

Also, I could not accept the possibility that due to death or separation I might one day get out from under my insane family and our problems. A life apart from the one I had always known seemed impossibly remote. That is, until the day I found my mother lying there motionless on the floor.

At thirteen, I was in love with myself and my horse, in that order. The phone was ringing as I came into the house after school. It was the same routine every afternoon.

"Hi, Meg! Do you want to meet me at Romano's in a half hour?" asked my friend Dara, wanting me to go riding with her.

Tony and Helen Romano had boarded my horse Lito since my father bought her for me three years before. I had named her *Celito Lindo*, which meant "beautiful heaven" in Spanish, but from the beginning, I called her "Lito." The Romano's farm was within walking distance of our home, so I could get there under my own steam. *Good thing,* I thought to myself. *Mother's passed out drunk again.*

I could tell when Mother had been drinking by the smell of the house, like something ancient and sinister was lurking there. My father was not home from the air base yet, and the house always seemed so dank and musty when there was liquor about. I knew the drill by heart. I would change clothes and let our dachshund puppy, Nicky, out. I'd grab a portable snack and look in Mother's bedroom to observe her sleeping there, passed out in a stupor, breathing heavily. I opened the bedroom door slowly and my trained eye fell upon the bed.

She wasn't there.

My heart pounded in my chest as I crept slowly into the room. I always felt like the boogey man would jump right out at me when I entered her bedroom while she was sleeping off a drunk. Or maybe I was afraid she would wake up and start screaming at me again. I would have preferred the boogey man. But I could not detect any movement at all in her room. I tiptoed to the open bathroom door. Nothing. I stepped across the carpet and peered over the bed.

There she was, lying in a heap, her head almost tucked into her belly. She was wearing her turquoise silk pajamas. It always amazed me that she could be too drunk to stand up, but she invariably changed into those stupid pajamas before she climbed into bed to sleep it off. Long before a bunch of older women got together and started wearing red hats and purple dresses, my mother had founded The Turquoise Pajama Society, with a membership of one.

It was then that I saw the blood, not much blood, but enough that I knew she had hit her head. It was trickling down her forehead in a little crimson rivulet, onto the off-white carpeting. She must have missed the bed and caught her forehead on the edge of the nightstand when she fell. *Was she breathing?* I stood, suspended in motion, staring at her. Rage and resentment crawled up my throat, threatening to choke off my wind. At that moment, I hated my mother and everything she stood for. I hated my life in my stupid, sick family, and I hated everything about the beautiful house my father had built. *It's not fair!* I choked back the tears. *Why my mother, why my family? Why me?*

And then I turned and ran out the bedroom door, out of the house, and straight to the stable where my horse was boarded.

My tears started, but I fought them back. At that time in my life, I didn't care if my mother lived or died. I truly believed we'd all be better off if she were dead. And nothing, not even the thought of her lying on that bedroom floor bleeding, was going to prevent me from taking my afternoon's ride. When we moved to Colorado, I had wailed and cried for weeks, begging for a horse of my own. Finally, my father purchased a beautiful bay mare, and I was hooked for life.

In those days, nothing was more pleasurable to me than feeling the rise and fall of Lito's smooth withers as I gripped her bare back with my legs. I never ceased to marvel at being able to direct an animal ten times my weight with just a few pieces of leather and a metal bit. To be one with this wonderful, caramel-colored steed meant I felt free of all my troubles. To feel and smell the cool, crisp Colorado mountain air as we wound through the trails up to the old Corley Road was the most tantalizing sensation I could ever imagine. The sky up there hangs the color of a cobalt blue glass bottle shimmering in the sun.

To me, riding was life itself. Me, my beloved mare, and the mountains, one and the same. Bonded forever, protected by the whisper of the wind through the ponderosas.

Riding was also my only way to feel independent from my demented home life, free from my parents and all their hassles. Right or wrong, I could make my own decisions, like riding in a thunderstorm with lightning crackling close enough to make my hair stand on end. I could set up jump courses high on a mountain prairie and sail my horse over the log piles past jagged granite slabs and swaying scrub oak that snapped to attention as we raced passed.

I could spur my horse close enough to the edge of a newfound mountain reservoir, close enough to see our reflection in the water. Then, WHOOSH! Off the ledge we jumped into the water, with Lito paddling as though she'd done it every day of her life. She swam all the way across that reservoir before she climbed out of the water at a sandy stretch of shoreline. From the trail above us, my friend laughed out of either joy or hysteria

It never occurred to me or to my riding friends how much danger we placed ourselves in day after day. To me, the adrenalin rush of horseback riding was far more enticing than what I had to face at home, with every conversation ending in a screaming match, and every day a new and different round of denial, frustration, and shame.

I didn't regret leaving the house every afternoon for the horse barn. It was what I needed to do to stay sane.

But as I wound my way back down the mountain and headed for home, the thought occurred to me:

What if Mother was dead?

Chapter 2
An Accidental War

An "accidental war," or "accidental attack" is described by the Armed Forces as "an unintended attack which occurs, without deliberate design, as a direct result of a random event such as a simple human error, or an unauthorized action by a subordinate."

Online Dictionary of Military Terms

I had not left my mother dead on the floor that awful day. When I came home from riding my horse, I entered the house slowly, by now feeling more than slightly guilty for leaving her the way I did. Seeing my father's car, I quietly let myself in the door and paused to listen to the "house noises." For the second time that afternoon, I tiptoed to the open door of my parents' room, and heard my father's voice. He was on his hands and knees, cleaning up the carpet.

He had found Mother there on the floor and moved her to the bed. She was lying in a lump with her face away from him, and I could see that he had cleaned the blood off her forehead and put a bandage there. He was talking softly to her, like she was a cancer patient. She was moaning something unintelligible as if she was participating in the conversation. It sickened me.

Going to my room, I changed out of my riding clothes. I sat downstairs in the family room until my father came in and told me Mother had fallen, but she was all right. I didn't volunteer that I had already seen her on the floor. I despised her and, at that moment, I hated my father too, because he insisted on playing this ridiculous game with her all the time.

Our family was engaged in a sick dance, where we all knew our parts by heart and each of us depended on the others to perform their part of the routine. But sometimes dancers just came up missing for a while—for a long while. We were still expected to keep dancing and just pretend that no one was missing. Step together, step together, turn, slide. I felt out of step and awkward when my mother was not in the dance. When she was, I resented how she was allowed to come back with no explanation or apology.

Slowly, insidiously, the "demon alcohol" infiltrated the very fabric of our beings until we were all working as a unit toward a common goal: Preserving the "look" of a happy, normal family at all costs. This team work was especially crucial when the head of that family was a high-ranking military officer.

My sister Barbara and I had no role models at home. We became our own role models. Because Mother acted like a child, we couldn't also be children, so we had to pretend to be adults. We weren't very good at it, so the circle went round and round. Failure was unavoidable. Feeling bad about ourselves was inevitable.

It's a terrible thing to compete for your mother's attention with a bottle of whiskey. I don't ever remember her being reliable. But I do remember my dad being there for me, in his own way, at least when I was small. My early memory is that he was kind and gentle towards my sister and me. I felt that I could count on him even when I was a teenager, but I could not count on my mother. In time, I just gave up playing the game of pretending she hadn't checked out of our lives (and her own reality) for weeks on end. She spent days—sometimes weeks—in bed, eventually even developing a bald spot on the back of her head.

Many years later, in my work with domestic violence, I heard a story about a frog in a pot of water. If the pot is placed on the stove and the temperature turned up gradually, the frog will adapt his body temperature to the water, because it is his nature to do so. Eventually, the frog will, quite literally, be boiled alive. Families in extreme dysfunction operate in just this way: the various members adapt to the daily changes that occur, and eventually, when things get really bad, they don't realize how far they've fallen. They would stare in disbelief if they could see what things were like in the beginning, compared to what they'd become.

I think what was most frustrating for my father, and perhaps what eventually drove him to his own level of insanity, was that he couldn't make Mother *do* anything. The military had prepared my father for every eventuality. My father learned to follow procedures, to pay strict attention to protocol. But there was no procedure or protocol for dealing with Mother's alcoholism. And no help of any sort was available from the military. In fact, at that time, the Air Force had strict rules about *not* dealing with "mental problems," which included all addictions. Military personnel facing mental health issues were simply asked to leave the service. For affected dependents, the family was told to seek help elsewhere.

I always speculated that there was more going on with my mother than just alcoholism. When I was younger, I didn't know much about alcoholism, and even less about mental illness. But it haunted me that she was so cruel, not only when she was drinking, but even when she managed to get sober for a while. When she was sober, she didn't hit or terrorize us or even really reject us. She simply didn't interact with us, not the way a normal mother would.

Her attitude of self-importance was all encompassing. I don't ever remember her displaying genuine interest in the things going on in my life. It seemed she always brought the conversation back to herself, if not by changing the subject altogether, then by reminding me that I failed her in some way. Once she demanded that I take a handkerchief or some tissues to school because I had a runny nose. While running on the playground that day, I fell into the path of a boy riding a bicycle. The boy literally drove his bicycle over the end of my nose, bruising it badly. When I came home, Mother screamed at me for five minutes because she thought my nose was red from not blowing it. I don't recall if she ever even listened to what really happened. It didn't matter anyway. The damage was done, not only to my nose.

Mother craved compliments but never gave them. It was as though her bucket had a hole in it and we all tried in vain to fill it for her, an impossible task because the hole was never plugged. When she got fed up with all of us not being able to fill that bucket to her satisfaction, she filled it with booze.

****

Growing up military had its benefits and its drawbacks. Because we moved about every three years, we had no normal childhood, no lifelong friends, no extended family. Other kids played with the same neighbor children throughout their childhood. We started over—new school, new neighborhood, new friends—each time we were transferred. Later, I resented the fact that we hadn't gotten to know my father's relatives in northeast Missouri, most of whom were kind and interesting and fun. We attended his family reunions once every three to five years, if we happened to be moving or we had an excuse to drive back to my father's birthplace in Bible Grove, Missouri. But we seldom visited Mother's family; they simply were not as connected as my dad's.

Psychologist and author Susan Forward said, "If Richard Nixon's Whitehouse staff had taken cover-up lessons from anyone in an alcoholic's family, Watergate would still be just a Washington hotel." That description fit our family perfectly. It wasn't enough that Mother never accepted her alcoholism because she believed she wasn't "one of those skid row drunks." We were so mortified to tell anyone about our situation that the "family secret" was treated like classified material. We gave security clearance to no one.

This huge, hidden "family secret" made it tough to make friends to begin with, and the frequent moves made things even more difficult. I was unbelievably naive growing up. I had never been to a funeral, an anniversary celebration, or even a wedding, except my sister Barbara's when I was fifteen. And hers didn't count because she walked me through every single tiny step since I was her only bridesmaid. How *she* learned about weddings, I had no clue. It never occurred to me that *all* weddings were similar in many ways. In college I was asked to be in a friend's wedding and didn't have any idea what that involved. I was so dumb I didn't even know that the rehearsal was held the night before the wedding. If the bride hadn't by chance called the day of the rehearsal to give me some small detail I would have missed the whole thing.

****

My father used military terms and concepts all the time, in a very formal and regimented way. We had "basic training for service brats" at a very early age. Barbara and I were told to answer the phone with, "Colonel Blaine's residence, Margaret/Barbara speaking." We addressed all female adults as Miss or Mrs. (there was no designation of "Ms." back then), civilian men by Mr., and military friends were addressed by their rank. Daddy was and always would be "Daddy"— even when my sister and I were grown and he was aging. And always, always, we addressed my mother as "Mother," not "Mom" or "Mama" or certainly not "Ma." Those endearments were for lower class families, not ours. She reminded us constantly that she was, after all, "a gracious lady," and even her children were expected to address her in a formal manner.

Besides all the military terminology we had to learn, our mother also expected us to learn all about etiquette and manners as if our very lives depended on it. In a way, they did, because she would go absolutely ballistic if we forgot some simple rule or acted in a way she decided was rude or uncouth.

When we stayed home sick from school, Daddy would say we were "goldbricking," the military word for loafing. We knew he was teasing, but of course, he never told Mother she was "goldbricking" when she was sleeping off the booze. Needless to say, Mother wasn't there when we were ill to feed us chicken soup or take our temperature. But when Mother was "sick," and Daddy was left alone to care for us, he would dash around the house with mops and brooms and dust rags, giving orders for us to "police up" the place.

When Daddy wanted to defer to Mother to make a decision, he would say, "You'll have to ask the War Department," until that joke ceased to be funny. By that time, Barbara and I had developed our own "field guide," a language we didn't share with our parents. Our house was a battle zone, and their fights were hand-to-hand combat. Frequently, my sister or I would scream at our parents to get them to stop arguing. In a few cases, one of us actually climbed on Daddy's back so he would be forced to let go of Mother. Sometimes we used diversion tactics, like distracting one of them to defuse the fight. They didn't always work because our parents were usually both on automatic pilot by the time we got involved. The fights usually ended with Mother retreating to the bedroom, many times crawling on all fours. Daddy slept in the guest room or on the couch.

My sister and I really wouldn't have had to try to break up their fights. But it was hard to stand by and watch without wanting to take some action. We were more like embedded reporters in a perpetual family war.

We learned to scrutinize our "distant early warning system," signs that meant trouble was on the horizon. Like that day I had found my mother on the floor, we would have noticed the signs: the car crooked in the garage, or her bedroom door would be closed in the middle of the day. Or perhaps she'd be on the phone chewing someone out when we got home from school. Or worse, she would be one the floor, passed out and bleeding.

The bathroom was a "demilitarized zone," where I'd go to get away from Mother, to stay beneath her radar. Sometimes I was so angry, I'd chew on towels—big, thirsty Fieldcrest towels—until I pushed my anger down inside me and I could control my outward self. Meanwhile the rage was boiling inside of me and doing serious bodily harm to my insides. One day Mother followed me in there. For some reason, she was angry about my glasses and she tried to grab them off my face. She'd never done anything like that before. I raised a hand to protect myself. Then, this little woman who could hardly stand up on her own because she was so drunk, hauled off and knocked me into the bathtub. Time was suspended for a few seconds as we stared at each other. I don't know which of us was more surprised. She stormed up the stairs, while I lay in the tub awhile, not believing what had just happened. Then I got up, locked the door and chewed on more towels. That was the only time she ever actually hit me, but now the threat was always there.

More than once, huge fights erupted over how much alcohol my mother had consumed. Whenever I went to see a movie, I used to imagine how the reporters in those old newsreels would have portrayed our family fights:

We are reporting from a war-torn region known as the Living Room, where the fighting has intensified in the last few hours. The political issue at hand appears to be a deep-seated and long-running disagreement over a Smirnoff bottle that is divided at the Vodka Parallel into two regions known as Above and Below. Fighting erupted quickly between the Father Field Forces and the Mobile Mother Militia over the unauthorized relocation of the Rubber Band, which is believed to have been placed in a strategic location by the Father Faction to indicate an acceptable level of consumption of the contents therein. Sources here say that the Father was on a routine reconnaissance mission undertaken to obtain, by visual observation or other detection methods, information about the activities of the Mother, to secure data concerning the geographic characteristics of said Rubber Band upon the surface of the Smirnoff Vodka Bottle. Visual observation led the Father to the realization that the Rubber Band had presumably been moved by the Mother, casting doubt as to whether or not the Mother had consumed more than the amount of the Smirnoff Vodka agreed upon, thereby violating the terms of the last of several Sober Treaties. The Father, clearly the more rational and conservative of the two factions, is demanding reforms. The question then becomes, "Was this simply human error or is it truly the unauthorized action of a subordinate?" The Mother, on the other hand, is quite obviously attempting to launch an organized movement aimed at the overthrow of the household through the use of subversion and possibly armed conflict.

****

As kids, we learned our survival tactics very well. Since I was younger, with nearly seven years between my sister and me, Barbara did a great deal of "search and rescue," trying to shield me from the craziness in our home. But try as we might, neither my sister nor I was ever able to crack the security code and understand why our father was so devoted to our mother. He kept plugging away at that marriage other men would have left long ago. As the years went by, he became more and more entrenched in Mother's web of deceit, denial, and derangement, and it was very painful to watch.

My father's military career took him many places and we had a wide variety of experiences. But the only combat my father ever saw was a mutiny of undefeatable proportions within the heavily fortified compound of his own home.

Chapter 3
The Charade

*The charade of the normal family' is especially damaging to a
child because it forces him to deny the validity of his own feelings
and perceptions. It is almost impossible for a child to develop a
strong sense of self-confidence if he must constantly lie about
what he is thinking and feeling. His guilt makes him wonder
whether people believe him.*

Toxic Parents
Susan Forward

"Happy birthday, Daddy!"

My sister Barbara was home from college, and there was a big
celebration going on in our house. My father had turned fifty that
June. Most of his twelve brothers and sisters had been born in June,
so it was a family joke that we all knew what my farming
grandparents were doing after harvest. My mother had invited over
an assemblage of new and old friends to celebrate the event, an act
that had made all of us a little nervous. Mother was, once again, "up,"
meaning she was temporarily semi-sober and back to the business of
being an officer's wife, with an opportunity to entertain. She was all
dressed up and prepared to be what she called a "gracious lady" once
again. Though none of us raised the question out loud, there was a
constant concern that Mother wouldn't be able to hold it together
until the guests had all gone home.

We all knew this party wasn't for Daddy's benefit. Mother staged
the party so she would have a house full of admirers. My sister and I
learned very early on that our family had two rules:

Rule #1: It's all about Mother.

Rule #2: If, for even a nanosecond, you mistakenly think that it
might be about anyone else, see Rule # 1.

A red-faced Air Force pal of my father's made a toast: "Here's to
ol' Mayhue, may he live well and prosper!"

The rest of the guests clinked glasses. "Here, here!"

"Happy birthday, Daddy," I chirped. "Happy half a century!"

Before I knew what hit me, my college-aged sister snatched me off the couch and marched thirteen year old me into our parents' bedroom. Even though I wasn't sure exactly what I had done wrong, I knew I was in trouble with her. She was my "substitute parent," and though she lacked the maturity or the knowledge to truly act like a parent, I was powerless to stand up to her. Years later, I read psychologist Susan Forward's wise words, "When a child is forced to adopt the role of parent, he loses his role models, threatening his developing identity." But at the time, I had no more idea of how to act than my sister did. Like the saying goes, negative attention was better than no attention at all. Bad or good, I was just glad somebody was trying to parent me!

"Don't you ever talk disrespectfully to our father like that again!" she shouted into my face.

"I'm sorry, Barbara, I didn't mean to be disrespectful!" I was crying and feeling about a foot high. "I was just joking, like all of Daddy's friends!"

"Well, don't ever let me hear you say that to our father again, do you hear me?" Her eyes were blazing, and I knew she meant what she said. I never knew quite how to take my sister. I knew she was just as disgusted as I was with our home life, and I knew she did not condone the antics of either of our parents when things got rough. But sometimes it felt like she was judging me–blaming me–for the things that went on under our roof. I loved her desperately, and I tried to take my cues from her about how I should act, think, and feel about our parents, and about life itself. But sometimes, more often than not, her signals weren't very clear. Once I called my mother a bitch behind her back, and Barbara was airborne before the word was out of my mouth. It wasn't until years later that I realized all of my sister's posturing was an attempt on her part to act grown-up. The terrified child inside of her was just trying to control whatever part of the situation she could, by whatever means she was able to employ.

After Barbara's little parenting lesson, we returned to the party, which by this time was getting pretty rowdy. As usual, my parents' friends were well into the liquor cabinet by mid-evening. It always seemed as if the earth slipped a little on its axis when the Blaines had a party. I remember most keenly the smells of party time at our house. The acrid odor of cigarettes, which back then everyone including me thought was sexy. The sickly sweet smell of whiskey and soda, especially after it had been recycled over someone's tongue and breathed back in my face. Everyone was always hugging and kissing me at these parties. I remember one man in particular who doted over me the entire time he was at our house. I don't know why I caught his fancy, but I knew my parents would consider it impolite for me to pull away from him. His breath smelled sour and his eyes were all watery and dull from the liquor. No wonder I developed a disgust for inebriated people that has lasted my whole life.

Usually, I would be in bed long before the guests left. That's when the fighting would start again, or at least I always hoped that it wasn't the fighting that caused the people to go home. It always amazed me how we existed with that unseen, unspoken thing living right there among us all the time, that awkward presence towering over everything in the household, but nobody dared mention it. Our family went on for decades without acknowledging the "silent intruder" called alcoholism. Today, in chemical dependency circles, they call it the "elephant in the living room." Thinking back to when I was a teenager, it's pretty clear to me that our living room had a whole *herd* of elephants being chased by a tribe of natives with high ball glasses in their hands.

In any case, the elephant remained with us for years to come. She was a member of our family as surely as any of the rest of us, although not flesh and blood like we were. Her presence could be felt almost all the time. No one said anything, but we all knew the elephant was there among us.

Chapter 4
The Gracious Lady

We were inclined to say, 'Look me over, boys. Pretty good, huh?' We had no humility, no sense of having received anything through the grace of our Heavenly Father.
Dr. Bob, Co-Founder
Alcoholics Anonymous

We never knew when my mother would come completely apart in public. It happened unexpectedly, except that we were always expecting it, most often directed at some innocent bystander, like a grocery store checkout person. My mother could go from calm, cool and collected, to a screaming maniac in about fifteen seconds, sharing her opinion about anything and everything with the hapless clerk, all while we were just supposed to be deciding if we wanted paper or plastic.

Once while my sister Barbara was learning to drive, a military police officer pulled her over at Fort Carson Army Base. Barbara had committed some small infraction, like failing to signal a turn. By the time Mother was done giving the officer a piece of her mind, we were all in the Provost Marshall's office. My father was summoned to come collect the entire lot of us. My sister was mortified. I was surprised she ever drove a car again.

When I was barely into my teens, my sister Barbara went off to the University of Colorado to study nursing. On the day we took her to the dormitory in Boulder, our mother was sober for once, or at least holding her own in the "appropriate mother behavior" category. It seemed like hundreds of other girls were moving into that dorm at the same time my sister was, and I don't know why she was so nervous. Barbara realized all at once, before the rest of us became conscious of the impending crisis, that some of the boxes with her stuff in them didn't have tops. She had a meltdown. She was not going to move into that dorm until we found some tops for those boxes—everybody else's boxes had tops—and she didn't want anybody seeing into her stuff. It took some ingenuity on my father's part to figure out how to cover up the contents of those boxes posthaste so we could get my sister deposited into her dorm room.

All I really cared about was getting my parents back home where I would now be an only child, at least until my sister came home for the weekend.

Barbara actually did pretty well at school. By the time she came home for a weekend visit, she was a full-fledged college coed, with a new sophistication about her. Being away from our parents for the first time was a very positive experience for her. Things for me didn't change much after she left, except that I missed her terribly. I ground along in my mundane life just like always.

****

I was not popular with the boys or the girls in school. In spite of the fact that my mother thought our family clearly headed up "the beautiful people of Colorado Springs," as well as the rest of the galaxy, I found myself sadly lacking in "cool" friends. I was impossibly skinny, and my honey blonde hair was straight as a string and baby fine like my mother's. To top it off, I had awful acne, which I began disguising with tons of make up when I was in my early teens. Colorado Springs was so permeated with military families that, even in school, there was a hierarchy of military rank. The generals' sons and daughters had a special status, while colonels' kids like me were a dime a dozen. It was plain to me that I was never going to run with the generals' kids.

In order to create what I thought was a normal teenage social life, I tried to hold parties at our home. I was happy with our house after so many years of moving around with the Air Force. Daddy had done so much of the work himself that it truly seemed to be the first house that had ever been "ours." And I had helped him too, with little things. Even as a child, I had a sense of color and design, just like Daddy. He always listened when I had an idea about this or that for the new house. He even built me a white board fence all around the backyard that was "dog proof and horse high," as he put it.

The fall of my sophomore year in high school, I was planning a party again. I had invited everyone who was anyone at Cheyenne Mountain High School. I knew they wouldn't all come, but some of them surely would. I loved to plan the decorations and the food, and I prided myself on my record collection. And the kids who had come before were never rowdy or out of line. Just good teenagers having fun. The party was just two days off, and I was in high spirits. But in the back of my mind, I knew plans of this sort were always a crapshoot because of my mother.

My father appeared in the door of the basement recreation room, where I was hanging crepe paper streamers.

"Margaret," he said quietly. He never called me by my nickname, Meg. I had chosen the name myself, in a childish game of "Little Women." My friends and I all picked which of the book's characters we wanted to be, but a teacher told me that "Meg" really was a nickname for Margaret, and it just stuck. My parents and my sister always called me by my legal name, which I hated. And when it was really serious, my father called me "Margaret Ruth." But it would have been disrespectful to challenge my parents on it. One thing "service brats" learned was respect for their elders, whether they deserved it or not.

"Hi, Daddy. What's up?"

He perched on one of the stools he had built to match the wet bar, a charming addition to an already "wet" home.

"Honey, I'm going to have to ask you to call your party off. Mother's really bad, you see, and we can't… "

"NO!" I spat the word at him. "I'm not calling off another party! Every time I plan anything, you just let her ruin it! It's not fair!"

"I know, I know," he said evenly. "You know I'd love to let you have your friends over, Honey, but we just can't risk having your mother make a scene."

I knew it was no use to argue with him, and I knew he was right. I threw the roll of crepe paper across the room, stormed off to my bedroom and slammed the door. I sat in the dark, alone, crying and wishing I had been born into any other family than this one. I envied the other kids I knew, the ones whose parents seemed so different. Other parents *cared* about their kids' social life. Once, by some streak of luck, I ended up going to a movie with several young people, including a general's daughter. After the movie, we decided to go for hamburgers. I was absolutely astounded when she had to find a phone and call her parents to ask permission to go someplace other than the movie theater. I envied her, having parents who actually gave her these boundaries. I had no boundaries, really, but I knew if I did something bad and my dad found out, I would suffer some very serious consequences. That was *very* different from *wanting* to do good things because I respected my parents.

When my father told me to cancel the party, I had to get on the telephone and start calling people. I made up every excuse I could think of, hoping that the kids wouldn't compare notes the next day. I told some of them my mom was very sick (which was true), and I told others that I was grounded for partying until the wee hours of the morning without my parents' permission (which was wishful thinking).

I finished the last of the phone calls and got into my pajamas and crawled into bed. I was too tired to cry any more, and my body ached for sleep. I missed my sister. She was the only one in my entire life who really understood how I felt. About the time I dozed off, I heard a loud crash above me. Throwing off the covers I ran upstairs, stopping in my tracks at the top of the stairwell. Mother was awake, and she had come up swinging.

Whenever Mother came out of one of her drunken stupors, our lives suddenly became like a hurricane or a tornado warning that had turned to an actual sighting. When Mother would go to bed for days on end, it was like a demonic storm brewing and stewing off the coast of our lives, and none of us knew exactly what course that storm was going to take. There was always a sense that we needed to board up our emotions, if not evacuate altogether. When she rose up out of that bed, it was like all the evil spirits of Hell had been loosed.

My dad, my sister and I must have looked like those weather reporters with our hair standing sideways as Mother whirled around the house flinging accusations at my father and shrieking at all of us for no apparent reason. *That's right, Barbara!* I could hear myself saying, *Hurricane Verel is expected to make landfall sometime within the next few hours! As you can see, the winds are already pretty fierce. The path of this storm is expected to track right up the hallway from the bedrooms and into the living room, but we won't really know for sure until it happens. Back to you in the news room, Barbara!*

My sister always said Mother's mind was like a file drawer because she seemed to have an endless capacity to pull the drawer open and withdraw a little mental card with some past infraction printed clearly on it, which she would use to chastise one of us at the top of her voice. This particular night, her satin pajamas were making their own fashion statement all twisted around her body, with one pant leg hiked up to her knee in clear defiance of the polished look she always sought. She had just attempted to walk down the hall from the bedroom to the kitchen, but had knocked most of her collection of bone china demitasse teacups off their glass shelves as she stumbled along. *How fitting,* I thought. *She always cuts a wide swath when she's drinking—with objects and emotions.*

Mother staggered into the living room and attempted to execute a three-point landing into the barrel-back chair by the fireplace. She missed the chair altogether and arranged herself on the floor, trying vainly to act like that's where she intended to sit all the time. "I am a *gray-shush lllllaady!"* she declared with her head swaying from side to side. We could always count on Mother reminding us that she was, in her mind at least, a "gracious lady" whenever she was inebriated.

I never really understood what my mother was so angry about when she was drunk. Her soliloquies ranged from upbraiding the Air Force for never giving my father a rank above Colonel to memories of her childhood in the shadow of Uncle Stanley. There was never a chance for discussion or an opportunity to dissuade her from her reveries. When she was drunk, she was a one-woman show.

Like most nights, I retreated to my bedroom and slept fitfully, with a big feather pillow over my head.

Chapter 5
Beaten, Hopeless and Angry

We who are in the family circle of an alcoholic suffer fears and frustrations; we feel beaten, hopeless and angry—with overtones of guilt.

> May 6th
> One Day at a Time in Al-Anon

*That to which your heart clings and entrusts itself…
is really your god.*

> Martin Luther

A very strange thing happened when I was in my early teens. My parents started going to church. I have no recollection of a catastrophic event, such as a death in the family, or a serious illness, which might have caused this change in protocol. I could see no emerging frame of reference in my parents' actions or speech that would have indicated a hope in God or a life beyond this one. No reason appeared evident to support the need for a spiritual commitment. Nevertheless, we started attending the big Methodist church in downtown Colorado Springs. This church was so big that, to me, its doors looked like the Gates of Heaven, and I decided the senior pastor looked like God.

Of course, I had no idea what God looked like, either literally or figuratively. Most of my life, our family was what are called "two timers" because we went to church twice a year, on Christmas and Easter. In my photo albums are stair-step pictures of Barbara and me dressed in our little starched dresses with little Easter bonnets and snow-white gloves (always gloves: it was a necessary part of my mother's "official gracious lady uniform"). Once we had little fur muffs for Christmas instead of the gloves. There would be a photo of my sister and me, and then the obligatory shot of my mother with us girls and then my father with us girls (my father was big on having a variety of poses). And when my sister got a little older and my father trusted her with his camera, Barbara took photos of our parents and me. By the time that I got old enough to take pictures, we didn't take pictures any more.

I can't recall if my mother was coming off of an especially bad bender at the time, but she began talking about the fact that she had been baptized many years ago by an evangelist who came to Kirksville. My Aunt Ruth had taken Mother to this tent revival, and because Ruth had "gone forward," Mother did too. I don't think she was very old at the time—maybe eleven or twelve. But nevertheless, she and Ruth got "dunked," as in, fully immersed in water in the old-time evangelist tradition. Now, when I was about the same age as she had been then, my mother was insisting that the dunking pretty much took care of things in the religion department for her. It was my father's and my turn.

"It's the least you could do, Mayhue," she pleaded. The way she said it caused me to wonder if my father had committed some unknown indiscretion and needed now to absolve himself in my mother's eyes. That theory seemed somewhat illogical, since she had, by now, at least a million infractions for which he could demand that she pay up. But then again, nothing ever seemed quite fair in our family's "rules of engagement."

He protested, saying that he also had been "dipped in the river" near his boyhood home of Bible Grove, Missouri. I knew my father's family members were all big church people; I had heard about them all my life. Daddy described how my Aunt Bessie had been saved at least six times, and how my Aunt Ruby played the pump organ in the Bible Grove church wearing a huge straw hat. This was all very confusing to me, since I had never had any religious training. But Mother's persistence paid off, and one day my dad and I went down to the big Methodist church, into the little chapel. I was disappointed since I wanted to be baptized in the big sanctuary that looked like the Gates of Heaven. We were baptized by the youth pastor—again I felt let down because I wanted the guy who looked like God to do it so maybe it would stick better. Since my sister was at college, she escaped this peculiar ritual.

Needless to say, I had no idea what baptism meant, and I wasn't sure my father knew either. We weren't required to take any religious instruction beforehand. But the fact that we got baptized seemed to please Mother, at least until she fell off the wagon again. Then she didn't much care what we did. A fairly good trade off was that I got to go on the church youth group retreat. The only thing I remember about the trip is that I got to lead the worship time the first night when we camped at Rocky Mountain National Park. I picked the only two hymns I knew at the time for the group to sing; "Fairest Lord Jesus" and "Holy, Holy, Holy." I got pretty worked up, thinking of what to say in the prayer I was supposed to lead. That was probably the first time it dawned on me that maybe all that beautiful Colorado scenery wasn't an accident.

When I look back, it seems odd that this was really my first introduction to Christian life. I remember trying to pray about my home situation, but I didn't know how to pray and nothing good came of it, so I decided I had better quit before I prayed something wrong and messed things up. I also tried to talk to the youth pastor about my home life a couple of times and that was my first introduction to the idea that not all grown-ups (even church grown-ups) know everything. I was very honest with him, which was not my usual modus operandi. I had become so used to lying about our family's situation that my little fabrications had spilled over into lots of other areas of my life. So although I didn't realize it at the time, I was really doing a little spiritual cleansing by speaking truthfully to this poor youth pastor. He was very sincere but I don't think he had the foggiest idea what to do or say to make me feel better and I think he was glad when I just stopped coming altogether.

Soon enough, our family stopped going to church altogether too. This had to do, in part, with the fact that we were no longer all living under the same roof.

****

My mother wasn't the only one who kept our home in turmoil. My father could, and did, scrap with her for hours. Once he almost killed her.

I was coming home from an evening play rehearsal at school. Besides riding my horse, high school drama productions were one of the ways I coped with my jumbled life. Playing some part in a theater production was far superior to the sniveling existence of my true life. I *became* my character, escaping, falling, transporting myself to another time and place. When I managed to get a part in a play or a musical at school, even a minor part, I put all of my energy into learning my lines perfectly and studying the character I was playing. My mother never came to any of my school plays, and my father came only occasionally. I could seldom count on either of them for a ride to and from school activities, so I usually relied on my friends' parents for transportation.

A girlfriend's mom was dropping me off. But as we approached the house, all I saw were flashing red lights. When I had left for the evening, Mother was sleeping it off again, and my father was reading quietly in the living room. What could have happened in the short time I was gone? Were the police and the ambulance summoned for her, or worse—*was something wrong with my father?*

I asked my friend's mom to drive faster and I was out of the car before she even stopped completely in the driveway. I ran past the ambulance and up to the porch. Just then, two paramedics opened the front door and began wheeling my mother out on a stretcher. I saw that her hands were restrained, and a blanket was tightly tucked in around her legs. There was blood on her face and her hair was matted down. She was screaming obscenities at my father, who stood, pale and shaking, in the entryway. I ran past her stretcher and clung to my father.

"Daddy, what happened?" I shrieked. "Did Mother hurt you?" I was sobbing. I didn't notice the police officers in the living room.

"I'm afraid it was the other way around," he said solemnly.

"Colonel Blaine?" An officer appeared in the entry. "We'd like to speak to you for a moment, please."

My father took my arms and pushed me away. "Go to your room, Margaret Ruth. We'll talk later."

"No, Daddy. What's going on here? What happened to Mother?" Now I was shaking too. I didn't understand what had happened. My parents had fought so often before, but it had never come to this. Barbara and I had pulled the two of them apart dozens of times, but they had never really hurt each other. The police had never come before. An ambulance had never needed to be called to our house. There was just drinking and fighting and then everyone slept.

I wished my sister were home. Barbara always made things better for me, at least. But with her gone now, I felt the suffering weight of responsibility on my own shoulders, like it was my job and my job alone to keep peace between my parents at all costs. This was a new development, to think Daddy couldn't control himself around my mother any more.

My brain hurt. I was at a loss to define what I instinctively knew, that things were getting horribly out of hand. It was as though

Mother's alcoholism gave off toxins into the air that infiltrated the entire family's collective bloodstreams, rendering each of us poisoned.

Since Daddy wasn't talking, I sneaked downstairs and called Barbara at nursing school. My father had called her earlier, before the big fight. What I learned from my sister first, and then from my father some time later was that my mother had been having an affair with another drunk, meeting him at a flop house hotel downtown. I didn't even know what an affair was. I didn't even really know what sex was! Barbara had come home once and, in great big medical terms she was learning in her classes, had tried to explain sex to me. I thought the whole thing was disgusting and I said I never wanted any part of it. So when she told me that's what having an affair was— and that my mother had been with somebody other than my dad—I got really nauseous. I never knew how my mother met this other man or how long they had been seeing each other. But somehow my father found out, and when he did, he went berserk.

My father was not placed under arrest. He was not taken to jail. This was, after all, just a little domestic dispute in the early 1960's. At that point in time, a man could pretty much inflict bodily harm on his wife and not experience any consequences. He had indeed "smacked her around a bit," as he told me later. He cried as he told me about the argument that had ensued.

"Your mother has a thread, Margaret Ruth, a thread of *good* running through her," he blubbered. I had heard the "thread speech" from him before and it was usually when he was feeling guilty. Of course, he left out the real reason for the argument - he wasn't about to tell me that Mother was cheating on him. I didn't want to hear any of it anyway. It was not for young ears, but my father had no true friends that he felt he could call. Being a military officer carried with it the expectation that family matters were kept strictly at home. Period. The Air Force had no alcohol or drug treatment programs, no battered women shelters, no intervention programs, no child protection workers to help us; we didn't even know if they existed someplace else.

During those years, I yearned to be free of all of the entanglements that had somehow grown so overwhelming. I often escaped into a bizarre fantasy where a handsome young man kidnapped me and held me hostage, but was really very good to me and I fell in love with him. Years later, it struck me very odd that I thought being forcibly removed from my family by some crazed and sex-starved pedophile was a wished-for alternate to my home life. In fact, the remembrance of that fantasy haunted me for years.

****

That night, because she was a military dependent, my mother had been taken to the Air Force Academy Hospital, a brand new, state of the art facility. No bones were broken, but they kept her overnight "for observation"—a nice way to say, "until they unraveled what was really going on." The determination was made that my mother's blood alcohol level had been somewhere near the national debt. The next morning, my father was summoned not by the courts or the doctors, but by some superior officer who told him to get his wife out of the military hospital because they didn't treat "situations" like that there. They gave him twenty-four hours to find someplace else for her to go, which for lack of another "appropriate setting," meant bringing her home. My mother called my sister at college and cut a deal; if Barbara and I would come to the hospital and see what my father had done to her, she would not press charges against him.

Barbara skipped her classes that afternoon, rode the bus home, and we drove silently to the hospital. We found mother's room, and we were shocked at what we saw. Her physical appearance was startling enough; her face and neck were badly bruised, turning lovely shades of purple and blue. Her left arm was covered with scratches. One of her eyes was swollen almost shut. Her hospital gown covered the rest, but we could see by the way she was moving that she hurt all over. She probably was not even completely sober, even then. But more disturbing than her physical appearance was the look in her eyes. I had seen my mother's eyes progress from jade green to dark storm with a succession of alcoholic beverages. But if the eyes are truly the windows of the soul, that day my mother's soul appeared to have been unleashed from hell.

"This is what your *faaaather* did to me," she hissed through clenched teeth. Then, always certain to be using her "gracious lady proper language," she added, "This is the man to whom I am married. This is the monster who calls you his children! This is what he did to me!" (This last was delivered in a less-than "gracious-lady-like" tone.)

All the world's a stage, I thought. *And Mother is going to assume the center of it.*

Chapter 6
Accepting the Unacceptable

Many children of alcoholics develop a high tolerance for accepting the unacceptable.

Toxic Parents
Susan Forward

My mother did not press assault charges that time. She came home with a complete set of multicolored bruises, but a mellower attitude, at least for a while. Surprisingly, life went on as usual for the rest of my sister's college years. Her senior year in nursing school, my sister met a young Air Force sergeant named Larry who had come to Denver on a temporary duty assignment. My sister had, by this time, lost two boy friends. One died in Viet Nam and the second more recent one was killed while she was in college. Mother was, miraculously, sober at the time, and she actually drove to Denver to pick my sister up and take her to the funeral, which came as quite a shock to me and provided a rare "rational adult behavior model" for my young and impressionable mind.

My sister had attended four high schools in four years and suffered her share of sadness. When Larry came along, I think even my mother hoped my sister would find some happiness. Despite my father's desire for both my sister and me to marry commissioned officers, my sister married Larry. The wedding took place with a minimum of hassles, and my sister and her new husband left in my dad's old gray Chevy for Seymour Johnson Air Force Base, in Goldsboro, North Carolina.

I was fifteen years old, scared to death, and not at all certain I could cope with our home situation without my sister.

****

After my sister got married, I missed her terribly, but I still had my horse and my friends. The friends I rode with were different than the ones I saw at school. Having a horse was a great leveler of the playing field, and kids who didn't normally hang out together would ride together after school and on the weekends. We had special sleepovers, just for girls who owned horses. Sometimes, if one of the girls kept her horse right on her parents' property, we'd even bring our horses along for their own slumber party. My "horse friendships" were a great distraction from my sorrowful home life.

In my years of riding, I developed an awesome respect for horses. I realized how much responsibility was being entrusted to me—not just to be a spoiled city kid with my own horse, but the accountability of caring for an intelligent, sensitive animal who was far more intuitive than I could even imagine. Lito taught me to love all animals, and to marvel at nature. When I left home for college, my dad said he'd give me the old Volkswagen beetle if I gave up my horse. I couldn't refuse his offer, but I never forgot that beautiful bay mare with her shining eyes the color of chestnuts.

****

In ninth and tenth grades, I began dating a little bit, though not the boys I wanted to date. I had a serious crush on a boy named Trevor McBride, who was at least civil to me, so I took that to mean there was a good chance he wanted to marry me some day. When it came to the opposite sex, I really had no emotional compass to help me discern what was a healthy feeling on my part and what was sheer stupidity.

Trevor was the only person I ever knew who got shot. He wasn't saving the world when he took the bullets, although I was convinced he could have. It was just a hunting accident, but he almost died, so he had been out of school for a whole year. When he came back, every girl in the school made over him, including me. He seemed so mature, having had such a close brush with death and bravely living to tell about it.

Aside from my prowess at horseback riding, I was clueless about athletics. I had been born with a curvature of the spine, but the Air Force doctors, who my father said got their medical licenses out of Cracker Jack boxes, told my parents "not to baby me." "Ignore her condition," they told my parents, and I would do fine. Because I rode horses, the muscles in my back became strong enough to support my crooked spine. In fact, I was probably in better shape then than many of the other girls in my high school who were cheerleaders or who played in one of the few girls' sports available at our school in the early sixties. But I was so clueless about sports that I found it hard to talk to the boys in my classes

I also didn't know very much about life. Due to the serious lack of adult direction at home, I set off in search of one or two surrogate parents at my school. When a guidance counselor signed me up for Home Economics, I thought that sounded like a good place to find a mother figure, while I'd also be developing my domestic skills, so that I could be ready when Trevor McBride asked me to be his wife. I was sadly mistaken, about several things.

On the first day of Home Ec, all the girls walked into the class and then we tried unsuccessfully to walk back out again. The new teacher, Mrs. Bisby, looked like she stepped out of a covered wagon. She was short and plump and she wore a dress she made herself, she proudly told us, out of one of those little prairie prints. She had a gingham apron over the prairie print dress, and lace-up granny boots long before they returned to being fashionable. Her gray-brown hair was pulled straight back into a bun, which was covered by a little crocheted affair that she told us was called a *snood*. We all thought Mrs. Bisby *looked* like a *snood*. I wondered absently if there was a Mr. Bisby, and a whole tribe of little Bisbys. I quickly crossed her off the surrogate parent list.

Amid giggles and apprehensive glances among all the girls, Mrs. Bisby (whom we quickly dubbed "Mrs. Busy-Bee") began to teach us things we would never use in our natural lifetimes. First, we had to examine the flour and sugar for bugs. Most of our upper-middle-class mothers would have just thrown out the flour and sugar if it had sat there since last spring, but Mrs. Busy-Bee made sure we knew how to sift through the canisters to look for mealworms.

Next, she taught us to make deodorant out of baking soda and water, a concoction, which she said we could just plaster under our armpits and we'd never have to worry about offensive body odor again. She didn't mention that we'd have to administer the homemade deodorant while we were hanging upside down so it wouldn't drip for the prescribed half-hour or so it took to dry like cement. We all thought Mrs. Busy-Bee should have taken her own advice about the prevention of body odor. She also taught us how to "glass" eggs, a method of preservation that went out with the invention of the electric refrigerator.

I moved on to the English teacher, a pock-faced, jolly fellow named Mr. Pandowdy, who also served as the drama director. I loved this teacher to death because he was even more dramatic than my family – and besides, he had a license to *teach* drama! It was probably with Mr. Pandowdy's encouragement that I was involved in every dramatic production my high school ever put on, from *South Pacific* and *Bye Bye Birdie,* to *Hamlet.* At his encouragement, I auditioned for the part of Ophelia, but instead I was asked to be Hamlet's mother, Getrude.

Mr. Pandowdy thoroughly embarrassed me when he asked me to read the part a second time because he said I did the best job of "reading cold with a British accent." He described my reading as "insipid." I rushed home and looked the word up, shocked to learn that he wasn't really paying me a compliment, but he was saying I had the whiney, wearisome and monotonous character of Gertrude down cold. Even after I learned what "insipid" meant, I felt like I had won the Oscar. I put my heart and soul into that performance of Hamlet, in spite of the fact that neither of my parents ever came to see one single production.

I recall one other memorable teacher, Agatha Farnsworth, who taught speech. Agatha had been trying for several decades to get her classroom and her facial hair under control, never having been particularly successful at either. Kids were constantly in this teacher's face. She came completely unglued at the slightest provocation, and most of the kids in her class wanted to see her do this repeatedly, like a monkey and an organ grinder. Once, the kid in front of me delivered a speech on the exact same topic I had chosen. When it was my turn, I got up and sort of apologized to the class and to Mrs. Farnsworth for unknowingly choosing the same topic. Agatha must have thought I was being a smart aleck because she lit into me in front of the whole class and asked me if I waned to deliver my speech or not. Her tantrums were very entertaining, unless you happened to be the object of her wrath. I told her I just wanted to deliver my speech so she shut up. I survived that day and the rest of her class. After I got out of high school, I heard that she gave the whole deal up and committed suicide.

****

About a year after my sister had left home, my father talked my mother into agreeing to go to Fitzsimmons Army Hospital in Denver for some sort of emotional realignment. My father insisted I ride along to take her there, for some reason that I could not fathom. So we were tooling along on Interstate 25, about half way between Colorado Springs and Denver, and Mother decided she was going to jump out of the car, presumably to end it all just like Agatha Farnsworth. She was crying hysterically and saying that if my dad didn't turn the car around, she would open the door and fling herself out. I smelled a rat right away. I was sitting in the back seat, behind her, and my dad started yelling at me to grab her. He was grabbing her too, while trying to bring the car safely over to the side of the road. He managed to get the car stopped and we had quite a little scene there on the shoulder in the dark with cars whizzing by and honking their horns. Then Daddy turned the car around and drove us home.

After that, my mother went on a really wild bender and ended up in the downtown hotel with her drunk lover, Stuart Webster. I remember the name like it was my own because my father used it so often.

"Your mother ran off with that *Stuart Webster*," he would say, over and over. "I can't believe she'd go off with a man like that *Stuart Webster*!" I couldn't believe it either, but I thought it was just fine. The more she was gone, the better my life was.

But inevitably, my father couldn't leave well enough alone, and one night he went to the hotel to find her and presumably bring her home. It was probably just as well that none of us saw the scene he made, because this time he got himself arrested. I couldn't believe it when he called me! *She's the one who should have been thrown in jail!* I said to myself. He told me to call my sister and tell her what had happened. I stayed at the house by myself that night, fanaticizing about being kidnapped by Trevor McBride, until they let my father out on bail the next morning.

His little fiasco at the downtown hotel cost a pretty penny. Besides the bail, he had court costs and the local paper carried a story about the incident on page five. I was mortified when Trevor McBride came up to me the next day in school and said he had seen the article. (Did he also somehow know about the fantasies? He did, after all, possess special powers.) He was very sweet and seemed to understand, which I took to mean he loved me desperately and wanted to take me away from all of this, just like in my fantasies.

But our troubles were just starting. My mother was enraged. She was determined to do everything she could to make my father regret what he had done. She obtained a restraining order that made life for my father and me fairly tricky. The court ordered my father to vacate the house. I chose immediately to leave with him and go to a small motel down the road from my high school. I had no choice but to go with him. He was the one I trusted, and I could not bear to stay in the house alone with her.

****

And so we hurriedly packed up a few things before my mother's cab arrived from the hotel. I bundled up the dog bed and food for Nicky, and threw in his leash since he would not have the benefit of a fenced yard. On a cold, crisp February afternoon, my father and I took up residence in a twelve by twelve efficiency apartment at the Silver Moon Lodge. A better name for the place would have been the "No-Tell Motel," a relatively sleazy looking place where you probably didn't want to know more about its inhabitants than was absolutely necessary. The entire motel was knotty pine—the furniture, the paneling, the sign out front.

In those days, there was no such thing as a "smoke free" room, so the whole place smelled like stale tobacco, sweat and dust mold. The sheets on the hide-a-bed where I slept were gray in color and kind of starchy. They scratched my skin when I rolled over. The room was furnished with a black and white TV, sort of like the very first one we had when I was little.

The woman who ran the motel was from the south, and all she said was "yes." Only she pronounced it with a southern drawl, so it came out "yea-us." When we asked her for an extra key, she said, "yea-us." If we wanted some ice, she said, "yea-us." We dubbed her "Mrs. Yea-us," and my father said he figured if he asked her to sleep with him, she'd say, "yea-us."

It was strange living with my father in such close quarters. He readily assumed all of the parenting roles, cooking for the two of us in the tiny kitchen, doing laundry in the motel's utility room. It was not like he had no experience in these areas, since my mother was no domestic goddess. Sometimes we went out to eat and once he took me to a movie. We saw *Lolita*, which I always thought was a strange film for him to take me to. I had been reading the book, and I mentioned that the movie might be good. I'm not sure he knew what the story was about until we saw it in the theater. Of course, there weren't any *real* similarities: he wasn't my stepfather, and he didn't kidnap me, and my father wasn't a letch. We didn't talk about it much afterwards. I think he was too embarrassed that he accidentally took me to a movie like that, and he just didn't know what to say at all.

****

Every afternoon when I got home from school and he got home from work, we made this strange little tactical reconnaissance to the house for the mail, sort of like the airlifts over East Berlin. The court order said my father could not come within a mile of the place, but he fudged a bit on that so I wouldn't have to walk too far. I don't suppose he really wanted to make me do this, but what choice did he have? A childhood interrupted by adult responsibilities. We set up our mobile reconnaissance headquarters in a park close to the house, and I prepared to conduct my ground operations from there while my dad maintained a vigil, in case, for some reason we needed to abort the mission. House key? Check. Flashlight? Check. Satchel for mail? Check. Destination: occupied territory. We synchronized our watches and *soon I was goin' in....*

The first time I went to the house for him, I felt like I was a brand new actor in a really bad action adventure movie. The house was closed up, with all the curtains drawn tight. I used my father's key to open the front door, pushing it open slowly as if some crazed executioner was going to leap out at me with a twelve-inch knife.

No executioner. Just the same familiar smell of my drunken mother. As soon as I entered the foyer, I picked up the day's mail that had been shoved through one of those little slots in the front door. I had reluctantly agreed with my father that I should probably check on Mother. I tiptoed to her bedroom door, which I found open this time, and I peered in. She was sleeping quite peacefully, under a mountain of covers. Nothing out of the ordinary. At least I could hear her breathing. I could do what I needed to do and stay beneath her radar. I proceeded to the kitchen. I was not at all prepared for what I saw.

On the counter top were three or four open cans of food—vegetable beef soup, green beans, blueberry pie filling, and something mushy and orange with no label. There were spoons or forks in each of them but no sign of a pot or a pan. No dirty plates or bowls either. My mother had been eating the food cold, right out of the cans. The mushy stuff was smeared all over the counter and down the side of the cabinet. In the corner of my mind, I clearly saw the elephant in the corner of the dinette, stuffing her pudgy face with peanuts. I covered my mouth and ran back to the front door, locking it as I let myself out.

The next day, things were worse. When I tried the front door, it wouldn't open. I had been denied access to my own home. I concluded that Mother must have heard me the day before and had locked the deadbolt sometime after I left. I had visions of her staggering around the house, having a little midnight can-snack and somehow sensing that I had been there. Could she have realized in her sodden state that I had been invading her little domain? Why did she care? She certainly was in no shape to take care of the mail.

I stood on the front stoop, feeling like a juvenile delinquent at my own door. *Think, Meg*, I told myself. *There has to be another way in!*

I walked around the house to the back door leading to the garage. I was in luck! We had always left the door unlocked in case we forgot a key, and Mother hadn't thought of that! I entered the house through the kitchen door, this time ignoring the stuff on the counter, and I quickly retrieved the mail. I could hear Mother snoring, so I concluded she was alive and that was enough for today.

Day three. I didn't even try the front entrance, but when I retraced my steps to the back of the garage, surprise! The door wouldn't budge. Clearly sabotage. I could see through the little back door windowpanes that Mother had moved our Oldsmobile forward, at a weird angle, until the front bumper pinned the door shut. In those days, an Oldsmobile 98 was about the size of a Sherman tank, with about as much maneuverability. I was thinking, *How did she ever get it into that position?* Her determination amazed me. But mine amazed me more. I was not to be outdone.

I ran around the backyard to my bedroom window on the lower floor, just at ground level on our sloping lot. While pondering the whole situation as I drifted off to sleep the night before, I remembered that I had opened the window a crack the day we left, for no particular reason, just to get some fresh air while I was packing. I had forgotten about it until now, and it was still open. I punched a little hole in the screen with the house key, tearing the screen enough to get my hand in. Then I reached through the open window, having just enough room to wind my arm through and turn the window crank.

During this delicate procedure, I was making a mental note to myself not to leave the window open like this ever again for the rest of my days, lest I fall prey to some maniac out checking for ways to break into houses. It had never occurred to me that this would be the only way I would be able to enter my own house. It never occurred to Mother either, and so in the days and weeks to come, I completed my little mail-mission by climbing in and out of my own bedroom window.

Chapter 7
The Family Chess Game

Our children are the first things to consider. Our attitude is the key to a successful family relationship – and their normal growing up. And above all… never use the children as pawns in any conflict.

June 27th
One Day at a Time in Al-Anon

Back at the Knotty Pine Motel, I was getting pretty bored with just my dad and the proverbial "elephant in the room" for company. A new family moved in with a son about my age, so that kept me interested for a while. I got home from school before my dad, so this boy and I would have a little rendezvous every day until my father put his foot down and said I wasn't to see the boy unless he was around. It didn't really bother me. The kid wasn't that cute, and he always smelled like lemons, except on Sundays when he smelled like his father's cologne. His family was building a new house across town and he went to a different school: chances were I'd never see him again anyway.

After about a month in the motel, we discovered that Mother was no longer staying at the house. My father was frantic, which of course baffled me. I thought this was a great turn of events. Maybe she had run away for good with her beloved Stuart Webster. I figured he could have her—what was left of her.

But my father wanted to know where she was, so he started calling all over town, to the police and the hospitals, and he couldn't find her anywhere. This went on for a few days until finally Mother called him and said she was living in a hotel in Pueblo, about forty miles south of Colorado Springs. The state hospital was in Pueblo, where everyone knew they took all the crazy people. My heart leapt when my father told me Mother was in that town. I thought immediately, *she must be in the state hospital*. I was certain she was never coming back now.

But Daddy explained that she had decided to take a room there and "think things over," whatever that meant. What prompted her to move and how she got there was always a mystery to me, if not to my father. As if this news wasn't bad enough, next he said that she wanted me to come down for a visit.

"You could ride the bus," my father was saying. "It'll be nice for you to see her, and she's really looking forward to it! She'll meet you at the station there and you can stay overnight in her hotel room." I sat on the Knotty Pine Motel couch and listened nervously as that pesky elephant peered over my shoulder. I could hear her breathing, but I told myself it was just my imagination.

Somehow I got the feeling *he* was wishing he could ride the bus to see her. I wanted no part of it, and I told him so. I felt like my father was moving me around the board game of his life with no regard for how I felt about the situation. Though I couldn't have verbalized it then, my father was clearly using me to manufacture involvement with Mother.

But of course, he won, once again, and the following Saturday morning he took me to the bus station with my little overnight bag. I actually felt pretty grown up as I boarded the bus. It was the first time I'd gone anywhere alone. Maybe it wouldn't be so bad after all. My fifteen year-old brain was thinking that maybe Mother would buy me something nice while I was visiting her. I sat back and watched the landscape roll by: endless miles of dirt and dust and gravel along the drab, gray highway. Occasionally, a tumbleweed bumped across the road in front of the bus. I thought I saw one lonely antelope up towards the foothills.

Someone once said that most of life is just showing up. If that was the case, my mother must have missed a good two-thirds of hers. When the bus pulled into the station in Pueblo, I started looking out the window for Mother, but I couldn't see her anywhere. When we stopped, I anxiously stepped off the bus carrying my overnight bag.

No surprise: she wasn't waiting for me. I searched the entire bus station, even looking in the ladies room, but she simply wasn't there.

My dad had given me directions to the hotel where she was staying, "just in case." (*Just in case what?* I wanted to know.) I began to walk slowly down the strange street. An old gentleman asked if he could help me, and when I showed him the name of the hotel, he pointed to a building in the next block. I thanked him and moved on towards the door of a very old building. *Is this a hotel*, I said to myself, *or a genuine flophouse?*

Inside, it was just like an episode of Twilight Zone, with a dingy lobby and a funny little man with pointy ears sitting behind a tiny desk with one bare light bulb hanging from the ceiling above him. Behind him were little wooden cubes all over the wall, with the room numbers on each of them, for mail or messages, I assumed. I approached him cautiously and asked if my mother was staying there.

"What's her name, Missy?" he said, looking at me out of the corner of my eye. I told him.

"She's in two twenty-three," he replied. "But I haven't seen her at all today. Is she expecting you?"

"Yes," I said, barely audibly.

"Well, you can go on upstairs and see if she's there, if you like." He pointed up the dark stairway.

I started up the stairs, with the floorboards creaking under my feet. I found the room and knocked softly, with my ear to the door. I heard a strange moaning sound that took my breath away. *She's drunk*, I thought. *She can't even stay sober long enough for me to visit her! I knew better than to expect anything from her – from her OR Daddy!*

I turned on my heel and ran down the stairs, past the funny little desk clerk, and out the door. I ran all the way back to the bus station and showed the lady there my ticket which was dated two days from then.

"Can you exchange this ticket for one that goes back to Colorado Springs today?" I asked, breathlessly.

"Why, yes, I can," she said, "but there isn't another bus for four hours."

Four hours! I thought. *What will I do for four hours?*

I exchanged the ticket and sat in the corner of the bus station until the bus came. The only time I got up was to go to the bathroom once and to buy a Coke and a King Size Hershey Bar at the soda fountain. I sat scrunched in the seat, watching all around to see if Mother would walk in. I didn't want to see her, and I didn't want her to see me. It seemed like an eternity until the bus came, and another eternity until it got back to Colorado Springs. I called my father from a pay phone and told him what had happened. He came and got me, saying how sorry he was. As far as I was concerned, there weren't enough words he could say to make me feel any better.

****

A few days later, a package arrived from Mother. It was a fake leopard skin coat, very flashy, but I loved it! A note said that she was sorry she had "missed me." I didn't care if it was a peace offering, I just wanted to keep it as a payback for what I'd been through.

My father snatched it out of my hands. "Nothing doing," he shouted. "That's not a very appropriate gift for a young girl! You'd look like a floozy!"

I felt mortally wounded. How could he say I was going to look like a floozy when it was *Mother* who was the floozy! I screamed and cried and carried on, *way* out of proportion for what a stupid fake leopard coat should have been worth, but I was totally out of control. I felt like he always wanted me to participate in this sick little family game he wanted to play with Mother, and I always came up holding the short end of the stick.

In the end, he insisted that the coat be sent back to Mother with a note to return it. I stomped out of the room and slammed my bedroom door. The stupid elephant was sitting defiantly in *my* room, on *my* bed, crowding me out of my own life.

Chapter 8
By Our Follies

'Tis by our follies that so long
We hold the earth from heaven away.
                    Edward Roland Sill

Love is a sweet tyranny, because the lover
endureth his torments willingly.
                    Proverb, Author Unknown

Since my mother wasn't at the house anymore, my father and I said goodbye to the Knotty Pine Motel and moved back into the house within a couple of days. Needless to say, our home was a mess. We scrubbed floors, washed clothes and bedding, and opened windows to air the place out. It didn't occur to me at the time that my father fully intended to bring Mother home. He never said what his plans were.

Obviously, I was shocked when, early in October, I came home from school one day and found my mother sitting at the kitchen table, like she owned the place, having a leisurely cup of coffee with my father.

Instantly I flew into a rage, screaming at my parents and telling them it wasn't fair. I was the one who was always the last to know what little schemes they were cooking up: they never asked my opinion or let me be in on the decision-making. (This, of course, was not very sound reasoning, but I was only sixteen and lacked the tools to make adult judgments. I also lacked *adults* who could make adult judgments.) Then I swore at my mother and called her the worst words I knew.

That's when my father became airborne. I knew he was furious by the look on his face: a look I had previously only seen directed at my mother. Until now.

Whirling around, I started running with my father in hot pursuit. I couldn't believe he was coming after me! With my heart thudding wildly in my chest, I took off down the stairs to the basement. Daddy had never done anything like this before. When he caught up with me in the laundry room, I crouched in the corner and covered my head with my hands. His fists pummeled my back as he screamed at me, "Don't you ever let me hear you say those things about your mother again!" It was no use to argue with him. His reaction completely amazed me. Honestly, I expected that he would be *glad* if Mother went away for good. How could this be happening?

When the blows stopped, I turned slowly and looked him in the face and saw that my father had tears in his eyes. He must have seen the disbelief on my face and somehow come to his senses. But he didn't say he was sorry—and we never spoke of the incident again. He turned and walked away, leaving me crying in the corner. He went back up the stairs and then I heard him and my mother talking softly above me. Not wanting to hear their conversation, I turned on the clothes dryer, leaning against it to feel the warmth, staying there for what seemed like a long time.

After awhile, I made my way to the downstairs bathroom and peered at my strange reflection in the mirror. Except for the dried tears, I really didn't look that bad. I could feel some sore places on my back, but when I lifted my shirt, I couldn't see any bruises. Going into my bedroom, I locked the door and lay on my bed for a long time until I was sure my parents had gone to bed. I heard the muffled conversation they made above me, the strange sounds that I realized many years later meant they were making up or making love. Or both.

After what seemed like two lifetimes, when I was sure they were asleep, I slowly opened my bedroom door. I crept into my sister's room to the telephone there, and with trembling fingers, I dialed her number in North Carolina.

****

"What's the big idea, Barbara?" My father was clearly annoyed. "Margaret is just fine. We just had a little misunderstanding."

I was listening from outside the master bedroom where my father had gone to talk to my sister the next evening when she called. All day at school I had been on pins and needles, wondering what would happen when I got home. I had awakened my sister and her husband when I called the night before, and she promised me she would get Daddy to let me come and live with them. She promised, but it wasn't going well. Once again, my parents were trying to sweep everything under the carpet and make it look like nothing was wrong.

"Yes," he was saying into the phone, "Mother is doing very well. Yes, your mother has quit drinking. What's that? Well, of course I'm sure! Everything will be just fine, Barbara, you'll see!" He spoke more slowly now, to make his point, as if my sister were six years old again and not very bright. "There's no need to uproot Margaret while she's still in high school. You never liked it when we moved you! What's that? No, she's gone to bed early," he lied. "I'll be sure to have her call you tomorrow."

"I haven't gone to bed." I said under my breath. But I knew it was futile to argue with my father—-and my protesting had brought us to a whole new level of insanity. Slipping down the stairs to my room, I locked my door again, even though I resigned myself to being back in the "Honeymoon Phase," and I would not be bothered again that night.

It was then that I decided to run away.

I dressed quickly, before I changed my mind. As I sneaked out the back door, I was certain I saw the ever-present elephant crawl out from under the family room couch, stretch at bit, and then assume a comfortable position amid the throw pillows.

****

The October night was chilly as most Colorado nights are. Luckily, I had grabbed a sweatshirt, but no gloves or hat. The tears were still trickling down my face as I crossed the backyard and climbed the wooden fence. *This fence is dog proof and horse high*, I said to myself. *How come Daddy doesn't make this house kid safe?* It never occurred to me that my father, upon discovering that I was missing, would fear that something bad had happened to me.

Letting myself out of the gate my father had built, I picked my way carefully down the hill behind our house, along the tiny path overgrown with scrub oak and chokeberry. When I reached the bottom, my hands were scratched up, but I didn't care. My rage at what my parents were doing to me and my life gave me courage to go when I would not have gone otherwise. "Where am I even going?" I asked myself out loud. "Who would even want to help me?" And then I knew, all at once, that I would go to Trevor McBride's house. I still had a crush on him, and every time I saw him he tied my heart in knots. Someone with his degree of maturity would surely know what to do.

I had never been to his house, but my friend Chelsea lived right across the street from him (a fact which cemented my friendship with her considerably more than our familiarity as classmates). The road below the hill from our house descended into another housing development, older than ours. The streets were all gently curving and friendly looking, even in the dark. By the time I reached the cul de sac where Trevor lived, the three-quarter moon was full overhead, casting a romantic glow on his house.

Stopping dead in my tracks at the end of the walk, I thought, *What am I doing?* But I was scared and angry and desperate. I was certain that the only known cure for this was to rush into the arms of this darling boy who even survived being *shot*, and have him tell me everything was going to be all right.

His father answered the ringing doorbell. I could have sworn I could smell Trevor's Canoe aftershave wafting out the open door. "Is Trevor home?" I managed.

"No, he's still at work."

Of course, I thought. I knew he worked at the Howdy Pard (short for "Pardner") drive in, mature man of the world that he was. My dad had even taken me there a few weeks ago just so I could say, "Thanks for the fries, Trevor," thereby using his name naturally in the course of everyday conversation.

"What time will he be home?" I asked this adult version of my heartthrob.

"Oh, not 'till about eleven. Do you want me to tell him you stopped by?"

"No, no," I said, trying to hide my disappointment. "I'll just catch up with him at school or something..."

And just like that, his dad smiled and said "Good night" and shut the magical door to the magical house where this magical boy lived. Looking at my watch, I realized: *Two and a half hours until he gets home!* I stood on the porch for a minute, trying to decide what to do, and then walked across the street to Chelsea's house, and sat down on the stone wall by her family's mailbox. And I waited.

Eleven o'clock came and went but my resolve was still pretty strong. *I'm not going home!* I hissed through clenched teeth. *Daddy probably won't even miss me.* A patrol car turned up the street, so I ducked behind an evergreen tree until it had passed. By eleven thirty I was beginning to wonder what Trevor could be doing that he wasn't home yet. His parents had left the porch light on, so I could see clearly that his car was not in the driveway. Was he in trouble?

Then, about ten to twelve, I got very nervous when I saw his car turning into the street and coming towards his house. *What if he doesn't want me here? What if he tells me to go jump in the lake?* Suddenly, I knew this was a really dumb idea. Soon he was in the house and all the lights were out. By now I was crying again. Then I just turned on my heel, walked out of Trevor's neighborhood and trudged up the big hill back to our house.

Surprisingly, both parents were waiting up for me, like we were some sort of normal family. My father did all of the talking. He said he had called all the hospitals and the police. He wasn't mad at me, just worried sick, he said with tears in his eyes. Did I want anything to eat, and was I awfully tired? At that instant I felt tired, so I told him I was going to bed. My mother never said a word to me that night—but it wouldn't have mattered if she had.

As I passed by the kitchen door, I thought I saw the family elephant unabashedly raiding the refrigerator.

****

My sister and I stayed in touch as much as possible in the coming months. She was concerned about me and wanted us to be together. She knew that I had absolutely no one—no other sisters or brothers, grandparents, no aunts or uncles, not even a pastor—to provide emotional support during the worst years of my mother's alcoholism. Although her husband, Larry, was from Pennsylvania and his own mother was a widow, Barbara convinced him that the next move they made needed to be near me. As soon as Larry was discharged from the Air Force, they packed up the old Chevy and drove straight for Colorado Springs. They took a little one-bedroom apartment, not too far from the Knotty Pine Motel.

My father had taken a job at a private employment agency after he retired from the Air Force. We probably could have lived comfortably on his retired pay, but with all the expenses involved with Mother's illness, Daddy may have felt he needed the extra income. With his help, Barbara got a nursing job right away, and

Larry took a position with the telephone company, using the electronics training he had received in the service.

My mother didn't stay sober long. Things went down hill pretty quickly, but this time my sister moved me into the little apartment she and her husband were renting. She didn't even discuss it with Daddy beforehand. She came to the house and helped me pack and left him a note. He didn't protest. I think he knew it was best for all of us. I slept on the couch at my sister's, and every morning Barbara took me to school on her way to work.

****

Although my father tired to keep his finances to himself, it was becoming obvious to my sister and me that he was concerned about money. The years of drinking and cracking up cars and running up court costs had begun to take their toll. For some reason, my parents (most likely my father) decided to sell the house they had built. I envisioned the elephant packing up her things in her imaginary trunk, ready to take up residence in the new rented house.

To put it mildly, my parents moved to a dump. Our big house sold quickly, and my father was wise enough to rent for a while until he could get his financial bearings again. The location was good for the time being; just a few blocks from my high school, but they were building a new school a couple of miles away by that time, so it really didn't matter. Also, the Romano's farm was way across town now, too far for me to walk. Since moving to my sister's apartment, I rode my horse only on the weekends when she could give me a ride. Although I had my driver's license by that time, Barbara needed her car to get to work.

The new house sucked. It was a cheap-looking rambler with a flat roof, with only a carport since the garage had been made into a master bedroom and bath. The walls were painted ugly brown and gray colors, and the linoleum in the kitchen looked like something out of an old Tennessee Williams novel. The interior had a musty smell from the day my parents first moved in. The basement was dark and damp and had none of the features of our previous house. I was glad I was living with my sister, at least for a while.

Part of this era that is somewhat fuzzy to me is how in the world my mother talked me into moving back home. Some bribery must have been involved. Mother got me my own phone line, and she let me pick the colors for my bedroom. Always enamored with the Polynesian culture, I chose some garish Hawaiian print. With flower print curtains and a matching bedspread, lots of fish netting and beads and paper lanterns, I could declare my room a genuine South Sea Island Disaster Area. I was starting to date some cadets at the Air Force Academy, so having my own phone came in handy for talking to them undisturbed.

My parents were thrilled that I was dating cadets. These young men were desirable marriage material, as far as they were concerned, and I was encouraged to attend the dances and social functions at the Academy. There were social directors, women who "fixed you up" with a date for an event. How much thought was put into "matching" you with someone with similar background and interests was questionable, but I got to wear fancy dresses and drive myself the twenty miles to the Academy grounds. It was all very formal, and Mother made sure I had beautiful gowns. Saturday I would spend hours getting ready for a date, doing my hair and my fingernails and toenails, putting on my makeup. My sister had never been one for this kind of fussing, but she didn't need to. She got the good hair in the family, and she had gigantic blue eyes that really stood out. Mine were small and close-set eyes that weren't noticeable at all until I lined them and brushed on mascara. Because of teen-age acne, very early on I started wearing what my history teacher referred to as "pancake mix" on my face.

Dating a fourth classman (military for freshman) in the beginning, he wasn't allowed off the Academy grounds. Eventually, I met a second classman and, unbeknownst to my parents, I used to pick him up and we would go to parties in town where alcohol flowed freely. Before I was seventeen, I was drinking scotch and soda like an old pro. But I thought it was okay because I was drinking with an upper class Air Force Academy cadet. Coming home, I would sit precariously on the toilet, hoping my parents wouldn't wake up and find me inebriated. The paisley wallpaper would climb up the bathroom wall, shimmering on its own as though it were alive, while I was contemplating whether or not to puke.

Neither of my parents ever gave me any sort of "talk" about dating (or drinking, for that matter). In fact, the only thing my father ever said to me was to "watch out for a boy when he gets a couple of beers under his belt." I was so naïve, *I thought he meant this literally*, and I just could not get my head around what it meant. To my knowledge, I never saw a guy with those bottles stuck in the top of his pants, so I figured my dad couldn't be mad at me for disobeying.

In high school and college, I had this perverse idea that if I could just find a boyfriend my parents approved of, our family would somehow be complete. It wasn't about what I needed or wanted or what was best for me. It was as though I was under some strange sort of spell, like a voodoo curse, and it was up to me to break the pattern my parents had set with their own relationship. If they could see me with Mr. Wonderful, it would somehow "heal" the bad feelings between my parents. Many years later, I read that children of alcoholics often have this impossible sense of responsibility; that it is *all* up to them to "fix" their parents' bungled lives.

****

Not surprisingly, Mother's drinking escalated again. Soon, my father was calling Barbara and telling her he didn't know what to do with Mother, a pattern that would repeat itself frequently in the years to come. Someone had suggested he try to have her committed, and he had spoken to a judge. "I just don't want to have her sent to Pueblo," he said. "I can't bear the thought of her being in a state mental institution!"

"What other choice do we have?" my sister asked. She was always the calm one in a crisis.

"Well, the judge said we could send her to Pine Tree Mental Hospital right here in Colorado Springs. It would be expensive, but at least it's not the state facility!"

Pine Tree Mental Hospital was probably *the* scariest place in all of Colorado Springs, at least to a kid my age. All the kids at school knew that Pine Tree was where they took anybody who was really crazy. We had all heard many wild stories about the things that happened there. If my mother would be going Pine Tree—that meant serious trouble to me. Simply put, I believed it meant that my mother would never be well again.

When I think back about how my dad must have reacted to the idea of committing her, I'm sure he felt pretty bad. Here was a man, totally unequipped to do anything about his wife's alcoholism, and now to top things off, he was told she needed to be placed in a psych ward. As low as my father had sunk, he must have truly agonized over his next step.

But he did take that next step. A judge signed a court order to take my mother out of our house and transport her to Pine Tree for a seventy-two hour hold. My sister, her husband and I stood across the street from our parents' house and watched as they brought my mother out on a stretcher. She was restrained, just like she had been the last time she left this way. She was screaming her head off, and before the ambulance rolled away, the entire neighborhood surely knew the Blaines were having another crisis. Barbara and I were mortified.

My father was beside himself with worry, guilt, sorrow, and shame. How had it come to this? How could he have done this to the one woman he loved and cared about? How could he have known at the time that the "therapy" she would receive there would totally miss the mark? He didn't know what might really be wrong with her, but I know he was desperate for help. He had next to no understanding of mental illness *or* alcoholism. The term "dual diagnosis" probably hadn't even been invented yet. For whatever Pine Tree Mental Hospital was, it was *not* what my mother needed at the time, and our family's money spent there might as well have been thrown off the top of a Colorado mountain.

****

"The snake pit," my father told me after his first visit there. "That's what they call it. She's in there with people who are seeing things and hearing things and thinking things that would scare the *bejesus* out of you." My father always used words like *bejesus* when he was really upset. Sometimes I thought he had to make up his own swear words for really important occasions because he used all of the regular ones in every-day conversation. He was pacing the floor and running his fingers through his hair.

There was no mistaking that he was devastated.

"But can they help her?" I asked tentatively, not really sure I wanted to know the answer.

"I don't know," he said. "I just don't know."

No one knew, it seemed. At that time, in the early 1960s, to our knowledge, there were simply were no treatment programs available for substance abuse, at least none that Daddy knew of or was told about by the "professionals" involved with my mother. Alcoholics Anonymous groups were available throughout the area, but it seemed the only way for a drunk like my mother to "dry out" was to go "cold turkey" on her own. The Air Force certainly didn't have mental health services as part of its coverage for those who served, much less for dependents. My father had been quite vocal about the cost of care at Pine Tree, and I knew he couldn't keep her there the rest of her life.

What kind of "help" (if any) she supposedly received at Pine Tree, I never knew. No one talked about it much. One day Daddy picked her up at the hospital and took her to a court hearing. All he told me beforehand was that it was a "commitment hearing," and, though my father never said anything of the sort, I fully believed my mother would be sent away forever, to the State Mental Hospital in Pueblo. I was thinking, *Goodbye, Mother! Good-bye, elephant! I hope you find some nice circus—or at least another family—to join!*

But the commitment hearing only resulted in my mother staying at Pine Tree for thirty more days. All my hopes of having her and her drinking out of my life for good went out the window, and I settled in for yet another period of uncertainty.

By this time, I was beginning to feel like a living, breathing yoyo, being bounced back and forth from our home to motels to apartments and then to a different home. I grieved for our old house, but I settled into some semblance of a routine, feeling pretty smug that now it really would be just Daddy and me. Mother remained in the hospital for about three months, during which time my brother-in-law's job took him to a small town in southern Colorado. I missed my sister immensely, but at least she was only a couple of hours away instead of across the country.

****

One night around this time, I watched my father frying up the pieces of beef liver he had bought for our dog Nicky, and I thought to myself that it was good he had Nicky. With all the chaos surrounding my mother's drinking, my father just didn't know where to put his feelings sometimes. He had always been an animal lover and we had always had a dog, even though my mother had no time for pets. I thought about how my mother would go berserk every time my dad would make that liver, for himself or the dog. Daddy and the dog loved liver just as much as Mother hated it, so he usually made it when she wasn't home. I watched him cutting it up into little pieces while Nicky danced around the kitchen on his short, squatty legs, yipping excitedly.

That night, my father took that little dog for a walk before bedtime, like he had every night since Nicky came to us as a puppy. Before Daddy realized it, Nicky found a stray pork bone at the side of the road, and he gulped the bone so fast, it lodged in his throat. My dad tried everything to get that dog to cough up the bone. Then he called the vet and rushed him to the emergency pet hospital. He came back a couple of hours later, without the dog. I was waiting up for him.

"He's gone," he said, trying not to cry.

I walked up and gave him a hug.

"Margaret," he said, not able to hold back the tears any longer. "Sometimes you've gotta get the bone away, even if they want it, you've got to get it away!" He was sobbing by now.

I knew in my heart that he wasn't just talking about Nicky and the pork bone.

My father was talking about my mother and the alcohol.

Chapter 9
A National Farewell

It was the Friday before Thanksgiving of my senior year in high school. Arriving in my drafting class early that day, I was sitting on my little drafting stool thinking about what a stupid Thanksgiving we were going to have because it was just my dad and me in that ugly house. We weren't even going to make a turkey.

Just then, Hunter Sardonis strolled in. The captain of the football team, Hunter was a typical Greek-god-athletic-type with blonde hair and rugged good looks. It was just he and I in the room, which didn't matter, I thought, because he hardly ever acknowledged my presence. This day, he glanced back at me on his way by my drafting table and said, "There's Meg Blaine of the tight-fitting clothes.'" He smiled and my face turned the color of a ripe tomato. At a loss to process his comment, it just hung there by itself in mid-air.

Soon the other students were piling into the room, all talking and jostling and making smart remarks. Hunter turned his attention to Toni Allen, the most popular girl in school (and also a general's daughter).

"Hey, Toni!" Hunter said, "How about that stupid President of ours? Look what he did now!"

Toni and Hunter had been having a running argument about John Kennedy ever since he was elected President three years before. Cheyenne Mountain High School had set up a "mock election," complete with voting booths and officials, and we all got to cast our votes for either the Democratic candidates, John Kennedy and Lyndon Johnson, or the Republicans Richard Nixon and Henry Cabot Lodge Jr. There wasn't even a discussion about any other candidates; it was assumed that the high school students would surely make an intelligent choice between these two parties. Hunter had been giving Toni a hard time ever since she told him she voted for Kennedy. Hunter was a staunch Republican, just like his dad.

"Yeah, Toni," he mocked her now, "it isn't enough that this clown gave millions to Cuba last year to get our own people out of there after the Bay of Pigs disaster. You'll never believe what he's going to do now!'

"Hunter, shuddup!" someone yelled from the doorway. "You're the one who doesn't know what's going on! President Kennedy was just shot in Dallas and they don't think he's gonna make it!"

We all froze in our tracks. No one spoke for several minutes. The teacher bowed his head. Some kids were starting to sob. Then the public address system squawked its warning that an announcement was coming. We held our breath.

"This is Principal Heimerl speaking. I am very sad to inform you students and teachers that President John F. Kennedy has just been assassinated in Dallas, Texas. He died at the hospital a short time after he was taken there by ambulance. Mrs. Kennedy is all right, thank God. Also shot was Texas Governor John Connally. The word is that the governor will recover." There was a pause, and then the principal added, "If any of you want to call your parents, you may do so, but the school will remain open for those of you who wish to stay."

My father was at his job at the employment agency, and I did want to be with him. Though he usually voted Republican, he was always very respectful of his "Chief of Staff," even if a Democrat occupied the Oval Office. After what seemed like eons, I walked to the office to wait in line to call him. Many students were crying, hugging each other. Hunter was crying himself, holding Toni and telling her he was sorry for the things he had said about President Kennedy.

None of us knew what to say or do, and we had no idea what it even meant. Assassinations happened in dark and distant countries full of crazy people, not the United States. I remembered the headline in my dad's newspaper less than a month ago when the president of the tiny Asian country of South Vietnam had been assassinated. But that was an underdeveloped country half way around the world. Would there be more attempts on the lives of U.S. officials? Who would kill our President? Was it a Communist plot? We were all scared to death of the Communists! We had learned in our Modern Civics class that the Soviet Union had built a fence around the portion of Berlin that they controlled, and a second parallel fence had been constructed, creating what was called "the death strip" in between. Anyone who tried to make a break from East to West would be shot on the spot.

My mom, my sister and I once visited my dad while he was the "Officer of the Day" at the Air Force Base where he was stationed.

He was supposed to be in charge of the entire United States Distant Early Warning System, an imaginary red line that the Communists weren't supposed to cross or we would blow them all to smithereens. After Daddy showed us around, my sister and I sat on the little cot in his quarters where he could get some sleep if the Commies were behaving themselves and an invasion wasn't imminent.

I asked him, "What would you do if they came over that red line?"

"I'd call the Sergeant and run like hell!" my father had said.

But it was clear now that our country was in peril over this assassination. I shivered as I thought of what it all might mean. Since my dad was retired now, somebody else's dad was the "Officer of the Day," but our safe world didn't seem so safe any more.

****

Daddy picked me up at school, and we spent a somber weekend at home. The radio stations suspended all regular broadcasting and played nothing but funeral dirges. Although my upbringing had left me devoid of the funeral experience, I knew it was a necessary thing to show respect for our President. Still, I missed listening to the Safaris and Leslie Gore and the new British group called the Beatles. My father was riveted to the living room couch, watching endless hours of coverage of the events on television. When I think back on that time, reporters and anchors seemed so much more genuine than those we see today. If they felt like crying on screen, they did, and when something shocking happened, they really looked and talked like they were shocked too, not like it was just another news story.

This was long before the days of "news advertisement," where you get snippets of the big stories throughout the day and evening, but you are held at bay until "details at eleven." And no one broke for advertisements for laxatives or sugared cereal.

More surprises were in store for us. On that dismal November weekend, Daddy and I sat in front of the TV in disbelief as the suspected assassin, Lee Harvey Oswald, was murdered in cold blood by Texas nightclub owner Jack Ruby, with dozens of law enforcement officers all around him. Historians continue to wonder and theorize about why these events took place. But that day, in our living room, my father had one constant thought.

"I wish your mother could be here with us," he said over and over. "She shouldn't be in a mental hospital during a time like this!" He visited her three times that weekend, and they talked on the phone nonstop. I shuddered to think of her being in that place where the patients were crazy enough when the country wasn't falling apart. Maybe the entire world was falling apart, including my family.

****

The television announcer gave a commentary about the late President as the horse-drawn caisson proceeded slowly from the capitol rotunda to St. Matthew's Cathedral. The reporters were mostly silent, allowing our minds, our entire beings, to be filled with the mournful sounds of drumbeats, bagpipes, horse hooves, and the cadenced steps of the military honor guard.

I couldn't take my eyes off those beautiful horses as they reminded me of the ones pulling Queen Elizabeth's coach at her coronation, only the Queen's were snow white and these were coal black. I especially watched the rider-less stallion, Black Jack, as he led the procession, with the boots turned backwards in the stirrups. Black Jack was a spirited steed, a magnificent specimen of form and motion.

My father said President Kennedy's funeral was exactly like the service for my Uncle Zip, a World War II hero who died later of leukemia. Instantly I was angry with Mother because she refused to allow me to go to that funeral when I was little—and for not preparing me for death at all. I was certain that I would be handling President Kennedy's death (not to mention my life) much better if only she had been a better mother. At that moment, I hated her intensely and I didn't feel guilty about it at all.

****

A few weeks later, I came home from school once again to find my mother sitting in the living room with my father. While my mother sat demurely avoiding my eyes, my father explained that the judge had, upon my father's request, released Mother to his care. The judge also ordered my mother to take a drug called *Antabuse*, which would make her deathly ill if she took even one drink.

This was something new. My mother had not been sober–really sober–for as long as I could remember. I didn't know what to think and didn't have any hope that she would remain sober, Antabuse or no Antabuse. She had always found a way to get her liquor, and at that point, I didn't believe for a second that this would work. But I knew enough not to protest. The last time I objected, I had unleashed my father's rage, and I didn't want to do that again.

In the coming weeks, a surprising thing happened. My mother's personality began to show signs of change. She no longer had the attitude of a self-proclaimed royal heir. She talked more softly and she smiled a lot. She seemed more genuine than I had ever remembered her. She even seemed to display a few traits of a true "gracious lady," which was a decided improvement over her previous phony act.

And she was sober.

Still, I was wary and could not find it in myself to trust her because she had let me down so many times before. Her sobriety was only as a result of the court-ordered *Antabuse*. What the drug did or how it worked, I didn't understand; I only knew it kept her from drinking.

What was most puzzling was how my father was acting. He was like a teenager in love. It seemed so odd that, after all the heartache my mother had caused each of us, he not only seemed to have completely forgiven her, but he acted as if there had simply never been a problem at all. I had never heard of words like *codependency* or *putting the cork in the bottle*. I didn't understand the significance of the word *denial* when it referred to untreated addictions or undiscovered family dynamics. Instinctively I knew that the family constellation had shifted dramatically. Where had this left me?

****

Sometime during this period of my mother's sobriety, after President Kennedy's funeral, I realized I was going to die. Not immediately. It just hit me one day that I was a *mortal* and was not going to live forever. Later I learned this is called "coming to grips with our own mortality." I grew terrified to drive a car or to be out late with my friends. At night I would lie there thinking, *If I go to sleep, I might not wake up...* I never discussed my feelings with either of my parents, or even with my sister. But several nights when I was just too freaked out to be alone, I crawled into bed with my mother and father and begged them to let me sleep there. They never said no, but my father would just get up and go into the living room. I would sleep like a baby beside my mother, trusting her to keep me safe in the dark.

My parents never once asked me what was up with a seventeen year old being scared of the dark. I don't know what I would have told them if they *had* asked, and shudder to think what words of comfort they would have offered me. Or not.

****

Because I now had my driver's license, the responsibility fell to me to practice my driving by taking Mother to receive her dose of Antabuse twice a week. Daddy had taught me to drive in the mountains, where I had ridden so often on my horse.

"Drive as close to the edge as you can," he would say. "I'll let you know when you get too close." I think he knew I would eventually do my share of mountain driving, so he thought the best way to reduce my chances of having an accident was to start right out having me practice high up towards the tree line. I knew how steep those ravines were; I had ridden Lito up and down them for years. I tried not to think about the car careening off the bluff and smashing into bits at the bottom of the canyon.

When I drove Mother to get her pill, I wasn't concerned about falling off the edge of the road, though by the look on her face, she might have been. We usually drove in silence, with me concentrating on the road and my driving, and my mother sitting stiff and unnatural, leaning hard against the seat of the car as though impaled there by some undetectable demonic force. Sometimes she cried. Many times she just silently stared straight ahead. I didn't understand that her entire body was probably crying out for just one drink of alcohol, just one warming, calming, satisfying shot of whiskey to calm her nerves.

Just one–and then another.

At her request, I would remain in the car while she went inside. She clenched her fists tight as she walked to and from the door of the doctor's office. She must have found it quite demeaning. It reminded me of a movie I had seen about a man on death row, walking to his execution. She seldom spoke after she was done, but one day my mother volunteered that the nurse made her open her mouth to make sure she had swallowed the Antabuse. And once, and only once, she also told me about being at Pine Tree Mental Hospital.

Frozen in the driver's seat, I listened as she related her experiences in "the snake pit" my father had mentioned.

"There were some pretty strange people in that place," she said, staring straight ahead and wide-eyed, as if reliving the experience. "There was a man who thought he was Adolph Hitler, and he marched around all day yelling things in German. And there was a young girl who looked a little like you," she said, glancing at me and smiling tenderly. "She seemed so lost…" Her voice trailed off.

She also told me about the dreams–horrible nightmares that she had most of the nights she was there. "They told me some of it was the D-Ts."

"What's that?" I asked, wrinkling my nose.

"The 'D-T's'? Delirium tremens–it's what happens when the alcohol comes out of your system. I thought I saw things that weren't there, like things crawling or climbing or creeping around in the night." *Like you do when you're drunk*, I thought to myself. "Even when I was awake, in broad daylight, I saw things," she added.

She went on. "I had the scariest dreams, too, mostly about when I was a little girl." She paused a moment. "I dreamed…about being so very unhappy as a child. I dreamed about the way my father dragged us all around the country and then left my mother all alone with Ruth and me. I dreamed about how scared I was all the time."

For one brief moment, I pictured my mother not as the "gracious lady" she tried to pretend she was, but as she must have thought of herself as a child: tiny, defenseless, terrified, and always, always, the child that no one wanted.

Part II

The House in South Missouri,
Where My Mother Lived
As A Child, 1919

Chapter 10
A Brief History: Haunted Chambers

One need not be a chamber to be haunted;
One need not be a house;
The brain has corridors surpassing
Material place.

Emily Dickinson
Time and Eternity

In the year 1919, Woodrow Wilson had just been elected to his second term as President of the United States. Important child labor legislation had been passed three years earlier, and railroad workers won an unprecedented eight-hour workday. These political advancements, coupled with Wilson's promise "to keep the United States out of war," secured the necessary votes for him to stay in the White House.

Verel was now six years old. She understood none of the politics that went into Wilson's reelection. She was more interested in playing with the new doll she received the previous Christmas. The most important things to Verel were her doll and the many farm animals that the family kept at their rented farmstead near her birthplace of Behler, in western Kansas.

Her father Walter's latest misadventure was the purchase of a plot of land in southeastern Missouri. He bought the land on a whim, when he was out on one of his mysterious excursions. The land was three miles from a wide spot in the road called Crocker, and seven miles to the nearest railroad station at Waynesville. That was where Walter shipped his motley herd of cattle by rail once the land had been purchased. By this time, Verel and Ruth's brothers were nearly grown, with the exception of Aubrey, who was just seventeen. When her mother, Birdie May, complained to Walter about another move, the argument became heated.

Finally, in a weak moment, Walter delegated the responsibility to young Aubrey to make a trip to Crocker and look the place over before the move occurred.

Aubrey was a shy boy, "the baby" among six brothers. He had not been given much responsibility until this time. Birdie doubted whether Aubrey could even successfully make the trip alone, much less be counted on to assess the conditions there, and report back with any useful information. But she agreed to let him go, hoping he would come back with more information than she already had.

Aubrey set out by train, and returned several days later.

"It's a right nice place, Ma," was all he said. He didn't mention the rocky land, or the steep hills. The boy must have thought it unimportant that the land had no well, and no creeks or streams running anywhere nearby. He neglected to note that the "house" was just a pieced-together shanty, and living off the land would be as unlikely there as on the surface of the moon.

By the time Aubrey returned with his less-than-detailed report, Walter had left again, according to him, to "take care of business" before the move. His instructions, upon his departure, were to have Aubrey escort Birdie, Verel and Ruth from the family farm to their new abode. With the meager herd of cattle entrusted to the railroad, Walter hitched up the horses, Ole Mike and Bessie, both of whom had seen better days, and rumbled down the country road and on to his next grand adventure.

There wasn't much to pack for the trip. The few household items the family possessed fit easily into an old steamer trunk that had belonged to Aunt Annie. Together, they had no more than a couple dozen items of clothing. Farm implements, garden tools and horse harnesses were hastily bundled together. Since Birdie hadn't yet seen the property, it wasn't known what would be needed there.

"We'll make do with what we have," she stated resolutely. She was accustomed to these surprise moves; her husband had been doing this to her for years. The fact she protested at all was a surprise in itself, but in the end, of course, she just resigned herself and went along. The older boys came to say their goodbyes, and Stanley tried unsuccessfully one last time to talk his mother out of going.

Though Verel would never have challenged either of her parents, she knew Birdie loved Walter in her own way. Birdie was smart enough to know that just because her husband always came back eventually did not constitute reliability on his part. Yet she pressed on, ever faithful, ever supportive. And she was always, always a good and kind mother to her children.

****

Whatever Birdie and her two daughters had conjured up in their minds about what their new home would be like, I am certain they were all quite surprised at what they really encountered. They arrived at the Waynesville rail station on a sweltering late July day, just a few days before Verel's seventh birthday, greeted by their father and the two faithful, but exhausted horses. The wagon, hardly fit for the trip from western Kansas in the first place, was now held together with bailing twine and prayers. The harnesses were dried and cracked, and the seat springs were rusted so badly, they threatened to give way completely with every bump. The few head of cattle, which made the trip from Kirksville in a car at the end of the train, were unloaded and roped together for the trek to the family's new land.

Verel sat between her parents in the front of the old wagon. Her older sister Ruth sat in back atop boxes and bundles, and Aubrey followed on foot behind the cattle. Though the ride was bumpy and dusty, Verel was both scared and excited. This was certainly different territory than Western Kansas! She gazed at the scores of dogwood trees, not knowing yet how she would grow to love their fragrant blossoms in the springtime.

The dirt roads through the prairie grasses gave way to uneven, rocky wagon trails, as they started up into the hill country. Verel turned around and saw that the road was getting steeper and steeper as they traveled. The horses strained against their riggings, snorting and shaking their heads up and down in protest. Her father slapped the reins against their rumps and shouted, "Git up!" She felt the back wagon wheels spin as they failed to grip the path. Wondering if the trip would ever end, she thought about her soft bed back in Behler.

It took eleven hours to drive the reluctant and worn team of horses, and the trip-weary cows to the place they would now call "home." "Home indeed!" Birdie muttered under her breath. Except for a small clearing where the buildings sat, the land was steep and rocky, generally unfit for farming of any sort. Aubrey joked that the plot was so steep, the horses might fall right out of the pasture! His father shot him a mean glance.

It was clear from the beginning that there was no living to be made there, neither from the dairy cattle they brought with them, nor from any crops that could be coaxed from the reluctant land. The cabin was nothing more than a tar paper shack, scrunched up against the mountain side, as if it was afraid it would topple down the steep slope altogether. The closest water was at Crocker, three miles away. The cattle and horses had to be driven there to obtain water for the week. By the time the round trip was made, the animals were so thirsty, they had all but consumed the upcoming week's ration.

Verel had one outstanding memory of the move, when they opened up a barrel and she found her favorite dolly hidden among the shredded newspaper. It felt like she could call this place home now that she had that doll.

After the family was somewhat settled, they discovered that the nearest school was at Crocker. Ruth and Verel had to walk the three miles each day, starting out at dawn and returning through woods that barely saw daylight even on the brightest of days. Often, the girls came upon men—laborers, loggers, moon shiners, and, quite possibly, crazed ax murderers—there in the thick forest. Ruth was old enough and smart enough to know that two young girls in the woods alone were no match for these men, should they be spotted. The girls quickly learned alternate routes as a means of protecting themselves. More than once they hid quietly in the underbrush until Ruth thought it was safe to go on.

At age seven, Verel didn't know exactly why they needed protection. After all, she had been raised in a houseful of rowdy men. Perhaps it was best that she did not understand until many years later what dangers lay along those Ozark mountain trails.

Birdie must have been naïve herself about the dangers because she had little Verel ride Ole Mike to the tiny postal station at a country store a few miles down the mountain to get the mail every Saturday. Verel was an excellent rider, along with her six brothers who had taught her how to handle these draft horse-sized animals when they lived on the farm at Behler. They had even taught her to "trick ride," holding her high in the air above their heads like a circus performer. She must have felt important; the star of the show, in the pasture on the rented land, even if her only admirers were the boys, her sister, and occasionally her mother, if she found a moment to put down what she was doing and watch. Perhaps young Verel thought of those happier times when she rode through the Missouri woods to retrieve the mail. Perhaps she spun tales in her tiny head of escaping the men her sister feared so much, of coaxing Ole Mike into a gallop, down the rocky slopes and into town, with her white-blonde braids flying from under her bonnet.

The family stayed in South Missouri less than two years. By that time, the money was gone, and Walter had long since taken off on his next big adventure. With a weary heart, Birdie telegraphed Stanley and asked him to come and get them. No one ever knew what happened to the land there. It was never clear if Walter had bought it outright or still owed money on it when they left. The important thing was that the South Missouri incident was really the turning point in Birdie's life, and subsequently in Verel and Ruth's lives as well.

When they left the mountain place, Stanley moved them to the northeast Missouri college town of Kirksville, where he and his wife lived. There, Stanley vowed to keep his mother from ever again having to follow his father's absurd and unattainable dreams. Birdie's sons pooled their money and bought a large old house across from Kirksville Teachers College.

And thus was born my grandmother's rooming house.

Chapter 11
Mrs. Rollins' Rooming House

Mrs. Rollins' Rooming House, as it came to be known, was much more than just a three-story building to Ruth and Verel. It was a place for them to grow and develop in relative physical comfort, as respectable young citizens in a booming college town. Their escape from the hillbilly life must have seemed so complete! In Kirksville the girls developed lasting friendships with classmates, something they had sorely missed while living in the southern Missouri hills.

The girls also eventually began dating. College students were always around—young men, mostly, who rented the rooms my grandmother had to offer. The renters were not just from Missouri, but also from places like Pittsburgh and Cleveland and New York and Chicago, arriving to study osteopathy, for which the college was known, or to major in science and engineering. The college students were smart young men and women, with a grand future ahead of them. Verel thought their eyes glowed in a special way because of all their knowledge. She longed to be like them: young, educated, worldly, and free of the typical teenage feelings of worthlessness. Aunt Annie's visits didn't help; the woman continued to refer to my mother as "the child that no one wanted" well into my mother's young adult years.

Verel, now about 12 years old, slept on a cot in the kitchen so her own room could be rented out. She was a good girl, and caused her mother little worry. She and her sister helped around the rooming house, but never for pay. It was expected that they would be as much a part of the operation as their mother. Although there were new child labor laws in the United States, most families still believed a child should help in a family business without pay. Stanley had trained as a builder, and he saw to it that all of his brothers had work in his construction business. Birdie never had to worry about fixing things around the property. The boys were always willing to help.

Like many tradesmen, my uncles all became Masons. Some also became Shriners, and their wives joined the Eastern Star. Verel remembered some of her brothers and their wives coming by the rooming house on occasion, dressed in their finery, on their way to a Shriners' Ball. Dressed in their best three-piece suits, the men wore their red fez hats perched proudly on their heads. Their wives were decked out in floor-length evening gowns, sparkling with sequins and pearls. Someone brought a camera once and recorded the event for the family photo album. Birdie admired the way they looked and commented that they all must be pretty successful to be wearing such expensive-looking outfits.

Verel remembered another occasion when her brothers came to show off their costumes, only that time they were sporting white robes and they carrying pointed hoods with eyeholes cut out of them. Neither Birdie nor her two young daughters understood what the outfits signified, but the boys and their wives were very proud of their snow-white garb. Prejudice grew in the family exponentially, and the meaning of the white robes insidiously wove its web in, around, and through the Rollins family. There were no cameras that night.

****

When Verel was young, her mother was no stranger to hard work, but working in the boarding house seemed different. This time, her efforts were her own. Verel loved how her mother created enticing dishes on the old copper-clad stove in the big open kitchen. Pies and cakes and cookies, and an endless supply of baking powder biscuits wove their spells around all who entered there. Though Birdie didn't serve meals to the renters, there were always enough good snacks for hungry college students on their way to and from class.

Verel liked the attention she got from those college students, especially the men. She was growing into a beautiful young woman, her white-blonde hair turning to a rich brown as she reached her teen years. She had dainty features and a flawless complexion. Her eyes were bright with expectation and her mind was filled with possibilities. She had been incredibly shy and self-conscious as a child, not surprising in a household of mysteries and denial. Not surprising, for the child of a deranged father who glided in and out of her life with false hopes and broken promises. Not surprising for the child of a mother who kept her husband's slippery secrets well.

Still, the words of Aunt Annie rang in her ears: "There's Verel, the child that no one wanted." But slowly, almost imperceptibly, young Verel was preparing to burst forth from her shyness and announce herself to the waiting world.

****

When Ruth was in high school and Verel in the eighth grade, a revival came to town in the summertime. All of Kirksville was abuzz, like when the Ringling Brothers circus had been there a few years earlier. A huge tent was erected in an open field, and "front men" came around to the churches to encourage participation.

On the first night of the revival, the steamy Missouri air was charged with anticipation as the townspeople flooded in to take their seats and see the show. Minstrels performed old-time gospel tunes, inviting the crowd to sing along. A seemingly endless parade of people took turns relating their personal stories of healing and victory. "Testimonials," they were called, all in the name of the Lord.

Finally, the evangelist took center stage and preached "hellfire and brimstone" for over two hours–longer than some could handle. Restless children gave in to sleep and stretched across their parents' laps. Some young people left to escape the discomfort the preacher's words brought on. Others remained glued to their seats, and when the altar call was given, dozens flocked to the front of the tent.

Among them were twelve-year-old Verel and her sister Ruth. The girls were given white robes and told to put them on in a smaller makeshift tent that served as a changing room. They were both taken out behind the tent to the "baptismal waters," a three hundred gallon stock tank filled with well water, with steps leading up to the rim. Then, one by one, all who wished to be saved by the cleansing Blood of the Living Christ took their turns being fully submerged—dying in Christ—and rising out of the refreshing water as "new creatures."

Perhaps it was the only bath some had taken in a long time. For Ruth, it was truly a turning point in her life. She remained among "The Faithful" for the rest of her days, attending church regularly, never touching alcohol or tobacco. She married young, and her mother sobbed when she and her new husband moved to Wichita, Kansas. She eventually became the state president of the Women's Christian Temperance Union.

Her sister chose a different path.

****

Verel soon discovered the college library. As early as junior high, she spent many hours studying in that library, often until closing time. She became an excellent student, graduating high school as valedictorian and as salutatorian of her college class. She completed her bachelor's degree in three years by taking course overloads and summer classes.

While studying at the library, she also spent time reading and studying books on etiquette: Emily Post's *Etiquette in Society, in Business, in Politics and at Home*, and *The Amy Vanderbilt Complete Book of Etiquette*. Which fork did one use to eat salad? How do you write a thank you note? When is it appropriate to call on a bereaving family?

Verel vowed to become just like the women she read about in those books. In fact, she spent so much time in the library and became so absorbed in reading about "the good life" that she eventually committed murder.

She was not assisted by Colonel Mustard nor Professor Plum, as in the popular board game. Her accomplices were Misses Post and Vanderbilt. There was no wrench or candlestick used in this crime of passion; her weapons were the words on the pages of those etiquette books. There, amidst the stacks filled with books about the world outside, Verel and her imaginary assistants slowly, methodically bludgeoned to death "the child that no one wanted."

In that child's place, Verel created a fantasy personality, a vision of a young woman who was ready to meet the world head on. The vision was of a *gracious lady*, of exaggerated achievements and imaginary talents. Young Verel made herself believe with all her heart that she was somehow "special" and that she should only associate with others who shared her sense of self-importance.

Eventually, Verel's narcissism completely engulfed her, rendering her incapable of any empathy. She entered adulthood, propped up with a sense of entitlement, blaming the world and not herself for any lack of success in her endeavors. With this metamorphosis came a complete lack of any responsibility for her own actions and the self-righteous expectation that others in her world were there only to do her bidding. Years later, when depression set in and she discovered alcohol to alter her mood, she unleashed her fury at her own family, forcing them to continue the desperate and futile attempt to make her happy.

After all, it was and always would be, all about her.

****

Birdie had no spare money to send her daughters to college. Verel worked part time at the five-and-dime store, but had little hope of ever earning enough money to pay tuition. Seeing great promise in her little sister's academic ability, Ruth gave all of her savings to Verel for her college tuition, an amazingly generous and selfless gift in those times.

The dark side of this era, again, was Walter, who still attempted to preside over the family activities when his travels brought him homeward. It was during this time that his mental health appeared to be at its worst, disrupting all the happiness and success the family had achieved whenever he entered the scene. Verel remembered him sitting in a chair, banging his head against the wall and repeating a word, such as "stupid," over and over again. His depression drove him to bed for days on end.

One summer day, when one of the brothers' wives brought over some ice cream, Verel drew the "lucky" straw, because she was his "favorite." She was asked to take some ice cream to her father as he lay in a dark bedroom in the back of the house. The shades were drawn tight against the window sash, and the musty smell of sweat and urine came from the bed where her father lay moaning.

Many mornings before she and Ruth left for school, Walter would play his "sympathy card" and tell the girls they needed to kiss him before leaving because he would not be there when they got home. Verel and Ruth never knew exactly what he meant by this; they were too innocent to understand his behavior as a symptom of depression or a possible threat of suicide. But they had to accept the fact that this was his only home, and he was a part of their lives, at least until his mood swung back to the frenzied side and he was off on another hapless quest.

Walter's adventures soon became few and far between. He was growing older, and his aging body could no longer follow what his lightning-hot mind tried to dictate during its emotional upswings. It must have been hard to watch him, like an ice-bound whale, wanting with all his being to pursue the next imagined thrill but being locked into a body that would not—could not—follow the mind's insane will any longer.

Chapter 12
Pilots of the Purple Twilight

For I dipt into the future,
far as human eye could see,
Saw the Vision of the world,
and all the wonder that would be;
Saw the heavens filled with commerce,
argosies of magic sails,
Pilots of the purple twilight,
dropping down the costly bales;
Heard the heavens fill with shouting,
and there rain'd a ghastly dew.
From the nations' airy navy
grappling in the central blue.

Alfred, Lord Tennyson
Locksley Hall, 1909

In June, 1909, a baby boy was born in a farmhouse near Bible Grove, Missouri. His parents were William Blaine and his wife "Altie," as she was called. They were of Scottish and Irish descent, with strong Christian values. The child was named Mayhue Delbert. Mayhue was number eight out of thirteen children, which means his mother was pregnant for nearly ten years of her life. Pregnant or not, she had a huge job taking care of all those kids.

William and Altie were good to their children and raised them in a God-fearing home. Altie still found time to help neighbors who were ill, and she helped deliver their babies (she had lots of experience with that). A strong supporter of education, William served on the school board for many years.

****

Orville and Wilbur Wright conducted the first recorded flight of a controllable, powered, heavier-than-air machine in 1903. After Wilbur flew a whopping 852 feet in 59 seconds at the reckless speed of 9.8 miles per hour, the world was introduced to the amazing prospect of "commerce in the air."

When Mayhue was a mere lad of seventeen, he fell in love with airplanes. In the county seat of Memphis, only about ten miles northeast of his parents' farm, was a tiny, fledgling business called the Pheasant Aircraft Company. Setting in motion events that never would otherwise have occurred, this small company changed the course of Mayhue's life.

The summer Mayhue completed high school, Pheasant Aircraft owner, Lee Briggs, was running a private "flying school" in Memphis and working on the production of a new airplane. Briggs was at the Scotland County Fair, demonstrating one of the planes he had purchased to train pilots. Mayhue was at that county fair and asked Mr. Briggs to give him a ride.

"It'll cost you two bucks, son," Briggs said, always the entrepreneur.

That was a lot of money for a young farm boy in those days, and Mayhue didn't know where he would get the two dollars. But he knew he had to have a ride in that airplane. He went home and begged his father to loan him the money. For three days, he followed his dad all around the farm place while they did their chores. He said he'd do anything his dad asked of him, but he wanted to ride in that airplane so badly, he couldn't stand it. After much protesting, his father finally gave Mayhue two dollars out of the household money, not exactly obtaining endorsement from his skeptical and fearful mother. She could not begin to fathom why her young son wanted to get into one of these "new-fangled flying machines." Travel on the ground was treacherous enough, and she thought it was foolishness at best, and insanity at worst, to want to fly in an airplane.

With the money in hand, Mayhue raced back to town after the chores were done and found Briggs, who was busy extolling the virtues of flying machines to a growing audience. Mayhue gave Briggs his two dollars and said, "Take me up in that plane, please, sir!"

The next thing he knew, he was sitting behind Briggs as he revved the engine and raised the old biplane into the air. As Briggs dipped the double wings to bank the craft into a turn, the plane rose higher and higher above the fairgrounds, above the townspeople, above the little dots that used to be sheep and cattle and horses and pigs. Mayhue felt the wind in his face and the plane wings lifting and dragging. Briggs was talking to him, explaining things, but he couldn't hear him because of the sound of the engine—a beautiful noise, my father thought—the most amazing sound he'd ever heard in his life. They were gliding now over the pieces of color that were Scotland County, the green of the corn fields, the brown of the drying beans, and the muddy gray of the Fabius River spreading out below them like the pieces of his mother's quilts. When they came down, Mayhue was still floating, and the feeling lasted a very long time. For a lifetime, in fact.

****

Altie was less than overjoyed when her young son announced his plans to attend State Teacher's College in Kirksville, Missouri. It wasn't that she was against college; quite the contrary, she valued education highly. But Mayhue's only reason for wanting to attend the college in Kirksville was to obtain entry into the Army Air Corps Flight Training School, at Kelly Field in San Antonio, Texas.

"I need three years of college to be admitted, Ma!" he pleaded. "After I finish, I'll have a good job either flying mail planes or passenger planes, or even staying in the Army Air Corps for the rest of my life!"

"What if there's another war?" she blurted out tearfully. She had lost her second son shortly after he enlisted in the Army, during the 1918 Spanish flu pandemic. She didn't approve of fighting and she didn't want to lose another child. "I don't want you becoming one of those dogfighters like they had in Europe during the World War!"

"There isn't going to be another war, Ma! We took care of all that!"

World War I was indeed called "The War to End All Wars." It proved to be a complete break with the "old world order" and the end of absolute monarchy in Europe. The United States became an "associated power" (as opposed to a full member of the Allies) in April of 1917. After a long and bloody conflict spanning several years, November 11, 1918 marked the Allies' armistice with Germany.

The brief period of prosperity that our nation experienced after Armistice Day was not felt by everyone—especially not by the Blaine family. Altie could not imagine how they would come up with tuition money for Mayhue. Although life at the Blaine family farm went on largely unchanged even when much of the nation plunged into poverty following the stock market crash of 1929, Altie had her hands full enough.

With help from the children, she managed to cook immense meals every day in her huge kitchen. She canned bushels of tomatoes and beans and corn, and dozens of cut-up chickens, plus my father's favorite, sausage balls. When Altie opened those jars of sausage balls midwinter, the aroma would knock you on the floor. The Blaines never went hungry, but there was no spare money for a college education.

****

Classes were starting soon at Kirksville, and Mayhue had to find a way to go to college in spite of his mother's protest. He knew his parents couldn't help him with money for tuition. He worked at odd jobs to pay back the two dollars his father had loaned him to take the plane ride. But he had no "get-rich-quick" schemes to raise more money.

Finally, he turned to his oldest brother, Cecil, who loaned him the money for his first semester at college. Mayhue found work in Kirksville, paid back every penny his brother loaned him and earned the rest of the money he needed to get through three years of school. He joined the Army Reserve Officers Training Corps. He excelled in math and science and studied all of his subjects intensely; he knew he would not gain admittance to the flight school with poor grades.

Chapter 13
The Importance of Flying

We welcome passion, for the mind is briefly let off duty.
Mignon McLaughlin
The Neurotic's Notebook, 1960

It was a glorious spring day, the kind that tugs at all of your senses simultaneously and beckons them to new life. All along the city streets in Kirksville, the flower bulbs had awaked from their winter slumber and now burst forth like brilliant jewels in colors of crimson, periwinkle and sunshine yellow. The birds' songs infused the air with music and put a spring in the step of all within earshot. Children, cooped up indoors far too long, ventured out to begin their annual love affair with the warm weather.

It was a day such as this in the year 1930, when Verel was standing on the corner of the college campus, across from the rooming house, talking to a friend. Young Mayhue Blaine walked by them as they lingered, exchanging comments about their professor. He tipped his hat to my mother. Later, in a letter he wrote to her, he described that encounter like this:

> "I many times see a rosy-cheeked, blushing little girl, in a bright-colored plaid dress that was modestly long for the day, standing on a corner, talking to her friend, while a dizzy-looking country lad caught her eye…and then immediately occupied his mind with airplanes. Remember? She is an awful sweet girl, you know?"

Verel's recollection of that day was a little more direct. Though she had never laid eyes on Mayhue before, she simply said to her friend after he had passed by, "That's the man I'm going to marry!"

Mayhue and Verel happened to meet again on a few occasions, and soon he mustered the courage to ask her out on a date. In those days, dating meant walking everywhere, to the movies to see *Anna Christie* starring Greta Garbo, and *The Big Trail* starring John Wayne; to the drug store to share a strawberry phosphate; or to the library to study. There were parties at Mayhue's fraternity house and dinners with Verel's honor society friends, not to mention football games and bonfires. Mayhue was three years older than Verel, and was in his last year of college that fall. Verel didn't date him exclusively at first, as her good looks and quick wit assured her of many suitors. Though she always thought her sister Ruth was the beauty, it was clearly Verel who drew more attention from the men. She was lithe and attractive with chestnut brown hair and a sweet face.

The two continued dating, and Mayhue borrowed a friend's car on several occasions to take Verel home to see his family. Photos of Verel during those visits show her to be dressed to the hilt, from her jaunty little hats to her well-coordinated dresses and shoes. All of the Blaine family thought this young woman was some sort of royalty, and Verel played right into their fantasy. She reveled in their attention.

Mayhue was completely smitten with Verel Rollins. Before he left Kirksville for flight school, they both knew this was more than a passing fancy. He promised to write to her, and did so faithfully, almost every day while he was in flight training.

****

In the fall of 1931, Mayhue arrived in San Antonio, Texas, fresh faced and starry-eyed, to begin the first leg of his trip to flight. All primary training was being conducted at the newly created Randolph Field. Mayhue dived into the physics of lift and drag, and the mechanics of operating the seemingly innumerable levers and knobs on the control panels in these early airplane cockpits.

In that group of young recruits (all men), Mayhue made many friends. One young man, Willy Taylor, became his best buddy.

"Willy was a cowboy in an airplane," was how Mayhue described him.

Indeed, it was Willy who got Mayhue to loosen up and have a little fun while he was in flying school. Willy was afraid of nothing, and he lived every day like it was his last. Both men even looked alike, with sandy blonde hair and slight builds. Willy was a little shorter than Mayhue's five-foot-nine, but his small stature didn't make him any less brave. It was Willy who, early in their training together, led the way to their first "bridge dive," flying *under* the area's river bridges instead of over them. In those days, there was really very little control over what the pilots of these aircraft were doing— except their own consciences. Though injuries and fatalities occurred with alarming frequency, every young pilot believed he was invincible and would never have to answer for his airborne antics.

Mayhue also challenged Willy, but in the intellectual realm. He far exceeded Willy's prowess in the technical side of flying, and tutored students in math and science at the college in Kirksville. "I just gave Willy an algebra problem and he is struggling vainly over it," he wrote Verel. "I like to stick it to him."

Soon the two men graduated from the Advanced Flying School at Randolph and were transferred to Selfridge Field in Detroit, Michigan. Willy also lived life to its fullest after hours. Mayhue wrote to Verel about Willy often drinking heavily at night and becoming involved with some "loose women." Once, they flew to St. Louis on a training mission and stayed the night.

"The flying was OK, but it was the party after we got there. The worst I have ever seen. Turned into a free-for-all. I got a skinned shin, but that was all. As usual, I was the light drinker, trying to be a good fellow and stay sober, and take care of everyone. But trying to rule a bunch of drunks is a tough task, and soon I became very unpopular. We were just lucky not to get thrown in the jug."

Another time after a night of partying, Willy brought a woman to the apartment the two men shared. Mayhue was shocked and indignant. But ever the caretaker, he fixed up the couch for the woman to sleep on. Willy passed out in the bedroom.

"A drunken woman is the most disgusting damn thing on earth!" he wrote to Verel prophetically.

Still, he and Willy never had any serious harsh words between them, and they remained friends throughout their training and for many years afterwards. In another letter, Mayhue described how he and Willy and the others would sit around between training sessions and talk about all the places they wanted to fly.

"Willy and I have flown all over the United States, and we are back again," he wrote, describing their flights of fancy. "That's a weakness or a virtue, characteristic of every flyer, to do lots of 'ground flying.' You know, we always do our best flying on the ground. But, at least it's a pastime that we really enjoy." The pilot's equivalent of singing in the shower bolstered the young recruits' spirits and kept them focused on their goals.

****

Mayhue also wrote Verel about the pilots who were killed during training. It must have bothered him as time went on, because he never failed to comment on it in his letters. He wrote her the names of each pilot who was killed, saying, "he got it," as if he couldn't bring himself to write the words "crash" or "fatality." One lieutenant he described was "flying blind in fog, and couldn't see the ground. He bailed out but he was too low for his chute to open."

Then, waxing philosophical, his letter continued, "Yes, Verel, you can, and must, caution me about being careful. Possibly I might heed your advice a little better than you think. Flying isn't all glory and glamour and heroics. It has its undesirable qualities just as does anything else. There are countless thrills and plenty of excitement, very true, but sometimes these qualities take on gruesome characteristics. I am seeing all sides of it quite frequently."

****

Mayhue actually crashed a plane at Pana, Illinois once. He wasn't hurt but he caused quite a stir among the town folks. He had the plane disassembled and shipped back to Selfridge Field, where he almost faced a court marshal for his actions. Even back then, the Air Corps conducted site investigations of crashes, which was difficult to do when the plane was safely packed in crates.

The following summer, he was out on a training mission near northeast Missouri, and he made a beeline for his folks' farm. He "buzzed" the farm for several minutes and then landed the plane (safely) in his father's cornfield. The locals came from miles around to see the plane and its pilot. The old timers in Scotland County talk about it to this day.

But in spite of the dangers, he continued to be enchanted with the entire idea of flight. Again, in letters to my mother: "I really like to fly. I am going to teach you someday. I flew an hour last night. Had a lot of fun. It was overcast, and I went up thru the clouds. The moon was shining and it was just as clear and sparkling as anything. Surely was impressive. I don't remember ever being above the clouds when it was any prettier. I thought of you, too, and wished you could have been along. Then I came home and dreamed of you last night."

****

Though there were stars in Mayhue's eyes, and in the skies he flew at night, the news of war in other parts of the world was having a sobering effect on the young pilots. In February of 1932, after hearing of Japan's invasion of Manchuria, he wrote: "It looks like things are pretty hot over there. China is making a good showing. I suppose time will tell. We haven't received any official dope lately."

And a few days later: "China and Japan are going like hell, and as soon as they succeed in killing off ten or fifteen million, I think they will quit. They need the room you know."

At that time in the early 1930's, it did not appear that the United States would be involved in the conflicts brewing in other parts of the world. And so, when Mayhue finished his commitment to the Army Air Corps, he applied for a copilot's position with United Air Lines out of Kansas City, Missouri. Willy applied there too and both men were hired immediately.

****

Meanwhile, Verel completed her bachelor's degree and accepted a position as a teacher in a one-room schoolhouse near Ness City, Kansas. One of her brothers was on the school board there and she lived with his family. Her salary was to be $50 a month, but because of the economic situation in the United States and the rest of the world at that time, she was never paid any money. She taught for room and board.

Actually, western Kansas was about the *worst* place to be during the Great Depression. Following several monstrous dust storms, a huge area of the western plain states of Kansas, Oklahoma and Texas became known as the Dust Bowl. Farmers were left with impossible conditions in which to plant wheat, corn, and other cash crops. There was little market for them anyway. Very few weathered the economic storms of that era, least of all the Rollins family. News came from New York City of stockbrokers who flung themselves out of top floor windows in despair. Hopelessness became a way of life.

When Verel wrote Mayhue of her living conditions, he was overcome with compassion and concern. Mayhue clearly wanted to rescue her from any more distress. In early December, he wrote to Birdie and asked permission to marry Verel. The answer was an overwhelming yes.

His actual proposal was less than romantic. He wrote to her: "If you want to, we can just as well go on with our plans and get married, though I do hate like hell to take on a wife with the possibility that I may go home and eat off her folks occasionally from necessity."

Mayhue sent her a train ticket and Verel came to Kansas City to join him when school let out for Christmas. She brought only a tiny suitcase and a small box of possessions, and no money. They were married the day after Christmas by a justice of the peace. Verel wore a simple, white lace, two-piece dress with a black velvet collar, and her groom wore his only suit. And thus began their sixty-eight year marriage.

****

During the early years of Verel and Mayhue's life together, there was no drinking in their household. The prohibition era ended the year they were married, but liquor was expensive and Mayhue knew not to drink when he flew.

Prophetically, two other men in the United States were struggling with alcohol addiction. Bill W. and Dr. Bob, as they are known today, began an organization called Alcoholics Anonymous in 1935. AA has helped countless numbers of people all over the world with alcohol addiction. Those with many other addictions have used its principles as well. It would be many years before Verel ever had need of the organization, and even then, AA would not be enough to help her break free from her addiction.

Chapter 14
Melancholy Days

The melancholy days are come, the saddest of the year...
William Cullen Bryant
The Death of Flowers

Needless to say, married life during the Depression was a challenge. Mayhue and Verel lived in what my mother always called a "cold-water flat," on the third floor of a dilapidated apartment building. They had a bedroom, a bath and a small sitting room, with a tiny "pullman kitchen," a kitchenette recessed into a wall and concealed by double doors. There were two dingy windows, both of which revealed a spectacular view of the brick wall of the building next door. The lighting was poor but my mother scrubbed and scrubbed until the apartment was at least clean and marginally livable.

Verel spent many nights alone in that place, listening to the tiny short wave radio Mayhue bought at a pawnshop. The words that were most precious to her ears were "Blaine over Kansas City," which meant he was approaching the landing strip and would soon have his United Airlines DC3 safely on the ground. Before long, he would climb the stairs and join her in the tiny apartment they called home.

Verel quickly discovered she was not as alone as she thought when her new husband was away. One night she heard scuffling near the icebox. When she went to investigate, she found a rat gnawing on a bit of bread that had fallen from the counter top. Too angry to be scared, she grabbed one Mayhue's golf clubs and killed the rat on sight.

Mayhue felt fortunate to have a good job, at least when he first started with the airline. But soon the Great Depression found its way to the young couple's doorstep and sorrowful times were upon them. Mayhue received word that all United Airlines junior pilots (himself among them) were being grounded and would be dispersed throughout the country to sell airfares door-to-door. They were astounded. Mayhue was a pilot, not a door-to-door salesman! They were struggling to make ends meet as it was. But the Depression respected no one, and within a month after they had married, he was sent to New York City to pound the streets.

He wrote Verel letters full of frustration. "We are to contact every office in each of these buildings. That means a building the size of the Empire State Building will require better than a week to work! In other words, we will be crashing offices, or attempting such, without any announcement or appointment! All in all, they have about six or eight months' work planned for us. Unless we can produce results in about a month, we probably will be fired." Then he added, "You can't make a high-pressure salesman out of a farm boy overnight."

Mayhue suffered through this period for about a year, with Verel eventually joining him on the East Coast for several months. But he was looking for options. Early the following year, he took a position as a copilot with Trans World Airlines, which like United, was headquartered in centrally located Kansas City.

****

Sad news arrived from Kirksville. Birdie had been diagnosed with breast cancer, and since both Verel and Ruth had moved away by this time, their brothers were calling the shots regarding her treatment.

"There were dozens of good doctors right there in Kirksville," Verel lamented over the years. "But the boys insisted they take her all the way out to western Kansas to those men they knew."

Verel never completely understood the medical facts surrounding her mother's cancer. All she knew was that these doctors removed both of Birdie's breasts using some type of cauterizing tool, leaving raw flesh exposed. The pain of the procedure and the subsequent recovery must have been excruciating. Verel was devastated but there had been nothing she could do.

The next brilliant family decision, made by the brothers, was to put the rooming house up for sale and propose that their mother simply move from one of her grown children's homes to another in a sort of "hospice-on-the-run" program. There were no affordable long-term care facilities in those days; most elderly people just moved in with one of their children. But the brothers' plan meant that all of the sisters-in-law, plus Verel and Ruth became rotating caretakers for a frail and desperately ill woman who hadn't the energy to walk across the street.   It wasn't so bad in Kirksville, going from house to house only a few blocks apart. But Ruth and three of the brothers had settled in various towns in Kansas, and Verel was in Kansas City, making a long train trip necessary for Grandmother to reach any of their homes.

Not surprisingly, she didn't make the complete circuit before the end came. When it was Verel's turn, she picked her mother up at the train station and took her straight to her own doctor. X-rays were taken. The cancer had metastasized to her bones. All Verel could do was to take her home and try to make her comfortable in the only bed in their apartment. Young Verel cleaned and changed the dressing on her mother's breasts and tried to get her to eat, but it was already too late. As usual, Mayhue was flying. Alone and frightened, Verel called a friend of hers who was a nurse. She came right over.

Birdie Mae Rollins died in Verel and Mayhue's bed early the next morning. Verel's friend knew she was gone, and called the coroner. It was hours before he was able to get there, so Verel and her friend sat quietly in the little parlor and waited. Finally, the friend had to leave too, so Verel sat alone. She didn't even leave the apartment to call her brothers on the phone downstairs until Mayhue arrived. Perhaps this was when Verel's psyche began to slip off its moorings. Fearful of death herself, she was devastated over her mother's passing, especially since it had occurred in her care.

"I heard the death rattle and I didn't even know what it was!" she would wail years later when she was drinking heavily. "And the first thing Mayhue did was to look in her wallet to see if she had any *money*!" This single action of her husband's, perhaps thoughtless, perhaps only practical, gave Verel ammunition with which to blast him time and time again, for decades to come. Family history was learned not by the events themselves, or the accomplishments of a lifetime, but by Verel's graphic descriptions of the heinous crimes committed by those involved.

****

Mayhue always said the runways at the Kansas City airport were tricky to land on because of the river. He said that the pilots, especially in the early days, sometimes made more than one pass at the runway before getting the plane lined up to land (perhaps the origin of the mystery aviation phrase, "final approach"). He always talked about the early system they had for what would eventually be called instrument flying. Before radar came along, the planes were equipped with a "directional beam," an unsophisticated device that could tell the pilot if he was on course. The problem was if he got off course, due to weather or pilot error, it was anybody's guess whether he needed to go up or down, left or right. That's when the pilot had to rely on his own keen sense of direction and balance. The expression "on the beam" came from this early navigational equipment.

In mid-October of 1937, Mayhue ran into his old friend Willy after not seeing him for several weeks. The two swapped the latest stories about their respective lives, Mayhue extolling the virtues of married life, while Willy (still single) insisted he wouldn't trade his freedom for a woman. Filled with bravado, Willy relayed tales of his airborne antics, even then. The two men bid farewell, and Mayhue went home to the little apartment he shared with his wife.

Willy was the copilot on one of United's "Mainliners," described in its day as a "giant luxury plane." His flight was to be from Kansas City to Salt Lake City, Utah. The plane made a routine landing in Cheyenne, picking up a few passengers. There was a snowstorm brewing over the mountains and visibility was decreasing. At 10:18 p.m., the crew lost contact with the control tower. Then, without warning, the passenger airliner slammed into the side of the mountain.

It was the worst air disaster since the invention of flight. All were dead: sixteen passengers (seventeen if you counted an unborn child), and three crewmembers. Willy Taylor was among them.

Mayhue mourned for Willy like he was a brother. The crash was a terrible event in the lives of all commercial pilots, and for everyone who worked in the pioneering jobs in the infant industry of commercial flight. Many, no doubt, chose to leave the occupation for something safer and more predictable. Others stayed, including Mayhue, but few forgot that, no matter how much they thought they knew about flying or how brave they might be, fate had a way of calling the shots. In the pursuit of the thrills and joys of flying, no one was immune to disaster.

Not even Willy "Cowboy" Taylor.

****

Whether or not Willy's death was a factor in the decision Mayhue made to rejoin the military, he never said. But in 1939, Mayhue accepted a commission back into the Army Air Corps, re-entering as a First Lieutenant.

Chapter 15
A Time to be Born and
a Time to Die

For everything there is a season, and a time for every matter under heaven:
a time to be born, and a time to die…
Ecclesiastes 3:2

God asks no man whether he will accept life. That is not the choice. You must take it. The only choice is how.
Henry Ward Beecher

It was early November 1940, and the rest of the world was at war. Mayhue had orders to take his wife and sail for the Panama Canal Zone immediately, but Mother was pregnant.

He was being reassigned from Mitchell Field on Long Island as an aide to an important general stationed in "the Zone," as it was called. He looked forward to his new post with a light heart. Though the United States was not currently at war, American forces were being built up around the world, in case they were needed at a future date. Mayhue was still optimistic about the United States avoiding involvement in another world war. He asked his commanding officer for an extension stateside until his baby was born.

"Well, I suppose the general can wait a few weeks for you to arrive," the officer said. "I'll extend your orders until December 20, but not a day longer! And don't come back asking me if you can go home for Christmas to…where is it you're from, Lieutenant?"

"Bible Grove, sir, Bible Grove, Missouri."

"Ah, yes, Bible Grove. What do they do there, grow bibles on trees?" The colonel laughed at his own joke. Mayhue tried to laugh, too.

"Good luck with that new baby, son."

"Thank you, sir."

****

Outside, Verel was waiting in their old Packard. The November wind on Long Island was cold, and the heater in their automobile didn't work very well. She saw her husband coming out of the administration building with a smile on his face. She opened the car door and stood up with effort. She couldn't believe this baby hadn't come yet.

When she found out they had been given another month, Verel shouted with joy. Maybe her child wouldn't have to be born onboard a cruise liner in the middle of the Atlantic Ocean after all.

And so it was that their first child, Barbara, made her appearance in the little Army hospital at Mitchell Field on November 16, 1940. The next few weeks for the young parents were full of the newness of the baby and the uncertainty of what lay ahead for them in Panama. Neither of them had ever been outside of the United States, much less to a country whose language and culture were completely unknown to them. But Verel busied herself packing for the transfer and saying good-bye to the friends they had made while living on base at Mitchell Field.

December 20th arrived and their belongings were being loaded onto the US Army Transport *American Legion*. As they stood watching with other military personnel and their families, crates of their meager furnishings were lifted up from the dock and into the ship's cargo hold. It was an exciting time, but also sad for them to be leaving. No one in either of their families had even seen their new baby girl.

Suddenly, a man wearing a Western Union uniform began searching among the people on the dock, repeatedly calling out a name. "Verel Blaine! Is there a Verel Blaine here?"

Amidst the confusion and general mayhem surrounding the deployment of troops, Verel heard her name and timidly raised her hand, unable to imagine why someone would be trying to find her here on this dock in New York Harbor.

"I'm Verel Blaine," she stated tenuously.

"Oh, Mrs. Blaine, I have a telegram for you, right here."

"A telegram? Who on earth would be sending me a telegram?" She took the envelope from the Western Union man and, with trembling hands, handed it to her husband. "Here, Mayhue, read it to me."

Mayhue, already fearing the worst, opened the envelope and quickly read the telegram to himself. "Oh, Verel," he said sadly, "I'm afraid it's bad news."

"What bad news?" she cried. After her mother's death, she didn't think she could take much more. "Is it one of my brothers? Or Ruth? Oh, please don't tell me something has happened to Ruth!" She felt the panic rising in her throat as she spoke.

"No, Verel," Mayhue said solemnly. "It's your father. He's…dead, Verel." The words found their way into my mother's consciousness, and she stood very still for several moments.

"Did he commit suicide?" she asked at last.

****

In fact, her father had not killed himself. Mayhue was able to telephone one of the brothers who confirmed that Walter had suffered what appeared to be a heart attack. And so, this man who seldom, if ever, revealed his whereabouts to his family during his long and mysterious wanderings—the "free spirit," the vagabond, the irresponsible one—was silent and still at last.

Although Verel cried few tears at her father's passing, it was as though she had old ghosts to bury, old wounds to bind. She spent time on the ocean liner walking the decks alone, when she felt she could leave her baby in Mayhue's care for a while. Perhaps she thought of her mother during those times, and how her mother had unselfishly stood by her father all of those years.

If Verel truly went a little insane when her mother died in her arms, then her father's passing had to have opened those floodgates of sorrow once more, not so much that he was gone, but that he had never measured up as a father or as a husband.

****

When the U.S. Army Transport *American Legion* arrived at Colon, Panama, Verel was especially anxious to get her land legs back. Spending the first few weeks of her first child's life on a ship on the high seas was not the ideal way to begin motherhood. The December waters out of New York were gray, cold, and unbelievably rough. Neither of them had ever sailed before, not even on a lake, so adjusting to the rolling and pitching of the ship was a totally new experience.

Mayhue, in his thirst for knowledge of all modes of transportation, spent much of the trip examining every aspect of the ocean-going operation. He pestered the crewmembers until they allowed him to tour the entire ship, from the top deck to the engine room. He asked dozens of questions; how the ship worked, how much it weighed, how fast it could travel.

Verel, on the other hand, was barely able to get through the days without being nauseous. When a fierce storm ensued around Cape Hatteras off the coast of North Carolina, she sat on the floor of their tiny stateroom, with her infant between her legs. She tried to keep her mind off the incessant action of the water, while soothing the baby to sleep.

In those days, even the troop ships kept strict rules about dining. But between the baby crying and Verel barely able to keep any food down, she never did wear all the fancy clothes she had bought in New York for the trip. She was most disappointed when little Barbara ran a fever the night they were invited to the captain's table; the gown she had planned to wear hung lifeless in the tiny closet, and Mayhue went without her. Instead of exchanging small talk with the other honored guests, she paced the stateroom floor with the, cooling her tiny forehead with washcloths.

Once the ship turned westward into the Caribbean Sea, the waters became smoother, but my mother was most ready to be done with sailing. When Colon, Panama came into view, Verel was greatly relieved.

Waiting for them at Colon was a friend of Mayhue's who also flew for the Army Air Corps. The friend said he had come to pick them up and fly them to the Army Air Base at Panama City, shortening their trip to the Pacific side by a day. The canal took about fifteen hours to traverse by ship, most of which was spent waiting for the lock chambers to fill. Though Verel was no more fond of flying than she was of sailing, she was happy to take Mayhue's buddy up on his offer and get to their destination a little sooner.

Of course, Mayhue said no. He was not about to miss the experience of moving through those locks on the ocean liner. He stood on the ship's fore deck, with the wind blowing through his hair and watched every drop of water fill every cubic centimeter of each of the three sets of lock chambers. Verel bravely accompanied him for a few hours, wearing a yellow gingham sundress and a huge raffia hat, bringing the baby along too, covered with a thin blanket against the scorching tropical sun. She was trying to come to grips with this new country, her new life. She had thought she would feel fashionable and cosmopolitan. Instead she was wide-eyed and fretful, and anxious for things to seem normal again.

Mayhue reported for duty at Howard Air Base in the Canal Zone. The United States was rapidly negotiating for leases and agreements on thousands of military sites worldwide; and "the Zone" was one of the most strategically important. Intelligence sources claimed that Nazi activities in Latin and South America were on the rise. Thus, an interest arose among nations of the Western Hemisphere to establish some type of joint defense. In spite of Mayhue's youthful optimism about a safe future, many world leaders feared that Japan or Germany might attempt to bomb the Canal, placing the United States' naval fleets, and those of our allies, at a disadvantage. When Verel and Mayhue came to Panama in December of 1940, canal defense was the first, and foremost, mission of the United States military forces stationed there.

****

Soon the couple was settled in their base housing, a small one-bedroom hut built on stilts to withstand the rain and the mud, and to afford some protection from the snakes and iguanas. They arrived right before Christmas, but with no evergreens to decorate, it was not going to be a Currier and Ives holiday. Verel unpacked their meager decorations, and they laughed about draping tinsel on an old banana tree just off their front porch. The rainy season was just ending when they arrived, and they had not yet experienced the scorching tropical heat and the stifling humidity that was to follow.

For the first time, Verel had domestic help. It took a bit of getting used to, especially with the language barrier, but soon she was enjoying this new privilege afforded to officers' wives. She took some Spanish lessons through the officers wives' club, and soon was able to communicate a bit better with the maid assigned to my father's household.

"Wash these diapers out for me, *por favor*," or "This soup is too spicy—*muy caliente!*" she would say. The maid would quietly do Verel's bidding for the hours she served the family, and then in the evening, she would go home to some small one-room shanty in the poor section of Panama City.

In the famous Broadway musical about World War II, "South Pacific," one of the characters sings a song called "You've Got To Be Carefully Taught." The lyrics tell how prejudice is begun at home when we are small, and how it becomes ingrained in us. Perhaps it was in Panama that Verel first began to think of herself as "better than" others who walked a different ethnic path than she did. Maybe her brothers' and their wives' involvement with the Klan had more influence on her than she would admit. However her intolerance and racism started, it flourished unchecked after Panama.

Some evenings, the maid would stay late and watch little Barbara while Mayhue and Verel went to the Officers' Club for dinner and dancing. It was on those evenings that they dressed in their finest tropical formal wear, Verel in full-skirted gingham or organza gowns with low necklines, frocks her daughters used for dress-up years later. There are old photos of Mayhue in his crisply starched white uniforms, which were probably unbelievably hot and sticky on nights when the heat was unrelenting.

On one such Saturday night, many couples attended a lovely ball held in honor of a general's wedding anniversary. The mood was festive, the champagne flowed and all the guests looked elegant, in what seemed like an enchanted moment in an equally enchanted life. How could they have known that the following morning, destiny would set the United States on its ear—and life as they knew it would change forever?

That night was December 6, 1941.

****

Sunday, December 7, 1941, dawned bright and sunny in the Canal Zone. Mayhue and Verel had gone golfing at a local course, leaving Barbara with friends. They then planned to have brunch at the Officers' Club. When they arrived at the gate of the air base, there were armed guards everywhere, and it wasn't long before they learned about the brutal attack by Japanese airships on Pearl Harbor.

The rest of the day, Mayhue spent in and around the base, processing what had happened and what it all meant. Briefings were held, communiqués were issued, and much strutting and sputtering was taking place at Howard Air Force Base. The American forces there were immediately placed on high alert. Life was about to change forever.

Chapter 16
No Unwounded Soldiers

In war, there are no unwounded soldiers.
José Narosky

"The Japanese ruined my life!" my mother said, over and over, all through the years. "The Japanese ruined my life!" Never mind what might have been going through the minds of people all over the world. Never mind that some devoted wife of a Japanese fighter pilot might have fancied herself as a "gracious lotus flower" until the United States dropped the atomic bomb in her backyard, and she watched her children's hair catch on fire and all of their skin slough off. War is hell for everyone…but never mind. It was my mother's life that had been ruined.

Remember the rules:

Rule # 1: it's all about Verel

Rule #2: if you think it's about anyone else other than Verel, see Rule #1.

Verel seemed to think she was the only one who suffered during those war years. In fact, Mayhue's sister, Ethel "Sally" Blaine, was one of the Army nurses in the Philippines who was captured by the Japanese and held in Manila for two years. Sally was brave and smart, a true war hero, caring for her patients in a makeshift hospital in the jungle on the Bataan Peninsula for weeks until her capture. As a charge nurse, she had her cot moved into the center of the "ward" when she contracted malaria and was unable to stand up. For years following the war, Verel resented her sister-in-law for the attention she received as a war hero. Verel's children were never allowed to get to know this amazing woman, simply because Verel could not stand to be around her.

Mayhue obtained a short leave, and he flew home to Missouri with Verel and Barbara to see his mother. William Blaine had died early in 1941, and Altie had three children in the Army when the United States entered the war. The whole family was gathered at Altie's home when word came that the Japanese had captured Sally.

When Mayhue and Verel returned to Panama, the orders were issued that all dependent military personnel in the Canal Zone were to be sent stateside immediately. "Immediately," in Army Air Corps language meant that no one left until at least March. There had been much confusion as to exactly what the role of the Air Corps troops stationed in Panama would be. Would they be mobilized to another location? Would they remain in Panama to defend the Canal? Was an attack on the Zone imminent, as many had feared even before the Pearl Harbor bombing? The days and weeks were uncertain for Mayhue, but he knew he had to make plans for Verel and Barbara to return to the United States soon.

When the day came, Mayhue put his wife and daughter on a commercial airliner out of Panama City. Verel and Barbara lived in Dallas, Texas, without Mayhue for eighteen months—not a long period for a wartime separation.

Verel hadn't forgotten her own mother's tactics on survival. She spent her money wisely, canning and freezing fresh fruits and vegetables when they were available. She busied herself with bridge games and afternoon teas with other war wives. Many had children, which gave Barbara some playmates. During that time in her life, my mother appeared to weather the storm fairly well, at least for a while.

****

Mayhue fared much better than Aunt Sally during the war years. Because he was promoted several times during his separation from Verel, she always said she never slept with a captain. Sadly, another woman stole that privilege. Soon Mayhue was not the man he had been before the war.

The details of this era have always been somewhat unclear. But somehow, some way, Mayhue told Verel that he wanted to end their marriage because he had fallen in love with another woman.

The woman apparently was English, but what she was doing in the Panama Canal Zone—other than pursuing married men—was never revealed. It was a mystery how Mayhue went from, "It's a nice day here in the Panama Canal Zone," to "Will you go to bed with me?" But he slid down that slippery slope and landed at the bottom without much concern for his family. In the words Mayhue would use decades later to describe the Bill Clinton/Monica Lewinski debacle, "he had zipper trouble." War is hell.

There must have been discussions between Verel and him about the matter, but how that took place, in person, on the phone, or by mail remained a mystery. In any case, Verel clearly felt that the Missouri farm boy had stooped about as low as he could go. She was devastated. An average wartime wife, her husband's infidelity crushed her spirit and left her barely able to cope.

This may have been when Verel's mental health took another serious plunge, when the demon was unleashed, or activated, if it had always been there. Until her husband's affair, Verel thought she was a real siren, that her beauty and her feminine wiles could woo the heart of any man, most especially Mayhue. When she found out she could no longer rely on this premise, it turned her world on edge. This, combined with the separation, seemed to have set in motion her need to fight even harder to maintain her façade as the "gracious lady." Later, she often quoted William Congreve's famous words, "Hell hath no fury like a woman scorned."

It is also uncertain how many times Mayhue came home on leave during the separation. Still, whatever was said or unsaid, done or undone, the marriage somehow survived the affair. The reconciliation was no doubt bittersweet, and the groundwork had been laid for a rocky trip through the remainder of their less-than-blissful marriage–all sixty-eight years of it.

****

Meanwhile, in early February of 1945, American troops retook Manila, freeing Aunt Sally and the other captives. She was quoted in her hometown Missouri paper:

"It was so exhilarating when those Texas boys of 'Skinny' [Lieutenant General Jonathan M.] Wainright's old cavalry division liberated us at {Manila} that we were intoxicated with joy for three days!"

Sally may have been intoxicated with joy, but as the post-war years went by, Verel continued to be intoxicated with jealousy–and eventually alcohol.

Part III

Barbara and Me, Christmas 1947

Chapter 17
My Arrival: Spirit Lodging and Milk Chocolate Hands

It is as though the body in which we have found our spirit lodged is at first strange to us.

Agatha Christie

Looking at photos of my childhood, there doesn't seem to be any hint that this child was part of a world gone mad, starting in her own living room. If I had been born twenty years later, I might have spent the first few hours of my life in an incubator in some neonatal unit. But without much fanfare, I entered this world on January 13, 1947, several weeks premature, weighing only five pounds two ounces. My mother had worn a form-fitting size-ten cocktail dress to a New Year's Eve party two weeks before, and only her closest friends believed she was really pregnant.

In fact, I almost didn't happen at all. When she was drunk, my mother told me the tale of my near demise over and over. After my father's little period of indiscretion, my mother sought help. There was no such thing as a marriage counselor in those days, or at least not that my family knew about. So it was a physician who advised my mother to get pregnant again to "save" her marriage. I have tried *very hard* over the years not to imagine the event that resulted in me. The mere thought of my parents having sex at all, much less during a time when my father had been cheating on my mother, is way too painful for me to visualize. But I'm pretty sure that I am the result of such a union, and I will be eternally grateful that Mother never described the union itself in graphic detail when she was inebriated.

What she did explain was that she almost lost me. "Do you know what happens when you have a miscarriage?" she would slur through the booze. The first time she asked the question, I reluctantly indulged her. After that, she continued anyway, falsely assuming my silence denoted spellbound interest.

"No, Mother. What happens?" I asked, rolling my eyes to the ceiling.

"Well, you begin to bleed…"

The part of the story that I did not know until years later was that the bleeding started because my mother was hit by a car. I believe she left this part out because it involved my Aunt Sally, who told me about it years later. In the fall of 1946, my father had been promoted to full colonel He was stationed in the nation's capitol to help in the founding of the National War College, where he later served both as an instructor and completed his bachelor's degree.

Mother was several weeks pregnant with me, and she and Barbara were crossing a street somewhere near the Pentagon. A car plowed right into my mother, knocking her onto the pavement. People stopped to help. My sister, who was nearly seven years old, was hysterical. Mother was conscious and gave someone my father's phone number at the Pentagon, but he couldn't be reached. Her next and only alternative was my Aunt Sally who happened to be in Washington too, with her new husband George, better known as "Zip."

After she had been summoned, Aunt Sally met the ambulance at Walter Reed Hospital and took care of my sister until my father arrived. According to Mother, the Walter Reed doctors recommended that she allow them to abort the pregnancy (I was not consulted), because of possible brain damage to the fetus (namely me).

"I told them I wanted this baby!" she would wail when the liquor took over her brain. And then, like clockwork, she would shoot me a dismal look and add, "You were the only way I had left to keep your father!"

And so it was that I became responsible for my parents' marriage surviving even before I was born. And people wonder where I learned about guilt and people pleasing.

✳✳✳✳

One of my very earliest memories is of the hands that cared for me: dark hands the color of milk chocolate with pink palms, the hands of my first black nanny, Lois. She was just a child herself, only about thirteen when she came to work for my parents. Those hands, it seemed to me, were full of kindness, always offering me something of worth: a yummy treat or a warm washcloth or a gentle touch. A teenaged surrogate mother, to be sure.

I was born in the base hospital at Mitchell Field, near Montgomery, Alabama, where my father was stationed at the time. Household help was cheap in the South, and almost all of the "help" was black. It was expected that the officer's wives would have "help" so that they could attend all the functions and committee meetings and civic projects available both on and off base. My sister wasn't old enough to take care of me, so we had Lois.

When I was only three years old, we returned to the Washington, D.C. area, and we brought Lois to live with us. It must have been a very hard thing for Lois to do, to leave her home and her family and travel several states away to live with this white family and the uppity woman my mother was rapidly becoming. I cannot say that my father was much better; for his entire life he was deeply prejudiced against blacks. He mellowed some in his later years, probably more because he always tried to keep his thumb on the pulse of our country's culture than because he had really turned his own thinking around.

Shortly after we brought Lois to Washington with us, my father took compassion on how miserable Lois was. He asked her if she'd like to go home. She shyly said yes, and he bought her a bus ticket and sent her on her way back to Alabama.

****

After Lois's departure, there was a succession of other nannies, mostly black—the labor force in Washington D.C. was almost as plentiful though perhaps not as cheap as Alabama. Strangely, I don't remember any of their names, but I do remember the care they gave me, and I remember that often that was the only care I got.

In our family, we didn't kiss each other goodnight, nor did our parents tuck us in. I don't ever remember my mother reading me a story, though my sister did on occasion. I don't remember ever getting an allowance or having the responsibility of doing chores. Little wisdom was imparted to us about how to live, how to handle finances and life's problems and people. We watched as our parents botched everything they tried to do for us as a family. Barbara and I were imbedded reporters—just there to observe.

Restlessness was an early feeling I recall having. I don't know where it came from, but I would feel a profound dissatisfaction with the way things were. Perhaps it was the beginning of depression, though it was much later in my youth that I began crying for no particular reason. I also recall having some awareness that our family had much to be thankful for; we were richly blessed by most standards. From the time I was quite small, I felt cozy on cold days because I always had a warm coat to wear. Our house was always well heated, making even the chilliest days seem bearable. One of my life's greatest pleasures was being outside in the cold, anticipating coming in to have hot cocoa and put my cold feet on the old steam radiators in our homes.

With my father away so much, discipline was most often meted out by my mother. I was completely smitten by the Good Humor truck and once I boldly disobeyed orders. With a nickel clutched in my tiny hand, I crossed the street without an adult. I didn't get caught, but I recall how that ice cream bar tasted different because I obtained it by breaking a serious rule. That time I lucked out and didn't get disciplined. I didn't understand until much later that reasonable boundaries imposed by caring parents help children stay secure.

****

I knew quite early that our family was not like others. Military families, by their very nature, tend to be isolated, most often having no extended family nearby and having to make new friends each time a transfer occurs.

We learned a number of important life lessons from Mother. One was never, never, *never* open Mother's purse without asking. Never. If you wanted something, like a quarter or a hairpin or a piece of gum, you brought the purse to her, and she got out whatever it was that you wanted. I thought this was about respecting her boundaries; but many years later that I realized it was because she always carried a flask in her handbag and she didn't want us to see it.

When I was about four and a half, my father took a most interesting job assignment that furthered our entire family's awareness of the lifestyles of the rich and famous. And, true to her manufactured persona, my mother embraced this time fully and flamboyantly.

My father was transferred to Ottawa, Ontario, Canada as Air Attaché to the American Embassy.

Chapter 18
The Royal Canadian Experience

Addiction and Recovery – The Jellinek Curve

Crucial Phase: Constant relief drinking commences...increase in alcohol tolerance...urgency of first drink...onset of memory blackouts...grandiose and aggressive behaviors...

When I learned to ride a two-wheeled bike at age five, my father was with me. We were right there on the street in front of our house in Rockliffe Park, a prestigious, older housing area in Ottawa, Ontario. It must have been in the fall because I remember leaves falling all around me as I pumped my spindly legs with all my might to make the bike's wheels turn fast enough so I wouldn't tip over.

"That's it," my father called to me. "You've got the idea!" He had been running alongside the bike, but I suddenly realized his voice was farther away than it was supposed to be. He wasn't beside me any more. I turned my head to check and see where he went, and the big bike skidded right out from under me.

Daddy picked me up and said more encouraging words. Though I wouldn't have believed it that day, I would learn to ride that old bike. It was an "American" bike, with thick tires and only one gear. The Canadian kids teased me unmercifully because they all rode "English" bikes. They called me "skinny with the fat bike," which did wonders for my self-esteem.

Aside from riding a bicycle, I was a quick learner, and I excelled in the progressive Canadian school system. One day, after I had started attending kindergarten, I burst through the kitchen door at our house. Puffing, I announced, "Mother! I have *one fair chance* to be in the first grade!"

It was true: I was ahead of my class, partly because Barbara had always taken time to help me learn my letters and numbers and how to read. I skipped two grades in the three years we lived in Canada. When we returned to the United States, though, I got put back a grade because I told the teacher that George Washington was the country's current President. They didn't teach much American history in Ottawa in those days! I knew far more about the Queen of England than I knew about American government. In fact, Queen Elizabeth was crowned while we lived in Ottawa.

****

The coronation took place at Westminster Abbey in London on June 2, 1953. Queen Elizabeth was twenty-six years old, a new bride, and a fairy-tale-come-true story for children around the globe. Commemorative souvenirs were being produced by the thousands. My sister and I each had a tiny metal coronation coach with six white horses that attached to the coach with a little hook. Barbara still has hers; I misplaced mine somewhere along the line.

That coronation will forever be linked in my memory with our first television, a Motorola. Daddy was so proud when he brought it home; a huge square wooden box, the entire bottom two-thirds of which was the cloth-covered speaker. The top third housed a fourteen-inch viewing screen, and it was on that screen that our family sat enthralled by black and white images of the Coronation Procession of the Queen of England.

My father also took time off from his late afternoon "duties" at the Embassy. In a festive mood, Daddy even allowed our domestic help to enter the living room and share the experience with our family. Canadian schools were let out the day of the coronation.

And so our family, only temporary residents of the vast land called Canada, came to identify in many ways with the customs of that nation. The Queen was as dear to us as she was to her many subjects worldwide. And, with all the attention Canada was giving to its new ruler, it seemed as though my mother's tendency toward her own self-importance fit right in. Mother would have agreed with the immortal words of children's book illustrator Mary Engelbreit: "It is good to be queen."

****

The house that the American Embassy rented for us in Ottawa was like something out of a scary movie. It seemed mammoth to tiny little me. The house stood on a huge corner lot that sloped down from the street. The driveway caused my mother problems right away the first winter. Having virtually no experience with winter driving, she couldn't get the car up to the street because of the ice and snow. She took to having the chauffeur, Thomas, drive it up the hill for her, and then she'd take it from there. Thomas must have thought she was a dumb southerner, which of course she was, at least about winter driving.

The entry to the house seemed like a castle gate. In the center of the main floor was a huge foyer in which my mother placed a large Oriental rug. The staircase curved all the way up to the second floor, and I could imagine a princess floating down it in a beautiful ball gown to meet her handsome prince, waiting for her at the bottom (a vision reinforced by images of the gala coronation).

Because of my father's position with the Embassy, my parents did a lot of entertaining while we were there. Daddy even told me once that partying is about all they did. The parties that were held at our home were spectacular affairs. Mother always said people came to *her* parties last because they were the best. She always served a huge ham and a large roast turkey, not just dinky little sandwiches and *canapes* like many other hostesses. The guest lists included embassy personnel from all over the world.

Mother would be in grand form for entertaining. This was her calling, her *raison d'etre*. Although my sister says Mother began drinking more heavily a couple of years prior to my father's transfer to Canada, I first remember her being "different" in the house in Ottawa. I'm sure I was too young to really understand that it was the alcohol that changed her personality, but it was very memorable when it happened.

At night, when my parents' party guests would go home, they would remain in the living room fighting. I remember sitting on the top step of that huge staircase, singing a song to myself that I had made up about me being a "little peacemaker." I couldn't shake the idea that somehow my parents' happiness was my responsibility, and one of my earliest memories is sitting on that step and trying to *will* my parents to stop fighting. Many years later, I would recall those times when I began to understand how early the entire family of an alcoholic gets hooked in as "co-dependents."

But it would be a long, long time until I would read such words of comfort as the July 23 entry in Al-Anon's *One Day At A Time*: "Probably there is nothing I can do now—this minute, this hour, today."

The reality was that all Mother and Daddy seemed to do in Canada was drink and fight. Every weekday after my father left for the Embassy, and my sister and I went off to school, my mother began a round of parties. There were "sherry parties" at ten in the morning, followed by "luncheons" with champagne or wine. Those led to "happy hour" at the officers' club, after which Mother poured herself into her car and sloshed home for highballs with Daddy before supper. And don't forget the *aperitifs* after the evening meal and the nightcap before bed.

Alcoholism is so cute in its infancy: funny, sexy, seemingly intelligent. I thought my mother was all of these things, in the beginning. I wanted to be just like her, to wear my hair like hers and put on make-up and sparkly dresses, and wear Channel No. 5 perfume which cost a whole lot of money even back then. I wanted to raise one foot when a gentleman guest kissed me goodnight.

I didn't understand then that my mother was really very insecure and intimidated by all the dignitaries she was entertaining. Even though she appeared to be at her best in the social scene in Ottawa, she truly was lonely and distrustful. The alcohol made her braver, and if "a little helped some," then she believed a lot would make her the most sought-after hostess in all of Canada *and* the United States.

****

Mother didn't have to cook in Ottawa. We always had domestic help, many times more than one person. The house we lived in "came with" a Latvian couple, Robert and Elizabeth. (I thought this meant that they were part of the house, sort of like a dollhouse that "came with" a family of dolls.) I doubt if those were their actual names; it was customary for the heads of the households to choose names for domestic help—thus withdrawing one more of these silent servants' ties to personal dignity. Though I wouldn't have dared ask them their real names, I imagined them to be something exotic like Boris and Natasha. They were there when we moved in, standing uncertainly off the big kitchen, in a hallway that led to their "quarters": a bedroom, sitting room and private bath.

Though we moved in during July, Robert had on olive green wool pants, a long-sleeved white shirt, and a plaid wool vest. Elizabeth looked like someone I'd seen in a storybook once. She wore a gathered skirt over her plump stomach, with a smocked top and a bright bandana tied around her hair. She bore no resemblance to the young queen of the same name. Robert and Elizabeth both stood, sort of proudly defiant, sizing up our family. My mother wasted no time giving orders about how she wanted things done.

I loved Elizabeth's cooking: lots of soft, mushy dishes with cream and gravy and butter. The kind of food that could make a child feel safe and secure just tasting it. Elizabeth didn't much like me hanging around the kitchen, and it became apparent soon enough why the couple had no children of their own. But Robert would smile at me with a sparkle in his eyes, and sometimes he'd tousle my hair as I rushed by on my way out to the huge backyard.

Barbara and I loved that yard. In the winter, Thomas would get a small tractor out of the garage and push the snow up into a huge pile at the end of the sloping driveway so my sister and I could build "snow forts." Each winter we lived there, Daddy built us a skating rink by putting up a little wooden barrier all around a flat area below the three-season porch. He flooded it with the garden hose, and it froze solid in half a day.

In the fall, my father would hire day laborers to rake leaves— there must have been a billion of those leaves, all brown and gold and red! My father would help the men, if he were home. Barbara and I would run and jump into the piles and laugh as the leaf dust and mold covered us.

A door joined my sister's bedroom and mine, the two rooms possibly having served as a nursery at one time, with quarters for a nurse or a nanny. Barbara used to lie in her bed on Christmas Eve and make "Santa noises," like "Ho, Ho, Ho," which would cause me to get up and run to her room (I wasn't sleeping anyway!). She would insist she didn't hear a thing, that I must be imagining it. I would reluctantly go back to bed, and then she'd do it again. It seemed I never slept the night before holidays like Christmas and Easter, and then my sister would get me up earlier than usual to go downstairs and see what Santa or the Easter Bunny had left. I invariably got sick from too little sleep and too much excitement.

In Canada, Barbara taught me to play games with her. Her favorite was the card game Canasta, and she always beat me, so I never wanted to play. Once, she bought a yoyo and tried to teach me how to work it. I was sitting cross-legged on the coffee table in the three-season porch, leaning over and trying to master that yoyo. I was just getting the hand of it when I lost my balance and fell headfirst onto the slate floor. Barbara yelled for our parents. Daddy scooped me up and carried me upstairs to their bed. Mother called the doctor, who came to the house right away. I had broken my collarbone and had to go to the hospital.

I remember going into the operating room without my parents and being scared out of my wits. A nurse put a funny smelling rubber cone over my mouth and nose and told me to count backwards from one hundred. I didn't want to count backwards. I wanted to get out of there. But in a few seconds, I had the sensation of falling into a great spiral, spinning down and down with bright, garish colors all around. I had nightmares about that feeling for years afterward, usually when I was ill, or when some smell or sensation reminded me of that old hospital.

I got out of school for a couple of weeks, and my classmates all wrote me letters wishing I would get better. I got my meals on a tray, usually in Mother's bed. I think Elizabeth thought this was absolutely the height and breadth of spoiling a child. She was pleasant, but I always had the feeling she thought I should be up helping with the chores (except we weren't required to do any chores!). I also got to lie on the living room couch and watch lots of that new television. There was "I Love Lucy" and "Ed Sullivan," and Mary Martin playing Peter Pan in a live broadcast.

****

In Ottawa, I had my first sleepover, at the home of my friend Patty. Her father was an officer in the Royal Canadian Air Force, and I thought his uniform was much more handsome than Daddy's dumb old blue one. Mother was good friends with Patty's mom, and I was looking forward to staying at their house.

I was in for a big culture shock. I was used to eating "dinner" with my parents and staying up to watch television until my bedtime, which was nine o'clock on the weekends. I was surprised to learn that Patty's family ate "dinner" at noon, and in the very early evening, about five o'clock, the children had "tea." This consisted of tiny little doll-sized sandwiches, a few carrot and celery sticks, and a glass of milk, followed by some doll-sized cookies. This whole "meal" was served to us in Patty's "playroom" at a tiny little doll-sized table and chairs, under the watchful eye of her British nanny, Emily (undoubtedly not her real name either). I knew enough not to be rude, but I must have been eyeing this culinary array suspiciously. Emily summoned Patty's mother, who asked me, "What's wrong, dear? Isn't this what you Americans have for tea time?"

"No, ma'am," I answered shyly. "We don't call it 'tea.' We call it 'dinner,' Ma'am."

"Is that so?" she replied sweetly in her Canadian accent. "And what do you usually like to have for 'dinner'?"

My reply, without a moment's hesitation, was "Rare steak and tomato ketchup!"

This sent both Patty's mother and her nanny into gales of laughter. I really didn't know what I had said that was so amusing. I felt my face redden. After they yukked it up for what seemed like eons, Patty's mom spoke again.

"Well, I'm terribly sorry, Margaret," she said, wiping the tears from her eyes and trying very hard to keep a straight face. "I suppose Cookie could find you a bit of cheese if you like." I wondered what Cookie looked like and what her *real* name was.

After the tea fiasco, Patty tried to entertain me with some of her hundreds of toys. We were just getting started playing "family" in her indoor, child-sized playhouse, when the nanny bustled into the playroom and announced it was bedtime. I looked at the wall clock and saw perfectly clearly that it was only seven o'clock. There must have been some kind of mistake. I knew we had at least two more hours to play, and I thought Emily had gone completely daft, as they say in Canada. My surprise turned to horror when Patty stood up, began putting her toys *away*, no less, and dutifully answered, "Okay, Emily!"

After I helped her pick up the toys, we trudged up a long winding staircase from the kitchen to the second floor.(Apparently, children and domestic help even had their own stairs.) Their home was of the same vintage as ours, and had a similar floor plan. Patty's room, just like mine, adjoined another bedroom with a door between. But the bedroom next to Patty's did not house a sister like mine did. It was Emily's room, and after she got us washed up and into our jammies, she tucked us into Patty's big bed and went into the other room and left the door open.

Patty fell asleep right away. I chose to stay awake and ponder my rapidly deteriorating situation. I couldn't fall asleep this early. It was Friday night and I was missing The Honeymooners on TV. Besides I was hungry. I could hear Emily in the next room, snoring loudly enough for all the world to hear. I began to cry.

Of course, this roused Emily out of her dead-to-the-world slumber, and before I knew it, she was at my side asking me what was wrong. "Nothing!" I blubbered. She persisted, and finally, I said I wanted to go home. Patty was awake by now, and soon her mother was there, too. Someone called our house and got my sister, who was still too young to drive. She told Patty's mom that my parents were "out," which was not really a lie. My father was chalking up flight time by going to White Horse in the Yukon Territory, where the pilots always stayed the night before returning home. My mother was passed "out" in bed. So Patty's family chauffeur, Gaston, who was French and spoke with a heavy accent and smelled like old roses and garlic, drove me home. End of sleepovers for a while!

****

The year we moved to Ottawa, Daddy bought a brand-new 1952 sixteen-foot Chris Craft Riviera motorboat. I loved that runabout, with its beautiful varnished mahogany finish that reflected the sunlight off the lake, and its red leather seats with white piping. We hauled it up to a lake behind my parents' 1952 gray Chevy coup, and I strained my neck to watch the whole way for fear the trailer would come unhooked and the boat would go crashing down some ravine. We always got there safely, though, and early the next morning, Daddy would launch the boat by sunrise and we'd be ready to go. Mother would load our round plaid Scotch cooler full of fruit, cookies, and sandwiches, "in case" we didn't catch any fish (which we always did). Soon we'd be cruising over the glass-like lake at a top speed of about thirty-five miles an hour.

My father always knew where to fish, and he always caught all the lake trout we wanted, enough to have a "shore lunch" and still take some home for the freezer. My mother and my sister would read or sunbathe on the runabout's front deck while Daddy fished. And I would go on imaginary ventures, pretending I was a French trapper or an Indian living in the wilderness. The hull of the boat was my teepee or my wilderness cabin or some other form of shelter. By lunchtime, I would work up quite an appetite from my make-believe quests.

Daddy would pull up to the shore wherever he could find a flat spot to beach the boat. After we all helped gather wood and my father built a fire, he would take the largest of the fish and clean it with his razor-sharp filet knife. Out would come the Reynolds Aluminum Foil, and Mother would use a piece of salt pork to grease it and add some flavor. Then they'd fold that whole fish, head and all, inside the foil and place it on the fire, turning it several times during the cooking process. Waiting for the fish to be done was agonizing. I would try to busy myself with more adventures on shore, but my parents didn't want me wandering too far off lest I encounter some unfriendly wildlife.

At last the fish would be done, and we'd have our feast. I have never tasted fish like that fire-roasted whole lake trout. When we were finished eating the meal, Barbara would break out marshmallows and Hershey's chocolate bars and graham crackers to make a new treat she learned about in Girl Scouts. To this day, I consider "s'mores" to be brain food. Before we left, we would clean up, with Mother using sand from the shoreline to "scour" the fry pan. We took all our trash with us back to the lodge where we were staying.

Those nights at the lodge, my bubble would be burst because that's when the drinking began. I recall one time in particular when some older man decided he liked me and kept hovering over me and breathing in my face. He must have been somebody important (maybe a general or something) because my dad didn't try to intervene. The man wasn't harming me, but it was the first time in my life I recall having little red flags go up, saying, "I'm not comfortable with this." I was very glad I wasn't left alone with this person.

This was also probably the first time that I recall connecting alcoholic beverages with bizarre behavior in people other than my mother.

****.

Back at the house one day, Robert came in to my mother and said, "Machine no work." The washing machine had broken down once more, and while he was fairly handy, he had been unable to keep it working for more than a day. This precipitated my mother blowing up at Robert and firing him and Elizabeth. Too much sherry that morning, perhaps. At any rate, Mother called the employment agency, and thus we began a period of revolving-door domestic help. No one suited my mother, and she sent a variety of help packing. The last person we had in Canada was a German woman named Hannah. Probably in her mid-twenties, she had come to Ottawa following Armistice Day. I never knew if she was from East or West Germany, because of course, she wasn't able to talk with us socially as my mother strictly forbade us fraternizing with the help. What I do remember is that when we came back to the Untied States, Hannah came with us.

Alas, the Canadian tour did eventually come to an end. The Air Force always took care of moving us, so Mother had no responsibilities except to hold court with the van line's employees while they got our "extra special important belongings" ready to ship. They packed up our furniture, clothes, toys, all the Gracious Lady fancy dishes and china and crystal that Mother had bought while we lived there, crate after crate and barrel after barrel. Before the containers were sealed, we slipped in several dozen more family secrets to take with us back to the States.

Chapter 19
Unreasonable Resentments

Addiction and Recovery – The Jellinek Curve

Crucial Phase (continued): ...Efforts to control fail repeatedly...unreasonable resentments...decrease in alcohol tolerance...onset of lengthy intoxications...

It was the summer of 1955 when our family returned to the Washington, D.C. area, where my father assumed the post of Legislative Liaison. This meant that he spent his days sitting in the U.S. House of Representatives, and then reported back to the Department of the Air Force about what the federal legislators were up to.

Of all of the tours of duty my father had during our growing-up years, my sister hated this second stay in the Washington, D.C. area the most. We moved from Ottawa right after Barbara's freshman year of high school. We first lived in a house in Arlington, Virginia, where Barbara started her sophomore year. Just when she was getting settled in yet another school, Daddy got the bright idea to move to Alexandria so that he would be closer to the Pentagon, the Capitol and the federal office buildings where the Representatives were housed. Although Barbara didn't know it at the time, the political winds would again soon shift for my father, and he would take a transfer to Colorado Springs within another year. Barbara would attend four high schools in four years.

On the other hand, I was fine with all of this. Or at least I didn't make it such a big deal as my sister did. I was younger and making friends seemed easier for me. My love of horses was continuing to grow, and I remember Daddy coming home many nights after his day at the Capitol and taking me down to a pony ring where I would ride a buff-colored animal named King while my father chatted with the proprietor. Truth be known, my dad was probably just trying to postpone the inevitable round of fights with my mother that, by this time, had become the principal evening activity in our house. The social whirl my parents had experienced in Canada had come to an end, and my mother had begun to fill the void by increasing her habit of drinking alone.

****

That first summer, Mother did stay sober long enough to take my sister and me on a "gracious lady training academy field trip to New York City. We packed carefully to make sure we had all the proper clothing: conservative dresses and stockings and patent leather shoes, and of course, white gloves. We boarded a passenger train at Union Station and rode in the dome car all the way to Grand Central Station in New York. We took a cab to the Waldorf Astoria Hotel. Our room was just about the fanciest thing I had seen in my whole life. There was a huge bed where my mother and my sister slept, and a long couch with a pullout bed for me. I could roll over three times in that pullout bed and not fall off the other side. The bedside lamps were ornate gold with fluted shades. The bathroom was equipped with thick white towels with the letters *WA* embroidered on them.

The first morning we ordered room service for breakfast, but Mother said we couldn't do that every morning because it was too expensive. They rolled a little table into our room already made up with a linen cloth and linen napkins in silver napkin rings. We had soft-boiled eggs in little alabaster egg cups imprinted with *WA*. The grapefruit halves had maraschino cherries in the center, and the sections were already cut up for us like we were these slow-moving rich people who couldn't get the pieces out without help. There were also some little cakes (Mother called them "tea biscuits") that were so light and fluffy, they tasted like spun sugar. Mother had coffee with real cream and sugar cubes, and we had milk served in fancy glasses.

I thought I had died and gone to heaven.

My sister sneaked a peak at the bill when Mother wasn't looking, and she looked horrified. I asked her how much it was, but she told me to shush.

The first day Mother was going to take us for a subway ride, out to see the Statue of Liberty. She hadn't lived in New York since Barbara was born, so she couldn't remember which train we were to take. We were standing on the platform with all the trains whooshing past us like wild animals just released from the zoo. I was mesmerized.

Mother said, "Stand still and don't move while I ask which train we take." She and Barbara turned their backs to me for just a second. I think some demonic force took over my brain. When the next train car stopped in front of me and opened up, I just walked right in. I was already in the car looking around at all the strange people and not realizing I was alone, when I heard my mother and my sister yelling at me. Then they dived right into the same car just as the door was closing. Fortunately, it was the right train. My mother took several minutes to regain her composure, and she kept saying, "You could have gone all the way to Brighton Beach!" over and over again. I had no idea where Brighton Beach was but I knew it must be a bad place, and I was really glad I hadn't ended up there.

After that, I paid more attention to where my mother was at all times—at least on the trip to New York. We saw all the sights in the Big Apple: the Statue of Liberty and Staten Island, the Empire State Building and the United Nations Building. We ate lunch at the Automat, something totally foreign to us at that time. It looked a little like a cafeteria line, with a long counter on which to slide your metal tray. There must have been *someone* back there putting the food into these little cubbyholes, but we couldn't really see them. Each compartment had a glass door and a place to put coins. You had to have the exact change, because nobody had figured out yet how to have a machine make change. There was a heated section for entrees and soup, and cool sections for salads and desserts. We made our selections as we moved down the counter and Mother put in the appropriate coins. By the end of the line, Barbara and I were begging Mother to let us put the coins in ourselves. It didn't take much to entertain us in those days.

We also went down to Radio Row, the warehouse district where the World Trade Center would be built decades later. There was so much merchandise to supply all the stores in New York City and the rest of the country that things spilled out of the doors onto the streets. I wondered what they did when it rained because it was clear they couldn't get all that stuff inside. We saw everything, from clothing to electrical appliances to toys to household goods.

One night, we went to Radio City Music Hall and saw the Rockettes dance with such precision, they looked like mirrored images all in a row. I fell in love with the music, and I remember getting such a thrill out of seeing people perform like that. They were all so beautiful in their costumes of sequins and feathers in all the colors of the rainbow. I wanted to be just like those performers when I grew up. But I was jolted back to reality by remembering that my father wouldn't allow music lessons or any instruments in our home. I never knew why. My mother had played the violin as a girl, but she said she was never very good. Maybe my dad had endured her playing in the beginning and didn't want to be subjected to his own children's practice sessions. He seemed to like to listen to music, so why did he feel this way? In any case, I knew it was futile to think I would ever be able to perform like the Rockettes.

The last night, we ate in the dining room at the Waldorf. The table setting was exquisite, with silver and china and crystal. It was a lot like our Gracious Lady Table at home. Mother had elegant table settings, and we often ate on the "good" dishes with the "good" silver. In fact, I was well into my twenties before I realized not everyone puts their condiments into cut glass decanters and crystal dishes. Mother would have practically denied us our inheritance if we ever set a bottle of ketchup or a jar of jam right from the refrigerator onto our table. She believed putting things in fancy containers was a law of the universe. Bread at our house had to be wrapped in a linen napkin, placed in a basket or on a silver tray. Each glass had to have a coaster under it, each cup had a saucer. We used only linen napkins, and of course gravy was served in a sterling gravy boat with its own saucer. No paper, plastic, Styrofoam, or cardboard was allowed, no chewing with your mouth open, *yawning* (with or without your mouth open), and no laughing, singing, or kicking each other under the table. No meaningful conversation between adults and children. No nonsense. No reality. No kidding.

That night in New York, my mother ordered lobster for all of us. When we came into the dining room, we saw a great big water tank with live lobsters in it, crawling all over each other like they were all trying to get out as fast as possible because they knew they were in serious trouble. My sister was gagging. She was always the soft-hearted one when it came to any of God's creatures. Mother asked the waiter to choose the lobsters for us—she remembered when we drove back from Canada through Maine, and Daddy got live ones to stick into a pot of boiling water in the kitchenette in the little motel room we rented. The lobsters screamed bloody murder when my dad put them in that water, and Mother, Barbara and I were screaming too. And then Barbara had thrown up right on the front porch of our bungalow. She didn't eat any lobster that night, so I'm not really sure why Mother wanted to reintroduce us to this delicacy now.

Mother didn't want to know any more about the food chain than she absolutely had to either. She was content to have the lobsters totally dead and cooked before they were brought to our table. The waiter obliged but we were still served these prehistoric-looking red monsters with bands around their claws. I poked mine a few times to make sure it wasn't going to get up off the plate and pinch my nose. Finally, we got down to using the little crackers and the skinny forks, and it tasted pretty good with all that melted butter on it.

Mother must have been pretty satisfied that my sister and I had acted appropriately for "gracious ladies in training." She behaved pretty appropriately on the trip too, and we all had lots to talk about when we got back home.

****

By the time we moved to Alexandria, our German maid/nanny Hannah was only working for us part time. She still lived with us, but my father had helped her begin the process of becoming a naturalized citizen of the United States. Part of what she needed to do was to get a job, so she became a carhop at a Hot Shoppe restaurant on the outskirts of D.C. It was a big treat for us when my dad would take us there to have her wait on us. My mother never went. We would have big, juicy hamburgers and thick chocolate shakes, which we ate in the car. Some people during that time said these kinds of restaurants were going to be the ruination of the nation. I thought this was surely the food of the gods.

My mother thought it was barbaric. Eating with one's hands was obviously for the lower class, not for our family. I think Mother never really liked Hannah either, because she was German. Mother thought it was criminal how European women had married American soldiers during the War, just so (in her opinion) they could get free passage to the United States. She would see them working at the base exchange or even in private businesses in the area, and she would be instantly infuriated at what she perceived to be their motives. Though this was not Hannah's situation at all, my mother was an "equal opportunity bigot," and her disdain for Germans included *all* German immigrants, no matter what their situation.

"Is better in Germany," Mother would say, imitating their accents, many times within earshot of Hannah. "They all want to come here and marry our boys, but they still say it's better there! Why do they come at all?" We never responded. My sister and I liked Hannah, and my father's job had acquainted him with the political importance of ethnic tolerance.

I wondered why the immigrants did come, with attitudes like my mother's to contend with. My family was presented with endless opportunities to explore diversity and different ways of thinking and living, but my mother's bitter prejudice seemed to thwart them all.

****

Many Sunday afternoons, my father took my sister and me with him down to the Pentagon where he had some work to do. I think it was when my mother was drunk, and he didn't want to leave us at home with her. He was gone a lot too. He had to fly planes for the Air Force to keep his skills honed, in case he ever needed to fly a plane for some real purpose like another war. On this particular day, we brought our schoolwork, but it wasn't too long until we decided to go exploring. The building certainly offered temptation, with more than seventeen miles of corridors.

The Pentagon wasn't very old at that time. Ground was broken on the site on September 11, 1942, exactly fifty-nine years before Islamic fundamentalist terrorists crashed into it after hijacking American Airlines Flight 77. The center of the pentagon shape was named "Ground Zero" during the Cold War because it was thought to be the most likely target in the event of a nuclear attack. Following the September 11, 2001 attacks, the site of the World Trade Center would later take that title away from the Pentagon.

Meanwhile, back to our Sunday afternoon adventure. My sister and I were well on our way to getting ourselves into a real fix by the time our father realized we were gone. We had been content to look around the area near his office for a while, but eventually, we rode an elevator to another floor and got off to see what we could find. We got lost quickly and tried unsuccessfully to retrace our steps. I was getting worried and tried not to cry. I trusted my sister, but I thought maybe we shouldn't just be wandering around the way we were. I wanted to blurt out something like, *"Hey, Sis, listen, I don't think we ought to try this on our own, really, without a military escort or a couple of small tanks or a miniature fighter plane or something!"* I thought I remembered from school that pentagons have some evil connotation, something to do with the Devil. Or was that pentographs? Or pentagrams? About the time I was going to ask my sister about this, we came around a corner and ran headlong into an armed guard who appeared to have no sense of humor.

"Stop!" he shouted at us. "State your name and what you're doing here!" I was mesmerized by how official he sounded; especially since it was pretty obvious we were just a couple of kids. I glanced over at my sister who looked at that moment like Dorothy in front of The Great Oz.

"We're Colonel Blaine's daughters," she managed.

"And where is Colonel Blaine?" the guard demanded.

I can't remember if my sister knew his office number, but she sure gave the guard Daddy's full name very quickly. The guard went to a phone, made some calls and then ordered us to come with him. We followed behind him, back into the elevator, off on another floor, down some halls until things started looking familiar again, and eventually into our father's office with the guard right beside us.

Because my father outranked the guard, we were gratified to see our escort snap to attention in Daddy's presence. *That'll fix him!* I thought to myself. Of course, Daddy said, "At ease," in his best military voice and apologized profusely to the guard before he dismissed him. We were not dismissed. We were made to sit quietly with our hands folded until our dad finished the work he had come to do.

****

All of our school field trips were to the buildings in Washington, D.C.: the Smithsonian Museum, the Capitol, the Washington and Jefferson Monuments. I was sick and missed school the day they went to Arlington Cemetery. The kids all said it was great. And later I thought I was going to have a chance to see it when my Uncle Zip died.

After Aunt Sally had gotten out of the Japanese prison camp in Manila, she met a dashing young Army Colonel named George Van Millett, Jr. Everybody called him "Zip." He had been in a German prison camp, so he and Aunt Sally had a lot in common. Uncle Zip was captured by the Germans but later escaped. All of these poor "heroes" and "heroines" were on a well-earned military leave in Hawaii, just trying to piece their sanity back together. Zip and Sally fell in love and got married.

Eventually, Zip was transferred to Lebanon. While he and Sally and their children lived there, Zip was diagnosed with leukemia, and quickly became very sick. Sally made arrangements to leave their boys in Lebanon, and she and Zip were trying to board a military transport to come back to Walter Reed Hospital in Washington so he could get the best treatment available. Uncle Zip died as they were boarding the plane.

Now, instead of taking him to Walter Reed Hospital, Sally was planning a funeral. She didn't have anybody to stay with in the D.C. area, so my father invited her to stay with us.

Bad idea.

The days before the funeral were sort of a blur, with people coming and going and the phone ringing constantly. It was interesting too, to see what people did when someone died. Because we moved so much, and because my mother was so weird about death anyway, my parents didn't go to many funerals. I was curious about what was involved.

Of course, we were all holding our breath again, hoping Mother wouldn't unravel before they got Zip safely in the ground. She was holding up pretty well, but she had a sort of edge to her that made you feel that she might decide all of a sudden that Aunt Sally had looked at her wrong or not looked at her, or whatever the case might be. And since my father was running around trying to be helpful to his bereaved sister, that made the situation doubly volatile.

The day of the funeral, Aunt Sally came downstairs dressed completely in black, including a black hat and a black veil. She looked tired, but in spite of all she'd been through, she was still a very good-looking woman. My mother looked nice too, in a smart but conservative suit. My dad was in his dress uniform, which made him look especially handsome. And of course, my sister and I were both dressed in our little "gracious lady funeral outfits," standing around waiting for the adults to tell us what to do next. My dad had prepared us for what we would see. He told us about Arlington Cemetery, how it dated back all the way to the Civil War.

When the relatives and friends were all assembled, and the big black cars came to the house to pick us all up, my mother looked at me as I stood inside the front door of our house. "Death is so sad," she said, holding my chin in her black-gloved hand. "I don't think you should go."

Our German nanny, Hannah moved onto the scene as if on cue, and encircled me with her arms. She had grown quite instinctual about Mother's behavior, and she always seemed to materialize out of nowhere to rescue us when something cataclysmic was about to go down.

"Let's you and me go have something to eat, *Liebling*," she said warmly in her still-broken English.

By the time I realized what had happened, everyone including my grown-up-looking sister was out the door and the black limousines were pulling away from our driveway.

Hannah and I spent a boring afternoon together. We played about two thousand games of cards: Go Fish and Gin Rummy and Double Solitaire. Then, I turned on the television and watched *Winky Blink and You*, a children's show on which kids drew on the television screen with special crayons and a clear plastic sheet that stuck to the screen. Winky Blink drew the designs from his side, one line at a time, and then the little kid (in this case, me) drew the same line quickly before Winky Blink made that line disappear. About the time this picture of a monkey was taking shape, all the black limousines had come back. Then the fun *really* started. It was time for cocktails.

****

I don't really recall when my mother got up a full head of steam that night. I was feeling really left out and scared because everyone else, including my sister, got to actually see them bury Uncle Zip. Barbara and Hannah both came upstairs and read stories to me before I went to sleep. The adults were actually behaving themselves in the living room, at least until Mother got past her point of no return. I know that Zip's parents were at our house for a while, and other people came and went all evening.

I don't know what started the brawl, but sometime in the middle of the night, my mother was screaming at my father about Aunt Sally and how did she think she could just waltz into our house and disrupt our wonderful life. Years later, my Aunt Maxine told me that Sally could be pretty strong-minded herself, but the fact remained that *Sally* was the one who had just lost her husband, and Mother could have *at least* tried to remain civil. I don't know where Aunt Sally was during the big discussion between my parents, but by the time I got up the next morning, Sally was long gone, and my mother was sleeping it off.

We never talked about what happened that night. In fact, we rarely talked about Aunt Sally at all. I know my mother held bitterness towards her husband's sister for many, many years. It wasn't until I was in my fifties that I really got to sit down with my aunt and hear her stories. And I did finally get to Arlington Cemetery many years later, when Aunt Sally herself was given a heroine's funeral with full military honors. She was a courageous and fascinating woman, and I regret not getting to know her better.

Chapter 20
Movin' West

"Margie, we're going to have to get you a little ball to squeeze!" my father said as he grabbed my nine-year-old hand in his.

He was referring to a silly habit I had developed, probably out of anxiety. I would "play" with my fingers in sort of an obsessive-compulsive way, running one finger around the edge of all the others, in order, and then doing the same thing with the second finger and the third, and so on, sometimes on both hands at once. I could not be interrupted or I'd have to start all over, which was what I did as soon as my dad let go of my hand. I was too young to understand that this behavior was probably one way I had of nurturing myself when no other nurturing was available.

The year was 1956. Elvis Presley was singing about people with broken hearts going to a hotel. The world was introduced to Eliza Dolittle as the Broadway musical "My Fair Lady" opened in New York City. Pakistan became the first Islamic republic. U.S. movie star Grace Kelly married Prince Ranier III of Morocco, and my father had been transferred again. The Air Force was moving our furniture and belongings, and we were driving our two cars in convoy across the country from Virginia. I rode with my father in the old Chevy, and Mother and Barbara drove the Oldsmobile.

We stopped off in Missouri to go to a Blaine family reunion, the first one I remember attending. My mother absolutely hated the Blaine reunions. For one thing, they were held *outside* in the summer and Mother lived *inside*, the year round. There was usually shade from trees or a picnic shelter, but all of the food sat out and my mother complained for years about the flies and the hot food getting cold and the cold food melting and running off the plates. She was very picky about what she ate at the reunions, and she tried to enforce what the rest of us ate too. Some of the food was eaten with our hands, which drove my mother right over the edge.

My sister and I just thought it was great to try all these home-cooked dishes: southern fried chicken, potato salad, six different flavors of Jello, pies made with lard in the crust, and all kinds of bread and rolls. The Blaines love bread. And corn on the cob, which of course Mother thought was just about the most disgraceful food to eat because you held it with your *hands*, for God's sake, and the butter dripped down your chin. We thought it tasted like yellow candy.

Mother also hated the reunions because nobody drank. Nobody. Well, I suspect some people might have had a flask someplace and made excuses to go kick the tires on their truck or duck into the woods to pee. But we sure never saw a bottle of booze anywhere in or around the reunion site. Mother must have felt like she was going cold turkey because she wasn't *about* to duck into the woods, and kicking tires wasn't exactly in her "gracious lady" repertoire. She would just sit on a folding chair looking miserable while Daddy's relatives made the rounds and visited with her until somebody relieved them so they could go have some fun.

But the visit to Bible Grove was over in a few days, and we were back on the road to Colorado.

****

I was so excited about moving to Colorado, I could hardly contain myself. I knew they had lots of horses there because that was where cowboys came from. All the way from Virginia, I played a game with myself picturing my imaginary horse, King, running alongside the car with his mane and his tail flying out behind him and his nostrils flaring. Never mind that King could never have run fast enough or far enough to keep up with an automobile. In my mind's eye, he was galloping for all he was worth.

Barbara, on the other hand, was clearly not happy. She was at an awkward age, a young woman with many wounds and scars already—and now she was going to her fourth high school in four years. I remember her as always having a soft heart with animals and people, especially children. My sister's caring ways were becoming more evident every year. I was grateful in my heart for her kindnesses, but I was not very good at telling her of my gratitude while we were growing up.

In a military family, moving is a fact of life, so my sister had to suck it up and try to make the best of her senior year. At first, we lived in a plain tract home, but my parents were building a custom-designed house that my dad had been dreaming of for years. Daddy planned to retire in Colorado Springs, after his last tour of duty at an Air Force Base there, so I looked forward to some permanency. My sister was just frustrated that she would barely have time to make a few new friends before she was out of high school and on to college.

****

My junior high and high school years weren't much more fun than my sister's had been. My friends were all "fringe dwellers," never the "in crowd." I longed to have something I was good at, so I could be proud of my accomplishments. I loved music and wished I could have music lessons, but my father wouldn't allow it. Once when she was drunk, Mother bought an old upright piano. I played it by ear when Daddy wasn't home, though I had no idea what I was doing. I thought maybe if I wished hard enough, I'd just wake up one morning and be able to play that piano like an old pro. But my parents fought about the piano so much that Mother finally got rid of it.

I was also good at art, and my father decided that I should be some type of artist when I grew up. I wasn't consulted. It was just understood that I would go to college and major in art, just like my sister was told she would go to college to become (choose one) a nurse, a secretary or a teacher. My father didn't think girls needed to get an education past high school, except "to have something to fall back on" if our respective "prince charmings" took an extended leave of absence or got killed defending our honor or our country—or both.

I began my freshman year at Colorado State University in Fort Collins, with a major in fashion design. My favorite class that year was American Literature, where I apparently wowed the professor so much he wrote a note on my book review of J.D. Salinger's *Catcher in the Rye*.

"You show great promise in writing," he scrawled in red pen, no less. "You have captured the essence of Holden Caulfield's personality. Care to meet me for coffee and discuss it further?"

I was so incredibly naïve, I stopped at his desk after class, heart thundering in my chest, and identified myself. We walked together to the student union and sat at a small table by the window. I noticed, in the harsh light, that the prof had more zits than I did. We spent an other-worldly hour discussing Holden Caulfield's depression, mental breakdown, sexual exploitation, impulsive spending, and generally weird behavior. Mostly the prof talked and I nodded my head.

"How many other Salinger books have you read?" he asked at last.

I cleared my throat. "Just the one. Sir." *Was I supposed to call him "sir?"*

He gazed at me like he had just been told I cheated on a test. I never did understand whether he was making a pass at me or really thought I had literary talent. In any case, the rest of the term went by without so much as a glance from him, in class or out. He did, however, give me an "A."

****

After one year at the State U, I transferred to Denver to be with a boyfriend. That ended on my parents' porch when he hit me following a date. At least I was smart enough to know that was not acceptable behavior from a boy. My mother happened to be on Antabuse at the time, and she heard the commotion. The only thing she said to me was, "Don't ever tell your father."

The truth was, Mother stayed sober for several years in Colorado Springs following her stay at Pine Tree mental hospital and her court order to take Antabuse to control her drinking. The year I received my bachelor's degree, my parents decided to move over the river and through the woods to Las Vegas, Nevada. They came to my graduation ceremony with the car packed. My sister was livid. She said she'd never take her children there to see their grandparents in that town. Though she eventually mellowed, we both always felt that Nevada in general and Las Vegas in particular was not a good place for my parents to settle. And, of course, at the time of the move, the big question I posed to my father was, "Will she still take Antabuse there?"

"Well," my father had said, obviously wanting to avoid the subject, "The court papers won't be *transferred* there, but I'm sure she'll be all right."

The weird thing was, she was all right, for a while. She stayed completely sober for nearly a decade. I could not have known at that time that *my own actions* would lead her to "fall off the wagon."

****

Around the time I graduated, I broke up with yet another guy. By this time, I'd been through quite a few boyfriends, and you would think that I would have gotten kind of used to these relationships ending. But I never did, and I got very maudlin and dramatic every time. This time was no different. I had "postponed" graduate school for this latest beau, which was probably my first mistake. He decided, with no input from me, that our romance was over, and though I tried to get him to change his mind, it was no use.

Lying in bed in my apartment, I was literally *forcing* myself to cry because I was supposed to feel bad. I mean, I *did* feel bad, but I had already been reaccepted into grad school and given notice to my employer. So I was moving on, and there wasn't any reason for all this commotion. But, at twenty-two, I knew no more about what a healthy relationship was supposed to look like (or not look like) than I had at fifteen. While I was staring at the ceiling blubbering away, I sensed a bright light coming from the hallway. Rolling over on the bed, I saw the most beautiful, soft glow. I would have been scared out of my wits, except the glow seemed so warm and inviting, and it was coming towards me, closer, closer, until I saw in the midst of the glow a robed figure that looked a whole lot like Jesus Christ.

Now *that* scared me.

Sitting straight up in bed, I threw a size six-and-a-half tennis shoe at the doorway. I told the vision to get out, go away, don't bother me, and I spewed out a few obscenities for good measure. And He vaporized into thin air. Eventually I cried myself to sleep, and when I woke up the next morning, I dismissed the whole incident as my overactive imagination.

****

In the fall of 1969, I went to Albuquerque and began the master's program in counseling at the University of New Mexico. Even though I had thrown Christ out of my bedroom, I had at least figured out that helping other people was a nobler career for me than to help relieve people of their hard-earned money to decorate their houses. The program at UNM was the shortest master's program I could find, and it did not require a thesis, only an oral final exam. I got a graduate assistant position in the dormitories which paid my tuition and fees, room and meals, and rendered about fifty dollars a month spending money–enough to get by, along with the small amount of savings I had. I learned a lot in Albuquerque, and I loved it there.

If New Mexico is the Land of Enchantment, my classmates and I were certainly mesmerized by the two department chairs for the counseling program. They were good buddies and more than a little weird. They taught us all the standard stuff: counseling theory, group theory, psychological testing, career development theory. But they both appeared to be stoned during most class periods, and their lectures were very disjointed. Fortunately, we had good textbooks, full of appropriate counseling concepts.

In order to graduate, we had to go through an all-night "group encounter" with a PhD candidate as facilitator. In our group were a couple of married men, three or four single women, a nun from Columbia, and the facilitator. It was an interesting night.

The nun kept asking us if we knew Jesus Christ as our personal Savior. Though her English was poor, she had *that* sentence down pat. We would just be making some sort of breakthrough where someone was really getting in touch with his or her pain, or childhood, or sexuality, or all three, and off the nun would go again. Finally, the leader who was Jewish, told her to shut up. I felt bad for her because she really was a gentle soul. Why she even wanted the degree, I don't know, but she was one of the first people I remember meeting who really could not be swayed from her faith.

Sometime after I graduated, I read that the two counseling department heads had moved to California and started a drug and alcohol treatment program based on the Gestapo Boot Camp Theory of Counseling (not part of our curriculum). Apparently, the program met with little success because they were subsequently both arrested for kidnapping and unlawfully detaining their clients.

****

By the time I had completed graduate school, my father tried to persuade me to move to Las Vegas and live with them. I had different ideas. I moved back to Colorado Springs.

Chapter 21
The Secret Place of Thunder

You called in trouble, and I delivered you;
I answered you in the secret place of thunder...
Psalm 81:7

After graduate school, I took a job as a vocational rehabilitation coordinator at a sheltered workshop and the west edge of Colorado Springs. My job was to coordinate services to physically and mentally challenged people who needed to develop job skills. The salary was lower than I wanted, but it was good to be back in what I now claimed to be my hometown, at the foot of Pikes Peak.

I rented a small apartment and bought a little dachshund puppy and named her Brandy for the color of her puppy fur. She went everywhere with me, and she was with me the day I drove up Cheyenne Canon in my little Volkswagen to search for scenery to sketch. I had not lost my interest in art, and although I was my own worst critic, I had begun sketching scenery and old buildings, and then completing the projects in watercolor when I got back home.

About halfway up the mountain, I pulled into one of the numerous parking areas. It was a gorgeous day in late June, still a bit chilly at the higher elevations, but that didn't bother me. I had worn a heavy sweatshirt, and I was ready for a great afternoon of art and relaxation. I gave Brandy a drink out of a plastic tub I had brought for her, and together we started up the mountain looking for a suitable scene to sketch. I chatted briefly with some picnickers there. Their children petted my puppy.

I found an interesting mountain scene, with the jewel-like sky just peeking through the mossy rocks, framed perfectly by some Ponderosa pines. I got out my sketchpad. Brandy found a sunny place on a rock and curled up for a nap. Time seemed to stand still.

I was struggling to get the sketch just right, and I became vaguely aware that I was losing light. *Almost done*, I said to myself. I was pleased that the drawing was turning out well.

Suddenly, I heard some branches crunching and a man jumped out from behind a large rock. He startled me, but I recall thinking he was just joking around. He had a green bandana tied across his mouth and nose. *What a jerk*, I thought to myself. Brandy woke up and raised her tiny head.

And then I saw the gun.

I dropped my sketchpad and pencil. The man grabbed my arm. The tectonic plates in the earth surely shifted as I tried to grasp the truth of what was happening. Movement slowed to a crawl. The sounds of the mountain forest became muffled, as though my senses were under water. The pressure in my skull threatened to blow my head apart.

"I've been watching you," he hissed.

Survival instincts kicked in and I heard myself say, "I'm with some people. They're over there." I pointed towards the picnic shelter.

"No, they're not," he said slyly. "They've been gone for hours."

"No, they'll be worried if I don't come back!"

"MOVE!" he yelled, propelling me forward up the mountain with one arm while pushing the gun into my back with the other. In the hand that gripped my arm, he also held a black drawstring bag with something very heavy inside. The bag bumped my arm as we walked. Brandy began howling in an unearthly way, making noises I didn't know a puppy could make. Her primal instincts signaled danger, and she tried her best to raise a ruckus.

"Shut that dog up!" the man said.

"Can I pick her up?" My voice was trembling, and I was suddenly very cold.

Amazingly, he allowed me to collect my dog, probably to keep her quiet. We walked a short ways up the mountain–the longest walk of my life–out of sight of the road, of anyone passing by, away from any chance I had of escape. My mind went numb. *Stay calm*, I told myself. *Don't panic.*

When we reached what the man must have thought was an undetectable location, he told me to put Brandy down. She wasn't howling any more. My holding her for a few minutes seemed to calm her down.

The man commanded me to take off my clothes. I did. At first, I thought he would make me lie down, and all I could think of was that it was getting colder–and I was feeling it. It was also getting dark. I just wanted to do what he wanted me to and get it over with. I thought he would get on top of me. But he had another surprise in store.

"Use your mouth!" he commanded. I don't remember what happened next. I must have kneeled in front of him. I did what he said. I remember vomiting when it was over.

Then he opened the little black bag that he was holding and took out a five or six foot length of log chain. That's when I thought I was going to die.

"What are you going to do with that chain?" I asked, feeling the fear rise from my toes.

"I'm going to keep you from telling anybody what happened."

He started dragging me towards a tree.

"NO!" I was shouting now. "DON'T CHAIN ME TO A TREE! IN THE NAME OF GOD, DON'T DO THIS!"

Looking directly at him, I saw eyes from Hell.

I saw him raise his arm but I was too stunned to react. The log chain came down and hit me on my right temple. I stumbled backwards, fell to the ground, felt the pine needles and small pebbles scraping my bare back.

"DON'T TALK ABOUT GOD!" he screamed at me. I held his eyes with mine. I was on to something.

"GOD, PROTECT ME NOW!" I cried, feeling a sense of momentary power.

"NO!" the man screamed. He covered one ear with a hand, swinging the chain at me again with the other. I rolled out of the way. And then he was gone–down the hill, running, jumping over rocks and branches. I lay frozen until I heard a motor start and then fade into the distance. I sat up on the ground, completely naked, trying to take in what had just happened. But at the same time, my mind tried to lock it out, to reject the occurrence as something too painful to be true. Even then, I knew on some level of my subconscious that what had just taken place was being etched into my memory with the hot soldering iron of terror.

But wait, something else was pressing on my consciousness: I had called on God's power, a God I didn't even really believe in, and He had delivered me. Of this, I was sure. Why? I had no clue.

Suddenly, I was in survival mode again. *I've got to get out of here!* Brandy was whimpering now, trying so valiantly to be my protector, doing what animals have done since time began, letting her primal instincts take over. I gathered my clothes and reached for her. At first she was reluctant even to come to me, but she let me pick her up. I hastily pulled on my clothes, no easy task, while carrying her and starting down the mountain. I was wary, looking all around, certain it was the man whom I had heard leave, but not ready to trust my instincts this soon. Would I ever trust men again?

By the time I reached my car, it was almost dark. Only a little bit of light remained in between the shadowy canyons. I thought of my art supplies, but I knew I couldn't go back for them. I sat in my car with the doors locked for a few seconds, but I quickly realized that I had to get some help. My head was throbbing. I reached up now and touched my temple. I found no blood. My hand was shaking. I HAD to tell someone what happened, anyone. Mostly, I just wanted to talk to another human being–a safe one.

Driving down the mountain, I saw no one for several miles. The parks and picnic areas were empty, no trout fishermen in the streams, no hikers enjoying their endorphin rush before heading home. Finally, I rounded a bend and saw a group of young adults loading their car. I pulled up along side of them and rolled down my window. *What do I say?*

"Help me please! I've just been raped!" I said. I watched as their faces went from happy weekend smiles to looks of terror and disbelief.

"Oh, my God!" said a woman. "What can we do?" asked a man.

What can they do? Nothing, I thought.

"Did you see anyone come this way? A man alone?" There was only one road, so I knew he had to have passed by.

"No," they said simultaneously. Then one of the women added, "Do you want us to drive you someplace?"

I thought for a moment. I didn't know what I wanted, but I was already driving!

"No," I replied. "I'll just drive myself to the police station."

I watched them for a moment in my rear view mirror. They stood, looking after me, as though stunned, unable to accept the horrible news that had just ruined their happy mood. The drive into town took forever but it gave me time to think and formulate what I could remember about the man. Height, weight, clothes. All I could see in my mind's eye was the green mask. *Think, Meg,* I told myself, *You've got to remember!*

At the El Paso County Sheriff's Office in downtown Colorado Springs, I carried Brandy into the building with me, and walked up to the desk. Everyone looked busy.

"Excuse me," I whispered weakly. "I've just been raped."

****

I have no idea what kind of treatment I expected. I had seen my share of detective shows on television, but none of them dealt with rape, or "sexual assault" as I later learned this was called. In 1972, households weren't ready for rape in their living rooms. So I really had no point of reference. And, as I realized years later, I was much more naive about things than I thought I was at the time. To put it bluntly, the treatment I received immediately following the assault was detestable.

After I waited for what seemed like hours, a detective came into the seating area and introduced himself. He took me into a little office area that held several desks. People were working all around him, so there was no privacy. He said nothing about my dog so I assumed she could stay with me.

"Tell me what happened."

So I did. He asked me several questions. The ones that stuck in my mind were: Is it possible you knew this assailant? No. Do you need medical attention? Possibly. What type of gun was he carrying? I have no idea..

The gun question seemed to pose the biggest problem for the detective. He wanted to know if it was a pistol or an automatic. I told him I didn't know the difference. The detective paused while my thoughts drifted someplace far away, back to the events of the day, to my life before, which I somehow knew was now gone forever.

Then the detective drew his gun, and for a moment, I thought he was going to point it straight at me, like in some cheap horror show plot where no one can be trusted. I conjured up a sinister look on his face, which wasn't really there at all. Perhaps he was going to morph into an alien being... Instead he laid the gun down sideways on the desk next to my trembling hand, with the muzzle pointing at the wall. "This is an automatic," he said gently, watching my face closely as investigators are supposed to do, to detect a glimmer of recognition in my eyes.

"That looks like the gun he had," I said evenly. At least I was sure of one thing.

****

After the detective was done questioning me, he said they would contact me if they heard anything. I didn't know what that meant, but I do remember thinking that surely they would find the guy. Yes, I was incredibly naive.

Another officer in a squad car drove me to my house to drop Brandy off. I ran inside and brushed my teeth; no one told me not to. Then the officer took me to the nearest hospital. I hadn't ever been to any of the hospitals, so I didn't know that my doctor didn't have "privileges" at the one he took me to, and I didn't know I had every right to insist that this hospital call my own physician if I asked them to. At the front desk, I was put in a wheelchair and taken to the emergency ward. A nurse helped me up on a gurney and told me to lie down. That felt pretty good. She looked at my temple that by now was beginning to throb. She told me there was a doctor on call, and they were trying to reach him now.

I tried to relax. I tried to think. I started to cry.

I lay on that stupid gurney for the better part of an hour. The nurse kept coming back to check on me, with a worried look. Eventually, she brought me a telephone and said the doctor was on the line. She had a look on her face that said, *This isn't right, but what can I do?* Picking up the receiver, I said hello.

"Hi. This is Dr. Bennett." He spoke very fast, like he had someplace better to be. "Listen, it's too bad about what happened... There isn't much I can do, you know. They explained the situation to me and because he didn't...well, you know, he didn't *penetrate*...there won't be anything to *prove* you were raped..."

About two decades later I finally understood what this clown was talking about. Today's forensic techniques most certainly could extract a semen sample from the mouth, and a DNA test could have positively identified the assailant—if he had a criminal record or could be caught. But in 1972, doctors could only look at obvious abrasions to determine if rape had occurred, and that wasn't foolproof. Lying in the emergency ward of that hospital, I grasped enough to know that this doctor did not want to leave his happy little life and come into the sad little hospital to see distraught little me. That I understood. And I was pissed.

"Hey, this guy hit me in the head with a log chain!" I protested, with the nurse cheering me on. "Don't you think we ought to x-ray my head or *something*?"

His tone changed but not for the good.

"Now, listen, Miss B-l-a-i-n-e." He spread the letters out when he pronounced them, for emphasis. "I think you're going to be just fine. You just go home and get a good night's sleep and contact your regular doctor on Monday, all right?" It wasn't really a question; more like a dismissal. Take two aspirin and call me when your sanity returns.

Then the doctor hung up.

****

In the first few days after the sexual assault, I tried very hard to return to what had been my "normal" life. But I found that the air I breathed felt jagged, like sharp rocks spilling down my throat and into my lungs. Breath that should have been life-giving choked off my sense of reality and banished any shred of peace I had developed thus far in my young adult life. In the space of a few seconds, my assailant had drawn a line in the sands of time and changed life, and me, forever. Forever.

Calling my parents was out of the question. I was a woman of the seventies, and I was independent. Instead, I called a friend, a coworker, on a phone the nurse brought me in the hospital. My friend asked me to stay with her and her husband and their two small children for a couple of days. She stayed up with me all night the first night. I talked, she listened. I stayed eerily silent, she still listened. I tried to sleep, with Brandy tucked under my arm, only finding that the second I would drift into unconsciousness, I would instantly see the shape of the assailant (not "my" assailant, as everyone wanted to call him) as clearly as if he were there once more. I cried but not enough. There were not enough tears to shed for me to express the horrendous loss that I felt. Concepts such as safety, trust, and security had been ripped from my tenuous grasp and flung to the farthest regions of the universe.

These same friends loaned me their Labrador retriever for a few nights. Brandy thought it curious that we had a houseguest, but she was happy for the canine company. She still eyed me suspiciously, and she crawled into my lap each time the tears came. She spent a good deal of time in my lap in those days.

I began to process my thoughts, slowly at first, then like torrents of muddy water coming through a hole broken in some great dam. I remembered most clearly that I had cried out to God and He *had* delivered me. I truly believed that. But why was I spared? I later learned that God doesn't give us trials He doesn't think we can handle, but why did He trust me so much then? I certainly wasn't ready to trust Him... Or was I? I recalled my vision in the apartment in Denver—how I had rejected the entire notion that Jesus Christ could or would appear to me.

Now, as when it occurred, I dismissed the vision as a product of my over-active imagination. Still, I remembered the eyes of the assailant and how he reacted when he heard my words. If I had not said them, would the man have chained me to a tree and left me there for dead? Would anyone ever have found me? How many hours, how many days, would I have endured the chilly mountain temperatures, trapped there, naked and terrified? Had the Lord of the Universe really just delivered me from a *more* horrible fate than I might have endured if I had not invoked His name? What power did the Name Above All Names hold?

And why did any of it happen at all, if I wasn't to lose my life, if I was to be left with only what *remained*, a threadbare and deranged psyche with no place to hide, no place to seek sanctuary?

These ideas tied my brain in knots. In the coming weeks, months, and indeed years, the thought of God's intervention on that day came to me on and off. But I could not grasp what I could not understand. Why did He not provide me with some way to decipher what had happened? What kind of God would deliver me from a fate far worse than I might have imagined, but leave me here, broken and afraid? And why was I delivered—and not others?

It tore me completely apart to view news reports about girls and women, boys and men, who were kidnapped, sexually assaulted, and murdered. Why them and not me? Lacking an interpreter, I put my questions on the back shelf of my life. Because I could not comprehend it, I chose to try to forget it.

Another thing I knew instinctively was that I was now a card-carrying member of the "society of persons who have experienced terror." There had been no monetary initiation fee, but seemingly the dues were never completely paid. I was only twenty-five years old, but I felt I had aged a thousand years or more in the space of a few dread-filled minutes. Before the assault, I would not have described myself as a particularly happy person, but I was getting by. Now it seemed as though now a new Law of the Universe was operating in my life. That law stated that, for as long as I lived, I could never *not* be the victim of this sexual assault. *Victim* was a word that now described *me* (though years later I would realize that I really was a *survivor*).

I was certain that I could never go through something like this again. I would rather die instantly–maybe commit suicide if I had to–than to suffer the way I was now. Even when I replayed in my head what *might* have happened–I could have been chained up, I could have never been found until it was too late, I could have even been shot and left to bleed to death, or had the life force beaten out of me in agonizing blows–I was unable to console myself with the belief that I was *lucky*.

Whether those acts which I now conjured up in my mind actually happened or not, they very likely *could* have, and the fear I felt was the same. Now that I had gone through this, I doubted that I would ever again feel totally safe again. Ever.

Besides just the terrifying remembrances, I began to notice differences in all of my senses. Time was no longer measured in smoothly flowing intervals of waking and sleeping, working and eating and playing. It was measured instead by jagged shards of fear and panic, endless periods of crying and stifling moments of not being able to summon tears at all. There were also false moments of euphoria, which would come on suddenly in the form of denial: *if I don't think about it or talk about it, it never actually happened….* But then my artificial calm would just as quickly be dashed to the ground by memory's harsh tugging at my frazzled senses. To deny the existence of the pain and fear was to deny the existence of myself. This unspeakable event *had* happened, and it had happened to *me*.

It goes without saying that the nights were the worst.

****

Within a few weeks of the assault, I moved, oddly, from an upstairs apartment to the main floor of a little house with an apartment in the basement. It was a move of necessity; my previous apartment had inadequate water pressure and almost no hot water, typical of many of the older homes in Colorado Springs that had been converted into rental units. I was fascinated with these old buildings, though they provided less-than-adequate housing, and this was my second move in a year. I traded the tenuous security of an upstairs apartment, with no water pressure, for a ground level, and thus more penetrable unit, in considerably better shape. The basement apartment of the new place was being rented by a young female college student, which seemed safe enough. We met only briefly. I wanted to say, "I've been raped (by this time, I had decided the term *raped* described it all), and life isn't safe!" Instead I said, "Nice to meet you. Let me know if you need anything."

Monday after the incident I visited my own physician. He and his nurse listened to my story, still so fresh to me it seemed I was telling someone else's tale. My doctor was incensed that the hospital physician had acted the way he did. He said he knew him and planned to write him a letter. That's when he told me he would have come to the hospital to see me himself if they had only called. He examined me and said I was okay physically except for a couple of bruises. (I would have decades of headaches, mostly emanating from the right temple where I had been hit. The fact that there was never any *medical* reason found for the headaches didn't make them any less real.)

My doctor prescribed something to help me sleep, but the medication did not stop the dreams. I was somehow always convinced that the rapist knew who I was and where I lived, that he would one day return for me and do me further harm. One night I awoke a few minutes after midnight to the sight of red lights flashing through my bedroom window onto the ceiling. A rising sense of panic forced me awake in spite of the sleeping pill. I flew to the window, trembling and fighting the terror.

Police cars were on the other side of my street, three or four of them, with radios squawking into the cool night air. Around the corner, they were loading someone on a stretcher. I took a deep breath, in spite of the rocks in my throat. There was no more sleep that night, pill or no pill.

The next morning's news revealed the answer. There had been a break-in at a pharmacy around the corner from my house. The pharmacist had been working way past ten o'clock closing. A burglar had surprised him, a scuffle ensued, and the pharmacist amazingly produced a small handgun. He shot the burglar just as a crowbar came down on his head. The burglar, not seriously wounded, limped out the front door and down the sidewalk where he collapsed, right across from my house. I was strangely drawn to the trail of blood left from his wounds—the first of many more such attractions in my "life past the line." It has seemed to me ever since that there is a fellowship of those who have lived through disaster. We court it again and again, perhaps somehow believing someone else's trauma, particularly one involving bodily harm, makes ours less real. Or more valid. I was never sure which.

An old grad school buddy, a positive and very compassionate person, became my roommate. I wanted her with me every second when we were at home, and would not rest a moment unless she was there. Once, I was taking a shower while she watched television. A total *Psycho* experience happened behind the shower curtain. I imagined she was *not* there, or that someone had entered the house and subdued her, and that the same someone was heading for the bathroom. Terror filled me, and I could not even bring myself to open the curtain. When I finally turned off the shower, I could hear the television and I could hear my roommate talking to Brandy. I grabbed a towel and wrapped myself in it and ran into the living room. My startled roommate did not ask why I was crying hysterically. She just put her arms around me and held me there, an exquisite act of love and friendship I will never forget.

The next week I asked her to move out, giving her no explanation. Was it because I was embarrassed at having been so vulnerable, or did I feel the need to be alone again to prove that I was okay? I am certain she was puzzled; I suspect she was very hurt. And so she moved as soon as she could find another place. We stayed in touch for a while, and then life took us to different places and we lost contact. To this day, I cannot hold back the tears when I think of those few brief weeks when she gave of herself for my sake. It was a long time until I understood my actions at the time to be more of a declaration of denial than a signal that I was moving on.

Denial hissed at me from other quadrants too. I began to see a therapist, a professional acquaintance who conducted psychological evaluations on some of our sheltered workshop clients. I called him in desperation because everyone said I should. Though I could endlessly extol the virtues of personal counseling to those I encountered in my professional life, I was stubbornly and insolently resistant to seeking help myself.

My health insurance company allowed ten visits, though the therapist informed me that there was usually an extension granted in situations like mine. I didn't want to be a "situation." All I wanted was my life back. Because I was well versed in how to play the game, I attended all ten sessions, crying appropriately and saying as much as I thought I could without going insane. At the end of the tenth session, I announced to my astonished colleague that I was "fine." Many times I have wondered why he did not see through my ruse and help me get to the bottom of my denial.

I was not fine. I stuffed my fear and pain as far down as I could. I returned to work only two days after the assault, fresh with weeping and dizzy with emotions I did not understand. Moving through the days as if in a dense fog, I really didn't hear or truly see what was happening around me. The "pseudo-survival," with which I had become so accustomed, failed me at times, leaving me flailing helplessly in the reality of what had happened. Each time, I chastised myself and dove deeper into my inner self, where I had suffered so many hurts even before the assault. *Why was this any different?* I cried defiantly, to no one but myself. *Life isn't fair. It never was.*

Before the assault, I had met a "nice young man" who was an elementary school teacher. We had been out a couple of times, and he went home to his parents' house for the summer. When he returned in late August, he asked me out. Debating about telling him of the assault, I decided that I should. If we continued dating, I reasoned, he would want to know. So I told him.

He never called me again.

This really came as no surprise to me. I had seen the same look on the faces of countless other soon-to-be-ex friends in my lifetime. If I told people about my screwy family, I became somehow "less than" in their eyes. Being a victim of sexual assault was just another notch in the same gun—when I shot it out there—-always seemed to send people packing.

∗∗∗∗

Before all of this happened to me, I had been observing my coworker Peggy, with a distracted sort of interest. Though many of the workers at Goodwill Industries professed openly to be Christians, Peggy positively *exuded* what I later learned was God's grace. My "friends" at work and I went about brightening our days with a certain sort of cynicism. After all, life *was* pretty comical when you were twenty-something and had no real responsibilities. But Peggy sat at her desk doing her job in silence. Not a priggish sort of silence. She smiled at everyone and spoke gently to each of us, and was always there to help when called upon. But during her lunch break, she did the most amazing thing: she sat quietly by herself in the corner of the cafeteria and read her Bible.

Though I had often noticed her doing this, I never really thought much about it until after the assault. But try as I might, I just could not get up the courage to share my experience on that mountain. I thought, *She couldn't handle it, she would run screaming if I tried to tell her about it.* And so, I continued to regard her silently, perhaps with even more curiosity than before. I didn't have the foggiest notion that this God of Peggy's was relentlessly pursuing me down the corridors of my life–and the chase was just beginning.

****

In the fall of that awful year, my parents came to visit, always an opportunity for disaster. My mother had continued in her sobriety after they moved to Las Vegas, but it always appeared to me that she was one sip away from a complete meltdown. We were far from close during that time. I trusted my parents very little, and they in turn seemed to grant me no permission to handle my life without them. We were, in counseling terms, stuck. There was nowhere to move forward, and we surely did not want to look back. If we had, it might have scared all three of us to death.

It was not surprising that I was able to keep the news of the assault from my parents. It was completely out of the question to believe they could help or support me during that time. I had not even told my sister. I was the tough one, the one who could pass through this life without accumulating any of the drudgery and sorrow that so many people displayed. I would fool Life itself. I believed it had worked for me for years, and I believed it would work now.

Then the bottom dropped from my world once again.

Chapter 22
A Blessed Thing to Mourn

*God has come to wipe away our tears. He is doing it; He will
have it done as fast as He can; and until He can He would
have them flow without bitterness; to which end He tells us it is
a blessed thing to mourn because of the comfort that is on its
way.*

George McDonald,
as quoted in *Our Daily Bread*

Sitting in the lunchroom at work, I was thinking of where I might
take my parents for dinner that evening. The place needed to be
obscure enough that, if there were to be a scene, no one would know
me or even notice this crazy family so at odds with each other. This
was always the way I thought when my parents were around, no
matter what outward appearances might indicate. There was always
the potential for a blow-up. It would ever be so. Avoiding the
catastrophe of a family feud was my chief goal whenever my parents
visited me.

It began slowly as the words across the table penetrated my brain,
but didn't really sink in. A volunteer who joined us for lunch was
telling an incredible tale, about a teenage girl and her mother, riding
horseback in the mountains. There had been a man, in a funny green
mask, carrying a gun, who had suddenly jumped out from behind a
rock. He made them dismount and tried to—*tried to what?*— assault
them, but the horses made such a commotion that he couldn't
overcome the women and they got away.

The words began to pierce my consciousness, slowly at first, and
then all at once, like a bucket had been overturned and spilled them.
The words lay at my feet and then they crawled up to my throat and
into my eyes. *"And the police caught the man,"* she was saying. *And the police
caught the man! AND THE POLICE CAUGHT THE MAN!* I was on
my feet and running past Peggy and her Bible, towards my office
when I heard the last of what she was saying. *"He's an MP. They have
him in the brig at Fort Carson."*

Slamming my office door, panic gripped me. *This cannot be happening! If they've found him, I have to come forward! I can't stuff this any more!*

I called the switchboard and had a coworker paged, the one I trusted the most. She knew about the assault, and she had been sitting at the lunch table beside me. The expression on her face when she knocked and entered my office told me all I needed to see. I knew in a millisecond where we were going with this.

"You've got to call the police," she said. "You know it's got to be him, Meg! You've got to let them know it's him!"

"No!" I shrieked at her. "My parents are here! They can't know what happened! They'll never understand!"

But I knew that I had to face the incredible reality that he had struck again. Amazingly, in an incomprehensible way, my life and the lives of these two new victims had crossed paths by chance. Now I had to see it through. *Perhaps I could help them*, I thought. *Perhaps they could help me.*

With trembling hands, I picked up the phone, and with my coworker's encouragement, I dialed the El Paso County Sheriff's office. Looking at my friend's face, as if the words might strangely be written there for me to read aloud, I stammered, "I think they've arrested the man who...who raped me three months ago."

Next there was an unbearably long silence on the other end of the phone–as though I had just stated something so unbelievable that the hearer was struck deaf and dumb at the very thought of it. I closed my eyes and waited. Finally, after what seemed like time stood completely still, she stated, "Let me put you through to the detective."

A male voice came on the line. More stammering, more dead space between my words and his. I managed to explain who I was and why I was calling, relaying the incredible story of how, by chance, I had heard of another assault. *Attempted* assault. Different but the same.

At last the detective sighed, a little too deeply, as though my report would add an unreasonable amount of work to his already horrendous day. Never mind what it meant for my day.

The detective instructed me to come to the sheriff's office to try to identify the man. Was this going to be a live lineup–the lineup of my nightmares? Shortly after noon, I arrived, trembling with the very thought of being in the same building with this awful creature. I was certain it was he–it could be no one else. The description was too similar. And by now, I believed they would have sent for him, transported him from the brig at Fort Carson, here to the sheriff's department for me to identify. After being ushered into a waiting room, I was told that a "matron" would come for me. Presently, a large, buxom woman in a uniform opened the inner door of the room and said, "You the one who thinks you can identify this guy?"

"Yes," I said timidly. *NO!* I had wanted to scream. *No, there must be some mistake! I'm not at all sure I can do this! I'll just go quietly and forget any of this ever happened.* This I said to myself, while my feet propelled me to the open door. I peered in anxiously, expecting the typical set-up I had seen in the movies, with a one-way glass wall. Instead of a lineup of scary characters bearing grudges and serial numbers, I saw a room filled with photo albums. My expression told the matron that I did not comprehend.

"You can look through these books and see if you see anybody that looks like him," she said matter-of-factly. She reminded me of an impassive flight attendant nonchalantly showing me how to survive, in case some life-threatening event occurred, while not believing for a second that anything remotely life-threatening could possibly happen on her watch.

"You must be kidding," I said. "There are hundreds of photographs here! How am I supposed to find this guy in here?'"

She eyed me guardedly. "This is all we got," she stated with finality. "Call me if you find him." And she unceremoniously shut the door.

Bewildered, I surveyed the dozens of books, some on shelves, some scattered on the table in this strange little room that seemed to hold the only key to getting this assailant off the streets and out of my life forever. Did I have any chance of finding him in all these photos? What I recalled of him, I realized now, was little of his face itself, behind the green bandana. Not a green bandana in any of these books, I imagined. What I recalled–his height, his weight perhaps, his gait, his mannerisms, his voice–none of those would be found in a mug shot, if indeed I could narrow the mug shots down in any reasonable fashion. I flipped through a couple of books and realized my efforts were totally in vain. Fighting the too-familiar tears, I stood and opened the door. The matron stood with her back to me and glanced lazily over her shoulder.

"I can't find him," I said, hiding my face.

Not a single word of encouragement. She neither stated the obvious (that it was an impossible task) nor offered me any other alternative (the live lineup I was expecting). She only shrugged and led me to the front door.

"Sorry," she offered, almost as an afterthought.

****

Years later, I learned from many professionals who work with victims of sexual assault that the law enforcement and hospital personnel with whom I dealt at the time of the incident were not only atypical but downright unprofessional and incompetent, even for the early seventies when the assault took place. I had every right to ask for a live lineup, and should have been assigned some kind of an advocate, volunteer or an attorney. And even if I had not been able to identify the man myself, I had every right to be apprised of his arrest, the investigation and the subsequent trial because of the similarities between the two assaults.

Instead, I walked through the fog back to my little Volkswagen. I drove around town until it was about time for me to be coming home from work, to avoid alarming my parents by arriving early (always the "good daughter"). I pulled into the driveway of my little house, and I went in and greeted my parents. I told them I had something I needed to tell them, and I asked them to sit down. To their utter amazement and obvious disbelief, I related the entire tale of the assault in terms I thought they could accept, being careful to leave out the unspeakable details. I ended with the day's events and stated that I believed they would call me to testify in some way and that, through my testimony, I believed this man would be punished for what he had done.

(Of course, I thought nothing of the sort, after having been dismissed so unceremoniously by the matron. But I thought, bravely, that this is what my parents wanted to hear.)

And then, the most amazing thing happened. My mother began to weep softly, and then not so softly, and I held her in my arms and rocked her to console her. Hearing of the rape was obviously too much for her to handle. While I rocked her, my father began pacing the floor of my living room, exactly like George C. Scott would do later in the opening scenes of the movie *Patton*. Then my father delivered a long and desperate oration about how he thought I ought to handle things from here, an impassioned father/officer plea. He told me (*ordered* me) not to agree to testify to anything because, once they got me on the witness stand, the lawyers for the defense would obviously ask me about every boy I'd ever kissed and I would be forced to tell all. (I suppose it goes without saying that my father considered me less than pure, which meant there was much to be revealed in a court of law, if not the family living room.) He told me to forget about the incident and move on with my life, like a good daughter/soldier–and there would be no talk of it again.

And there was not, from that day forward, any talk between my parents and me about the rape. I just stuffed it farther down, into my socks, until one day I found what I thought was an escape.

I ran away with the circus.

Part IV

Me on the Drums, 1984

Chapter 23
The Backside of the Desert

Take off your sandals, for the place
you are standing is holy ground.
Exodus 3:5

Over the years, I have come to believe that there are people in this world who use love wisely, like a well-honed tool, to demonstrate their ability to interact intelligently with other people, particularly the person they choose as a life partner. When I was younger, I was not one of these people. Instead, I used love like a pickaxe, swinging away at relationships without much thought about my aim and certainly without consideration of what these relationships might have in store for me. And, like many who are unskilled with a certain tool, I ended up being bloodied, not winning the right person's heart, but in the process, pulverizing my *own* heart and watching it be shredded into a near-lifeless mass of writhing red muscle on the floor of my life. Ka-thump.

Therefore, I was not surprised when at twenty-six, I ended up running away with a road musician. I had always wanted to be in show business, a dream never dimmed by the fact that I was only able to secure bit parts in theater and music throughout high school. Plus, because of my father's disdain for music lessons, I could not play or read one note of music. But to discover that, not long after meeting said road musician, I was playing trap set drums with a traveling show, and eventually even singing an occasional solo–this was perhaps the greatest surprise. Though the price I paid to get to that point was steep, I believe it was all part of a plan greater than I could have imagined.

When I left Colorado Springs, my parents had a meltdown. My mother said, "I can see why someone in your situation would do what you are doing." *What did that mean?* I wondered. *Was she referring to the fact that I was somehow "damaged" because I had been sexually assaulted, or that I was a "spinster" in my mid twenties? Or both?*

Then she said, "If you do this, it will not make your father and me very proud of you," to which I responded, "You've done plenty of things I'm not very proud of!" After a very pregnant pause, she answered in her best "gracious lady" tone of voice, "We are *not* in competition!"

My father just gave me his standard, "Why don't you come home now and we'll discuss this" speech. I didn't come home, and it was a long time until my parents accepted what I had done. At that point, I didn't care. But because my new love disliked my little dog intensely (was that red flag No. 1?), I convinced my parents to take Brandy off my hands, and she lived with them for the rest of her life.

In his book, *Combat Faith*, author Hal Lindsey talks about the difference between an *academic* award called a Bachelor's in *Divinity* degree and a *God-given* training program called a "backside of the desert degree." As I embarked on this next phase of my life, I did not understand that this God that I had only briefly encountered during times of crisis—this "foxhole religion," this Christ I chose to ignore and throw shoes at—was about to make Himself visible to me–again! Like Moses, I was being sent to the "backside of the desert" for the sole purpose of preparing for The Coming of the Lord.

****

I don't dare write too much about my first husband, whom I will call Rex, because, to paraphrase the old Carly Simon song, "he'd probably think this *book* is about him." We met in Colorado Springs when he was playing keyboard with a Polynesian revue (though he was of European descent and hailed from the farmlands of Wisconsin). I'll call the musical group Kai Kahoku and the Lahaina Sisters. I fell hard for this Wisconsin farm boy, though years later I realized I had confused true love with a way to remove myself completely from the harsh reality that had become my daily life. I anticipated leading a glamorous lifestyle, rubbing elbows with the rich and famous, and having more money than I could imagine.

After nine months on the road, we decided to tie the knot. Because my parents lived in Las Vegas, we were married in a little plastic wedding at the little plastic Chapel of the West on the Strip. I should have been suspicious when the pseudo "minister" showed up in a panel truck with the words "Dominici Taxidermy" on the side. At least he wasn't an Elvis impersonator. The logic behind the panel truck became more apparent at the end of the ceremony when he gave us a blessing on us. "Dominici Taxidermy," he said, making the sign of the cross, "and if you throw rice, it's extra."

The reception was a small, catered affair held at my parents' home. As we planned the wedding, the subject of having liquor came up. Rex, who had by this time demonstrated a keen interest in alcoholic beverages, stated emphatically that we could not have a wedding reception without at least some bubbly on hand. Having made it a personal policy not to drink in front of my parents, I tried unsuccessfully to put my foot down. My mother had been sober for nine years (four without the aid of Antabuse), and I wasn't about to be responsible for placing the opportunity to fall off the wagon in front of her. Rex insisted. I spoke to my parents and asked if they could handle abstaining if we "just" had champagne. They assured me they could, and we bought a case of Cold Duck.

When the best man asked everyone to toast the bride and groom, I looked over at my parents. And there was my father pouring himself *and* my mother a glass of bubbly. Years later, she told me, "Don't blame yourself. I would have found some other excuse to start again."

****

If you go on the road with a musical group, without a strong set of personal values, it is next to impossible to develop them while traveling. For one thing, we were completely surrounded by only two types of people: those who perform and those who think those who perform are some sort of gods. Since I didn't fit into the first category, I suppose I fell into the second, at least initially. I certainly was in awe of the performers, including Rex, for the first several months. But living in close proximity to the members of "our" show soon demonstrated that they were just average people too, with good points and hang ups and unresolved this and that. I suppose you could say I was a "fringe dweller," sort of basking in the limelight of other people's notoriety. Probably not a bad place for me to hide for a while. Soon I was wearing false eyelashes as long as Elsie the Cow's, and I even bought a "Dolly Parton" wig since my hair was never as fabulous as most famous people's. Gone were the jeans and cowboy boots of my youth, gone were the mini-skirted attempts at playing professional, and in their place, I wore softer, more feminine styles in richer fabrics and jazzier colors. It was the height of the psychedelic era, and I was, as they say, making a statement.

Besides enhancing my wardrobe, I also blossomed in another way: fabricating the truth. Harkening back to the "innocent" lies of my youth, I was now involved with entertainers who could stretch the truth with the best of them. When these folks got together and swapped stories about their "gigs," it was anybody's guess which tales (if any) were completely accurate. (Red flag No. 2.)

We schlepped around the western half of the continental United States for a year or so–though never to exotic places like Hawaii or Tahiti, where every tour bus driver and souvenir shop clerk had a band. Soon, several South Sea Island drummers had come and gone, and I jokingly said I should learn percussion. The bandleader thought it was a great idea, and we bought a small set of trap drums. I took some lessons and practiced day and night, placing towels over the drums and cymbals so we wouldn't get kicked out of the hotels.

My debut was at the Commercial Hotel in Elko, Nevada, where guns were legal as long as they *weren't* concealed A woman of questionable reputation had recently become the mayor after a landslide victory over one of the town's most upstanding citizens. (She abdicated her throne quickly, stating that she really only wanted to prove a point. Which point, no one was sure.) Elko was not what you would call the "big time," but many stars had started there. So the first night I was to perform, I dutifully stepped over the drunks in the hallway outside the dressing room and took my place on the stage.

On our first break, I was so nervous I downed three straight shots of whiskey to calm myself. The second set went better, and the third wasn't half bad, though I will concede that the booze altered my perception a bit. I still had a long way to go, but my entertainment career had been launched.

The more I played in that band, the more I began to realize that I was coming out of my shell, overcoming my shyness and my self-loathing. I adopted the phrase, "Second Set Syndrome," to describe the euphoria entertainers experience by the middle of the night's performance, when we'd perhaps had a drink or two (or six or eight), the audience was eating out of our hands (at least in our own minds), and we were playing fantastically well (or at least we didn't stink). It was the entertainment industry's equivalent of the runner's high. We believed we were, in a word, invincible.

The marriage, however, appeared doomed to failure practically before it began. To say that Rex and I were from two different worlds was putting it mildly. Midwest-only-child-farm-boy-musician meets neurotic-well-educated-Air-Force-brat. I knew nothing about relationships with anybody, much less one that was supposed to last a lifetime. The men in my life were expected to be not only mind readers, but also to run Spell Check and Grammar Check and maybe even Intention Check every time I opened my mouth.

I dealt with the differences between us in the way I was brought up: I yelled and screamed. Soon, I was not the only one yelling and screaming. Rex always said I taught him how to fight, but I think he grossly underestimated himself.

****

Alas, a couple of years into my budding career in the entertainment business, Rex's mother died suddenly, forcing us to get off the road and return to Wisconsin. Since Rex was an only child, it seemed appropriate to him to make the move home, to sustain his father in his loss. Whether my father-in-law needed sustaining, particularly by us, was a matter of further disagreement at the time.

We eventually took up residence a couple of miles outside Rex's hometown that I'll call Whitewater. At the time, it all seemed like another grand adventure, like we were sacrificing this incredible career in show business to return to his birthplace and make our home there instead of in some five-star (or one-star) hotel playing to a capacity house of devoted fans (well, sometimes to a few drunks at the bar). We began playing casual band jobs, Rex on keyboard and me on drums, and soon we had bookings every weekend. We got a lot of mileage out of our stint on the road with the hometown folks, and for a while, I was pretty impressed with myself. Once again, exaggeration seemed to be important: if we played a VFW club just over the border into Minnesota, we were on "an extended tour of the Midwest." If we played just over the border into Canada, we suddenly became an "international sensation." A rumor even got started that I had once been a Las Vegas showgirl, and I admit I didn't try to set anyone straight. If my goal had been to reinvent myself, I was surely accomplishing that.

One of the things that impressed me the most about living in Whitewater was the people. When his mother died, neighbors came in and cleaned his father's house from top to bottom. They kept "the casserole brigade" going long enough to feed us for a month. Since being involved in funerals had never been part of my mother's "gracious lady training,' I had no experience with how these people just showed up and tried to make it easier for us, without our even asking.

As I got to know the townspeople and my husband's relatives, I learned that small town people could be very thoughtful, generous, wise, funny, and most appreciative of life. They could also be opinionated, bigoted, stubborn, and negative. And I began to see that how you viewed things was a choice you made. I also realized that perhaps my own prejudices needed revisiting and untangling, but my family had not prepared me to do that.

****

Somehow, I had gotten the impression that Rex had a college degree. Once I learned that he had only taken "a couple of classes," I realized I was the only one with "marketable skills." Since the band jobs were not generating quite enough income, one morning as I was heading out the door, he asked where I was going. When I said I was going to look for a day job, he came unglued. (Red flag No. 3.) He didn't want "any wife" of his (which led one to wonder just how many wives there had actually been before me) getting a real job before he had one. He was content to live from pillar to post. I wanted *stuff*: a home of our own, two cars, modern appliances, things like that. In spite of his protests, I found a job as a county social worker, with a caseload of disabled adult clients.

On my first day at work, my supervisor briefed me on the job and its duties. As he was leaving my office, he said as an afterthought, "Oh, by the way, you'll also have 'battered women' as part of your responsibilities." At that time in our country's history, the subject of domestic violence as a social problem was, really, little more than a hidden issue. I knew little about the topic, but I was always up for a new challenge.

As I look back on it now, being involved with survivors of family abuse during those years did more for me than provide a paycheck. I was humbled by my clients' stories and their courage, and I learned an expensive lesson: not all abuse is physical, but it is still abuse. Sometimes, abuse comes in the form of intimidation, or extreme lack of respect, or driving family members around when you are stinking drunk, or cruelty to pets, or even making fun of you because you could not watch violence against women on television.

And, eventually, I learned that women–including me–could maintain incredibly serene outward appearances when not all was well at home.

****

What I thought I knew about life was put to the test over and over in those early days, most especially my attitudes about alcohol. To say that alcohol isn't an occupational hazard in the music business is like denying that coal miners are susceptible to black lung disease. When we were on the road, our Polynesian employer was pretty strict about us drinking on stage, but our breaks and days off were another story. Suddenly I had found myself immersed in a lifestyle that not only condoned heavy drinking, but in fact applauded it. Musicians were *supposed* to drink. And smoke dope. And spend hours and hours doing this, accompanied by the telling of equal-opportunity offensive jokes. In other words, anyone and everyone were their targets, and all inhibitions were thrown out the window. (Red flag No. 4.)

Now that we lived in Wisconsin, our drinking got totally out of control. We also quickly learned that our neighboring state, Minnesota, was not only known for its lakes. The state has jokingly been dubbed "the land of ten thousand treatment programs," a leader in facilities designed to sober people up and restore their lives to sanity. However, in both Wisconsin and Minnesota, it seemed to me that people drank for just about any reason: birthdays, holidays, graduations, weddings, funerals, baptisms, peewee hockey–you name it, there probably was at least a keg there, if not a full bar. My mother's constant companion for most of my life had been her booze, but she had always tried to hide what she was doing. I had never lived among people who openly included alcohol in as many aspects of their lives as those in the rural Midwest.

At different times, in the early years of my marriage, I tried to drink and party along with the rest of our social crowd. After all, I had been consuming alcohol since I was sixteen without any ill effects that I could see, other than occasionally studying the inside of a toilet on my hands and knees, or suffering through the hangover from hell for half a day. I accepted these inconveniences as part of adult life. I believed I could handle drinking with the best of them—or the worst of them, however you choose to view it.

Our band followers did their part to make this extremely easy. I remember once having thirteen Harvey Wallbangers lined up on my drum case, all sent to the stage by adoring fans. This led me to the conclusion that perhaps I should switch my drink of choice to something that didn't have two shots of liquor per serving. I took to drinking wine, and probably got just as drunk, but at least I felt less guilty.

Unlike the extended engagements of the Polynesian group, the band jobs in the Midwest were almost all one-night stands. We would be hired to play at a club or for a private party, generally no more than a hundred miles from home. This meant setting up and tearing down all of the musical equipment each time we played. Most often we played only on the weekends, but at certain times of the year, we might play during the week as well. One holiday season, we played twenty-one one-night stands between Christmas and New Years. Rex worked at day jobs off and on, but for nearly two decades, I worked at my job every weekday *and* played every band engagement.

The parties were insane. It was nothing for us to end up driving three hundred miles at the drop of a hat to go to someone's bash: a fan of the band, or someone we had met at the last Oktoberfest. We frequently ended up at people's houses after band jobs, for breakfast and more booze, often not getting home until the sun was up. More and more partying was going on, with less and less attention being paid to life's responsibilities. I pondered how some people seem to grow up and get married, and others get married and then grow up. Still others get married and *never* grow up. It was clear we were not growing *anywhere* together: up, out, towards one another, or inwardly.

As our lifestyle got crazier and crazier, I woke up one day and had this sort of mini-epiphany. Memories came back to me of my mother talking about her father being so irresponsible, chasing pipe dreams at the expense of the entire family's well being. I had long feared that I would turn out just like my mother, but now I had an even greater problem on my hands. Rex wanted to live in the moment. I wanted to be more pragmatic.

I realized that I had married my grandfather, the dreamer and schemer.

****

My concern about drinking and driving had been growing, and at some point I concluded it would be safer for me to transport myself to the band jobs. This was no small feat, since Rex took particular umbrage at my actions, and many jobs were over an hour's drive away from home. One night, I had driven myself to the job, feeling confident I could get myself home as well. Only I hadn't counted on the fact that my own drinking got a little out of hand. To be truthful, I was completely and totally smashed, and after the obligatory screaming match while we tore down our equipment (by now a guaranteed part of the evening's entertainment at no extra charge), I set out for home in a mood of righteous indignation.

It didn't take long for me to realize I might be in a little bit of trouble trying to drive. Rex had taught me how to drive home on back roads, to avoid encountering the "right arm of the law." I was tooling along some dark and narrow gravel path, probably going no more than thirty-five or forty miles an hour, though I felt like I was qualifying for the Daytona 500. Fear began to envelope me–a cold, slippery feeling that I might not be able to get myself home at all. I sat straight up and gripped the wheel, trying to focus on the road and watch for rural landmarks.

OK, I said out loud, *There's the Schultz farm, so I turn just past their driveway. And there's the old schoolhouse, just beyond the fork in the road. Don't-have-an-accident, don't-have-an-accident, don't-have-an-accident!*

My brain was so foggy, it took a while for the emergency lights up the road to register. Ahead of me was an explosion of red lights, flashing, flashing, lighting up the black sky. *How nice,* I thought, *they're already here waiting for me, with an ambulance and everything.* I slowed down to a crawl and pulled a little closer. *How did they know when I'd be here?* I wondered out loud.

And then I came to my senses (sort of). *They aren't here for you, Dummy!* By now, I was close enough to see that there was indeed an accident up ahead–but it was somebody else's accident. The alcohol-filtered scene was surreal, blurry, dripping down my consciousness like a Salvador Dali painting. There were several county sheriff's vehicles, an ambulance, a first responder truck and two very mangled cars. Rescue workers were loading someone onto a stretcher. I saw a small form, probably a child, lying in the ditch with a white-clad adult hovering above. Even with all the liquor in my brain, I knew this was not just a simple fender bender.

I made a sharp right turn and took another way home, making the rest of the trip safely in spite of my condition. The next morning, I woke up with a violent hangover and a sense that things in my life needed to change. I had no idea how or why, and I certainly didn't expect it to be easy. But I knew my life was not going the way I hoped it would.

****

As I look back over the years of my first marriage, I am amazed at how the "old ghosts" from my past kept coming back to haunt me. I had always thought of myself as an intelligent person, and I was truly disappointed that I allowed myself to be trapped in circumstances that seemingly perpetuated my demise. For all of my education and experience, I didn't seem able to function as a responsible adult in my own life. In the words of T.S. Elliot:

All our knowledge brings us nearer to our ignorance.
Where is the wisdom we have lost in the knowledge?

But although my earthly coping skills were definitely lacking, my heavenly Father was still hanging around. He had more than a few surprises in store for me. That *Holy Ground* was beginning to shake under my feet, and *The Great I Am* was preparing to lead me to a mountaintop.

Chapter 24
My Gracious Lord

If you look me in the heart, you'll see that I'm changing,
If you look me in the heart, His holiness shows,
For underneath this mortal frame, the Lord is reigning,
You will see it if you look me in the heart…
                    "Look Me In The Heart"
                    Wayne Watson, Christian Composer

The gymnasium at the Whitewater High School had terrible acoustics, but it was the largest venue around for the traveling evangelist who was to appear there. Rex said he wanted to go to hear the music, so on that frosty October night in 1976, I followed him into the school, not really knowing what to expect. I had visions of it being like my mother had described, when she and Ruth went to the tent revival so many years before. In many ways, I expected the "show" probably wouldn't be much different than the one they attended, except the music might be more "contemporary," and I couldn't see any kind of stock tank like my mother said she and Ruth had been dunked in when they were baptized as teenagers.

We had to climb up high on the bleachers because most of the lower seats were taken. Rex knew a lot of people there so he was introducing them to me. A few asked what *he* was doing there, perhaps prompted by another prejudice about musicians all going to hell. When it was time for the music to start, we turned our attention to the makeshift stage.

The tunes were like country and western songs with church lyrics. I could play this, I thought, and then I felt a little ashamed, since I thought myself too unworthy to ever be involved in something like a gospel group. When it was time for the sermon, I had the distinct feeling most of the people were somehow riveted to their seats. The evangelist spoke for no more than thirty minutes, but I remember his words like it was last night. He began talking about what's important in our lives, what drives us, and what we treasure. He talked about wheels, how he started out as a young boy with a hoop and a stick. He said he could entertain himself for hours with that hoop and stick, perfecting his skill in rolling it down the country roads, imagining it being everything from a locomotive to an ocean liner if he wanted it to be. When he got a little bigger, all he could think about was a bicycle he had seen in the Sears and Roebuck catalog. He wanted that bike so badly, and finally his mother and father went to great length to get him that bike for his birthday. From the bicycle, he went to wanting a motorcycle, and then a car, and then a bigger car, and so on, until he had completely outgrown everything he used to think was the absolute limit. And then he discovered that he was unhappy.

Next, the evangelist began to tell the crowd how the Bible teaches that we are all born in sin and that we'll never find satisfaction with earthly things. I thought I would mentally check out at this point, like I had when my college friend Alice had stuck a circular under my nose and said she'd pray for me after I had joined the band. Alice had "gone Christian" on me after her first baby almost died and some holy rollers prayed for her family and the baby got well. But this night, sitting on the bleachers, the message seemed different, like something I could relate to on a personal level.

The evangelist was saying we can try to become better people, but that we have no hope of salvation without God, who is merciful and gracious to all who come to him. There was that word, *gracious*. I had heard it all my life, from the sodden lips of the woman who *gave* me life. "*I'm a gracious lady,*" she said, over and over. But now the word *gracious* was being used with an entirely different meaning. *Now* this guy had my attention.

From there, he described how Satan (a real, living being) went about trying to mess up our thinking and get us to separate from God. But God had a plan, this preacher said. God provided a way we could be reconciled to Him through the death of His only Son, Jesus Christ. Jesus took our place, He died for our sinful nature, he said. But the best part of the story is that Christ defied death and rose again, promising that those who believe in Him will have eternal life.

I had never even heard the term "altar call" before in my life, but by the time that evangelist invited people to come forward that night, I was in an emotional place where I couldn't stay on that bleacher. When I stood up and said, "I'm going down," I distinctly remember Rex saying, "Oh, man!" I asked him to go with me, but he refused. He did agree to wait for me, but I wouldn't have cared if he hadn't.

At the stage, I was met by some "counselors," whom I later learned were lay people who had taken some training to assist us new "converts." Jessie, the woman who took me aside, was a young mother who I thought had the face of an angel. She prayed with me, and I asked Christ to come into my heart and my life and to be my Savior. I told her my marriage was on the rocks and had been for some time. Then she spoke some words that I accepted as the gospel truth for nearly twenty years after that night. "Divorce is not an option," she said simply.

"Divorce is not an option." That became my mantra, repeated frequently to myself when things were particularly bad. I believed at the time that it was a true statement, always—no matter what. I was not at all sure, even then, that it was God's will that I had married Rex in the first place, and it was a very long time until I allowed myself to consider the possibility of ending the relationship. I knew that night that I had embarked on a life-long journey of faith, and I believed it was my duty as a new Christian to preserve my marriage at all costs.

But at the same time, I began to see that I no longer needed *earthly* relationships to measure my self-worth. Nor did I need the approval of mere humans to validate *any* relationships I had. Now, finally, Somebody was there to comfort me, Someone had already written all the love letters I could ever need, promised to be with me forever, and would never, ever, forsake me. And best of all, I learned His ways of coping were far superior to mine.

I felt like I had come home.

****

That night, I dreamed of a dove descending and landing on my head, before I even knew the dove is the symbol of the Holy Spirit. The next day I picked up the King James Bible my sister had given me when I was thirteen years old. I read it like a child's primer, suddenly having insight to understand much, though not all, of what I found. It was as if I was listening to a beautiful symphony for the very first time, hearing each of the instruments individually, but also beautifully blended with each other. A few nights later, I dreamed I was eating the pages of that dusty old Bible, not knowing until much later that the prophet Jeremiah had been commanded by God in a dream to eat the Scriptures. Two months later, I heard the words of those old familiar Christmas carols in a new way. When I sang "To save us all from Satan's power," it was no longer just a stanza from a silly outdated tune; it was about me, and I was the one who had been rescued. One of my new Christian friends showed me a passage in the Bible, I Thessalonians 1:5, that expressed so perfectly what I felt:

> *For we remember how the Gospel came to you not as mere words, but as a message with power behind it, the convincing power of the Holy Spirit.*

I realized that performing in the band had filled a void in my life, but that void was where God should have been, not my own ego. Another scripture passage I learned was from II Corinthians 4:7:

> *But we have this treasure in clay jars, so that it may be made clear that this extraordinary power belongs to God and does not come from us.*

I was that clay jar, and the power I felt surging through me was like nothing I had ever experienced before. I began to be more discerning in my contacts with others. I would study people I knew who, by all outward appearances, were strong and sensible and exuded self-control, and I would seek to learn why they were the way they were. Although I had periods of personal relapse into the very persona I was trying to leave behind, I later realized that many regarded me as such a person. Only the light of Christ shining through me could have given anyone that impression about me. Underneath, I was in great turmoil, but that was just the point: the Holy Spirit had always been at work in me, every day, all the time, whether I realized it consciously or not.

What a blessing!

****

Jessie became my "sponsor." She called me the day after the crusade and we had lunch. Then there was a Bible study with other new Christians as well as some older, wise ones as leaders. Since the evangelist had encouraged people to worship in the local churches, I went to the pastor of Rex's home church, the one where his mother's funeral had been held. It was a tiny church, begun in his great-grandparents' living room over a hundred years earlier. I spent hours with the pastor discussing my newfound faith. He even held an "adult confirmation class" just for me; all the others in the class just came to review the old material and cheer me on.

"You are a new creature," the pastor said. And indeed I was. I hardly knew what to do with myself. I felt so many changes going on inside me and the more I learned, the more I knew I had to learn about God and the Bible and how to live with this new set of rules. As one of my new friends put it, I had swallowed the Holy Spirit, feathers and all.

****

Soon I began to realize that there were two distinct "kinds" of Christians: born-again (like me) and those who had been raised in the church and believed the same way but maybe weren't as vocal about it (like Rex). I also learned the term "charismatic," which depending on whom you talked to, could be a good thing (on fire for the Lord) or a bad thing (crazy holy rollers). I quickly decided I preferred the *charismatic* Christians to the *automatic* ones, but I was still struggling with how we all function as brothers and sisters in Christ. Jessie told me a story that helped it all to make sense. She didn't remember where she had heard it, but it was right up my alley.

"Think of it as being like two young horses that need to be tamed," she said. "One horse was born right there at the master's farm and has never known a day when the master wasn't around. The master begins handling the little foal at birth, and so she's used to his touch. Pretty soon, he puts a rope around her neck, and she gets used to that. Next comes a halter and then a bit in the mouth and a bridle, maybe a blanket and then a small saddle, and when she's big enough, the master climbs right up onto her back. She never knows the exact point in time when she gave her will over to her master, but she definitely knows she has. She knows he's not only the boss, but that he can be trusted."

As I listened, Jesse watched this sink in, and then she continued.

"Now take the example of a *wild* horse who has been running around with a whole herd of wild horses for all of her life. She has absolutely no idea what the master looks like, or smells like, or feels like. Maybe she's seen him in the distance sometimes but she doesn't even think about him because she doesn't think he's important. One day she wanders into the master's corral, and he decides to tame her. She may do everything possible to try to throw him off—kicking and bucking and running all over the place—but eventually she gives up. And she definitely *knows* at what point in time she gave her will over to him."

Suddenly, I was able to envision the difference in how Christians can be from totally different backgrounds, but the end result is the same. As I read the Bible and other Christian books like Hal Lindsey's *Combat Faith*, I realized more and more that this *free gift* of grace was totally unconditional and undeserved by me or anyone else. And yet it was there for the taking. It wasn't like my mother declaring herself a "gracious lady" because she thought she was somebody special or she believed she had done something important. It was about accepting *God's* grace because *He* loves *you*, just as you are.

Knowing God became like having a designated driver for my life: I never knew I needed Him until I did. Through reading the words of the Apostle Paul in the Book of Acts, and Christian stories like *The Hiding Place* by Corrie ten Boom, I wondered if I could survive being imprisoned for my faith. I knew the likelihood of that actually happening was slim, but in a way, I was imprisoned, by my fears and by my self-doubts, and by the rage that had been building inside of me for years. I had been a captive of my own thoughts, and I turned to God to set me free.

****

As time progressed, I saw that joy was the necessary ingredient for Christians to be motivated. Those people I met and read about who seemed to glean the most from their Christian faith had a distinctively positive outlook on life. I knew about Pavlov's experiments with dogs associating feeding time with a bell ringing. Now I realized that God really does want His children to react to His signals and "rejoice always," no matter what.

I think what helped me learn the most about God in those years was the music. The little church Rex's family attended only had a tiny, traditional choir that I'm sorry to say did not move me much! At that time, contemporary Christian music was just getting off to a roaring start, and churches like that one did not embrace the movement. Groups like the Imperials and the Bill Gaither Trio, and singles like Sandi Patti and Amy Grant, were just coming into their own. Those songs, written from the heart of believers just like me, fed my inner being and helped me develop as a new follower of Christ. One song that kept me focused was a Twila Paris tune called *The Center of His Will*. The words of the song made me realize that, if we seek Him, God will walk with us and keep us on the right path. During my early years as a believer, I was certain I had one foot firmly planted *outside* God's will now and then, but I knew He would always be there to welcome me back when I finally saw the error of my ways.

I had a small tape player that I strapped on when I took walks in the park on the lake near our home. I sang out loud as I walked and imagined playing the drums to all those old songs. I longed to play drums for God, but I knew that would never happen at the church we attended. I wished we attended a more contemporary service, but I consciously chose to remain at the small rural church. If I had found Christ while attending that little church, then I believed that was where He wanted me to remain, at least for now. Another scripture God had revealed to me, which convinced me to remain at that church, was Matthew 6:33:

> *Seek first His Kingdom and His righteousness, and all these things will be given to you as well.*

But studying the Bible and listening to Christian music were only the toy trucks of my growing faith. It was my prayer life that allowed God to bring out the earthmovers.

****

Many years after I accepted Christ, I came across the words of author Annie Dillard, which made me realize just how important prayer can be:

> *Does anyone have the foggiest idea what sort of power we so blithely invoke? Or, as I suspect, does no one believe a word of it? We as the church are children playing on the floor with chemistry sets, mixing up a batch of TNT to kill a Sunday morning... We should all be wearing crash helmets. The ushers should issue life preservers to us; they should issue signal flares; they should lash us to our pews.*

After my conversion, I would sit on the lake bank, in the park by our house and spend hours in prayer, just being with God, and really getting to know Him. I imagined a golden cord attached to the top of my head, leading all the way to Heaven, pumping power to my soul. There was an old boathouse on the edge of the water, crumbling and slated for demolition by the county park system. While it was still there, it became my "prayer point." I sat on the old cement stoop facing west towards the lake, watching the light play a myriad of patterns and sequences on the water's surface, marveling at sunsets, in awe of nature's incredible beauty and order. It was there I felt the

Holy Spirit moving in me like a huge glowing bubble in my chest, and it was there I first understood the passage in Romans 8 about "groaning" in prayer with words we cannot understand.

Someone along the way shared with me a comparison of prayer to the electrical outlets in our houses. We might actually have thirty, maybe forty or more different outlets we can access. But most of the time, we don't have something plugged into every one of those outlets. And some outlets, in rooms and areas we use frequently, may have extension cords and light strips and junction boxes plugged in all over the place, so we can get current for several gadgets at once. Prayer, I learned, is like that. We have this huge source of energy, which is God, and sometimes we just don't plug into the existing outlets to access that power. Maybe one day we pray with only one outlet plugged in, and others days we have three or twenty or a hundred. And some days we don't pray at all. But that doesn't change how much power is there, waiting for us to access it.

****

Now that I was "a new creature," Rex immediately considered me suspect. He knew me as "my old self" and was more than a little apprehensive about what this all meant. And, as is typical with many new "converts," I was expecting life to be much easier now. I felt that I would certainly be able to rid myself of all of my bad habits, like lying and swearing and gossiping and criticizing others. I challenged myself to be able to communicate effectively in love with family and friends, to maintain a positive outlook on life in spite of adversity, and to balance my checkbook to the penny.

I recalled all those years of anguish over my parents' situation, and I concluded that God was in charge of them, too. It was no longer up to me to bear the burden of guilt. God not only cared about what happened to every living creature, but He had taken *all* my sins and dumped them into the ocean.

I began to think I was living abundantly, and life was good. In the beginning, I didn't understand that Jesus didn't go to his death on the cross just to make crabby people become nice people. We all need salvation, whether we choose to be happy or sad. It's the choice to believe in Christ and what he did that brings that salvation. Once we accept that Christ died for us personally, we should all *want* to become nice. But that's not a *criterion* for salvation. I still had much to learn, and the Great Teacher was incredibly patient with me. This wasn't nearly as easy as I thought it would be.

I did immediately change my manner of speech. I no longer spoke the Lord's name in vain, and I generally cleaned up my use of swear words. I read in the Bible that I was supposed to "edify," so I went around trying to say nice things about people and to people. But I soon discovered that not everybody in my life was coming along for the ride. Many of my personal obstacles were still right where they had always been, in my way. My marriage didn't improve after my conversion, and neither did my relationship with my parents. I continued to feel like my blood was never far from the boiling point; I could still become angry at the drop of a hat. I didn't understand where all my rage was coming from.

By now I was beginning to feel the effects of working a day job and playing in the band several nights a week. I was becoming overstretched and stressed out. In many ways, I was still unhappy, and I was still crying a lot, almost every day. I was beginning to realize that having Christ's peace is not achieved by simply putting on a smiley face. Martin Luther said in his *Small Catechism*, "I believe I cannot by my own power come to the Lord Jesus Christ, or believe in Him, but it is the Holy Spirit who calls, gathers, and enlightens." It had not yet really sunk in that my conversion was not produced by my own strength or desire, but by a Power greater than all the world.

****

Because of my newfound faith in God, I began to try to look at my marriage through God's eyes. One "new" value that began to poke its little head into my consciousness was that becoming parents might improve our relationship. I mistakenly thought this was coming from God. It hadn't worked for my parents, so what on earth made me think it would work for us? But then, I was looking for miracles…and I took a chance that it might work out.

When Rex and I first met, we agreed that we would not have kids. He had a daughter from a previous marriage, and I had such a horrid upbringing I didn't trust myself to raise a child. I had gotten off birth control early in our marriage because of the side effects, and I had never gotten pregnant. So we were both surprised when I was thirty-five, I found myself with child. I was surprised because I was happy about it. Rex was also surprised—and furious. (Red flag No. 76.) He didn't want the baby, he said. What was I thinking? Of course it was my fault that I had gotten pregnant.

Right from the start, I was very sick, and I remember telling a neighbor, "If this is the way it is to be pregnant, I don't want any part of it." And I got my wish: I lost the baby at eight weeks, the night before the annual musicians' bash that we hosted every year. I sat propped up in a folding chair in our shed, watching about three hundred of our "close personal friends" come in and congratulate my husband, and then watching their faces fall when he told them I had lost the baby.

For a brief period, Rex felt bad about the miscarriage. I thought this was also a sign from God. Clearly, I was in the infant stages of recognizing when God was speaking to me. In between fights some years earlier, we had applied to adopt, but our file had gotten misplaced and thus we were never matched with a child. We went back to the agency and agreed to take a thirteen-year-old girl. Shortly after she was placed in our home, Rex's first wife sent his fourteen-year-old daughter to live with us for her remaining years of high school. If ever there was a couple that shouldn't have been raising kids, it was probably us. But I put my heart and soul into it and did a whole lot of praying.

Now, on my walks to the park, I prayed for both of our girls for the various trials they were going through. A scripture passage came rolling over me one day, *I believe, help me in my unbelief"* that I later found in Mark 9:26. The story is about a man who comes to Jesus to heal his child who is not present. When Jesus asks him if he, the child's father, believes, he replies with that statement, "I believe, help me in my unbelief." Then a miraculous thing occurs: Christ heals his child *because of the parent's faith*, not the child's. When I realized that Christ was inviting me to pray boldly and to expect my daughters to experience peace and wholeness, that's exactly what I did.

I know I made some mistakes, and the arguments between Rex and me probably didn't help the girls feel secure in their new home. Still, we plugged away at that marriage for longer than we ever should have, managing somehow to get both girls through high school and somewhat out on their own.

During that time, I prayed constantly that my marriage to Rex would survive. Not all of my prayers in those early days were answered with a yes. In my mind, I was certain God waned to do what I thought was "right." My prayers needed to develop into an expression of my acceptance of God's will, not in my own estimation of the "correct" outcome. A hard lesson for Christians, at any stage of this walk.

****

If I had possessed even a lick of sense, I would have given up the band and the booze at the time I accepted Christ, but I didn't want to. Though we were big fish in a small pond, performing in small venues as we were, the rush I got from performing was even more intoxicating than the alcohol we consumed. Early in my Christian life, I could not seem to differentiate between what the Lord was doing *for* me and what the band was doing *to* me. I was experiencing a new sense of self-worth, but where it was coming from was still clouded. At Bible study, I was reading that the God of the Universe had chosen me and named me to be His own. On the bandstand, I felt the warmth and high regard of the people who came to see us perform. I couldn't get my head around the difference. I was trying to serve both God as well as the false god of popularity, and it was causing me trouble. More than once, I said to Christian friends that God had given me only mediocre musical talents in percussion and voice to keep me humble. But sometimes it wasn't working.

And just when I thought I was struggling to get a handle on the realities of my "new creature" existence, another zinger came my way.

Chapter 25
Joy Through Pain

O Joy that seekest me through pain,
I cannot close my heart to thee;
I trace the rainbow through the rain
And feel the promise is not vain
That morn shall tearless be.

O Love That Will Not Let Me Go
Lutheran Book of Worship #324

I was in my late thirties when it began. It wasn't the pain that I noticed first. It was the fatigue. Initially, I passed it off as too many hours of work, and I even bragged about being "super woman," balancing so many commitments with so little sleep. I tried to sneak in naps when I could—naps after work, naps in the van on the way to band jobs, naps on Saturday and Sunday afternoons. But then I started napping in the middle of the workday. As a county social worker, I'd be out visiting my clients in their homes. Then I'd pull off on some rural road, lock the car doors, and fall sound asleep sitting straight up. I knew I was tense all the time too, but I figured that was just heredity. My entire family made a career out of being agitated. Besides, I had every reason to be rundown; each of our girls seemed to be battling her own set of demons. Rex was not coping well with either girl's situation. And me, well, I felt like I was mothering the whole needy world. It was as if, in my spare time, I was running my own private mental health unit.

Finally, doctors were consulted. My first diagnosis was Fibromyalgia, a syndrome characterized by chronic pain, stiffness, and tenderness of muscles and tendons. In addition, a curvature in my spine was beginning to cause problems that I never felt when I had kept my body in shape riding horses. The discs in my back were beginning to collapse; several joints would soon follow. I was way too young to feel this old, but I had to admit, my lifestyle was not helping my health.

Embarking on a life-long journey through chronic pain and exhaustion, I was becoming depressed and anxious. The pain grew more intense as time went on, and my body reacted by becoming guarded and constricted. My muscles felt like stones; my joints became rigid. Sleep evaded me. I would try to get sufficient rest, but it was like a cruel joke to lie in bed and not be able to drift off, or to begin to feel sleep taking over and have a muscle cramp jolt me back to reality. I tried everything: prescription drugs, the "over-the-counter" alternatives to prescription drugs, earplugs, a white-noise machine, even a pillow over my head. When I had dental work done, I stockpiled drugs they gave me because the dental work was a picnic compared to the other pain I had. I discovered the medicinal properties of alcohol, giving myself yet another excuse to drink. Nothing helped. When out of sheer exhaustion, I did sleep, I awoke not refreshed but weary and distressed and void of energy. I dubbed this brand of repose "mean sleep."

Needless to say, I went to prayer over this. At first, I was simply not willing to accept the suffering. God had met me on a Colorado mountainside and delivered me from the jaws of death; could he now do less than remove all of my pain? But as time wore on and the pain remained (manageable at times, but never *not there*), I looked for answers in different ways. Someone suggested I read the Book of Job, which was somewhat overwhelming. Others (bless their hearts) suggested there must be great sin in my life that I needed to deal with before I could be cured. But I learned that there is a great difference between being "cured" and being "healed." and in the end, I would eventually—finally—accept the healing that comes from simply letting the Indwelling Christ have His way with your life.

It also occurred to me, though not right away, that Christ bore this pain as well. No, of course He didn't have Fibromyalgia, or any other human disease or medical condition. But when He went to the cross for my sins, He also bore my pain. When He was broken and bleeding, hanging there like a common criminal, I believe He *felt* the pain that *all* of us have *ever* felt. Not just the pain any human would feel being crucified (which in itself is unthinkable), but *all* of the pain *all* of us have ever felt and *ever* will feel, from the beginning until the end of time. That's the sacrifice He made, and He made it for me.

As I meditated on God's Word and tried to the best of my human abilities to "make peace with the monster," I was given a great insight. God showed me that it was important for me to have a better reason to get up in the morning than just feeling good, or I would never get up at all. Jesus didn't feel very good on that cross, but He went there because He loved us. Could I do less, when my pain wasn't even a fraction of what He endured? I began to examine the true purpose for my life, pain or no pain, and that purpose, like the passage in Matthew, was to further the Kingdom of God.

It was clear that I was faced with an earthly challenge of huge proportions, but this awesome God never once left my side.

****

After I found out why my body hurt so much, I felt like I had to shut down all incoming stimuli and try to cope. It was a time when I should have felt fulfilled. In my early forties, I held a job as a counselor at a small two-year college in Whitewater. My colleagues statewide recognized me as being a leader within the two-year college counselors' group. By now, I had done a good deal of public speaking on the campus where I worked and at civic groups around the area. Another woman and I put together a conference on self-esteem and career choice for young girls, held annually for several years. I even took the conference on the road and visited high school classrooms full of tenth-grade girls. I planned other statewide conferences for student leaders and professionals, I wrote grants that helped bring money into our school. I honed my counseling skills to the point where I felt I was pretty good, and my students seemed to agree. I had attended many training sessions and developed a good deal of expertise on many topics, domestic violence and sexual harassment being among them.

Among my "other duties as assigned" at the college, I was the Sexual Harassment Compliance Officer, an emerging position in the '80s that appeared on more and more campuses every day. In light of my accomplishments, I was truly feeling comfortable in my professional role, more so than ever before. In my chosen field, under my particular set of circumstances, I had, as they say, "arrived."

Oddly, throughout my career, not one student who had experienced sexual assault came to me. That seemed very strange, since statistically a large number of sexual assault victims fit the demographic profile of the students at the college where I worked. Maybe God knew that being faced with another victim whom I was to counsel would cause me to have a meltdown, and He, graciously, had spared me having to deal with my own thoughts about that fearful topic.

Sexual *harassment* (unwelcome sexual advances, requests for sexual favors, and other verbal or physical conduct of a sexual nature that tends to create a hostile or offensive work or educational environment) was different. I seemed able to distance myself from my emotions, hear everybody's side, and assist administrators in dealing with these situations. But I still could not watch violence against women on television or in the movies, and even reading books or articles about the topic of rape made me uncomfortable. I had developed what I thought was a thick skin in that area, but really all I was doing was avoiding any stimuli about sexual assault. I thought I was doing just fine

****.

In the very early spring of 1989, I signed up for a workshop on sexual *harassment*—or so I thought. I was running late, and while I drove the hour and a half it took to get to the lecture hall at the University of Minnesota in St. Paul, I remember hoping that I would learn something new. Having been to so many of these sessions, I was getting complacent about the content. I wanted something different, some innovative ways to deal with the situations that inevitably arose, or to educate people, in an effort to prevent the harassment in the first place. There was a saying among compliance officers (mostly women) about the harassers we dealt with (mostly men; there were those who didn't get it—and those who didn't get it *right*. Perhaps there was a third type of male who got it, but didn't *care*. It wasn't that we were into man bashing, but these were the formative years of sexual harassment policies in the United States, and the concept of gender equity was still very new.

Realizing that I was not going to get to the lecture on time, and that by now the donuts were probably all gone and the coffee was as thick as mud, I became anxious once again. Besides, it was snowing lightly and the freezing temperatures made driving a slow process. It took forever to find a parking place, and by the time I walked into the lecture hall, the introductions were over and the main speaker had taken the podium. I could see no place to sit. Spotting one seat in the middle of the third row, I said, "excuse me" about twenty times as I tried not to step on anyone's toes. My brain was already trying to absorb the words coming from the female speaker. I knew how disappointing it was to have latecomers interrupt your delivery. When I finally sat down, it hit me that I wasn't in Kansas anymore.

The speaker was talking about the brutal sexual assault she had experienced several years before. As I tried to settle in and listen to what she was saying, I knew this was not where I wanted to be.

My palms became sweaty, and suddenly I had an intense pain in the pit of my stomach. My pulse increased to the point where I thought my heart would surely pound right out of my chest. My neck and face flushing, the tears began coming, like a small tsunami wave, threatening to engulf me completely. All of the emotions I had experienced so many years before during the assault on that Colorado mountainside were being played out in living color right before my mind's eye. I wanted out of there. Instantly.

At the time, I didn't recognize what I was going through as a panic attack or a flashback—or maybe both. I was in too much distress to figure out what was happening. Standing up, I stumbled my way past the others in the row, the same ones I had just disturbed three minutes before. I seemed to be propelled by some unseen force. I ended up in the ladies restroom, in a stall, sobbing huge, body-racking sobs. Shaking like a sapling in a hurricane, I felt the flight-or-fight response kick in as the adrenalin flowed.

"I think I've got some unfinished business here," I said out loud to myself, to God, to anyone who would listen.

****

That day I left the workshop immediately and sat in my cold car trying to sort out what had just happened. Re-reading the flyer telling about the topics for the day, I realized I had read it wrong. The meeting was not about sexual harassment; it was clearly about sexual assault. Was I in total denial when I read it? Regardless, I knew I wasn't ready to go back into that building. Realizing I didn't have to listen to that speaker any more gave me some sense of calm. Driving home, I stopped for coffee to clear my head. It began to dawn on me that, in spite of all my education and experience, I was powerless on my own to deny these old demons raging in my head.

There is a story about a Christian woman who puts all of her trust in God. When a flood comes and engulfs her house, she climbs up on the roof to wait for God to help her. She turns away two men in waders, then two more men in a boat, and finally two *other* men in a helicopter. She insists God will save her. Finally, she drowns and ends up in Heaven. She asks God why he didn't save her when He promised He would. God replies, "I sent six men to help you, and you ignored them all."

The moral of this story is that sometimes we need other human beings to help us out of a jam.

****

The next day, I called a therapist a friend recommended. Hannah practiced in a suburb of Minneapolis. I was afraid to go to anyone in Whitewater because I didn't want to be seen there. More important—I didn't want to see *myself* there.

Seeing Hannah was like having my psyche intubated—it was like having oxygen restored to my soul. Calm and reserved, but very skillful, Hannah did not openly profess to being a follower of Jesus Christ, but she clearly acknowledged the importance of my faith. We also agreed that I needed to deal with "old ghosts." Another revelation; we agreed that the marriage I was in was probably wrong for me, and that I had indeed jumped into the relationship as a means of escape. Where Hannah and I differed was in our view of divorce. She wanted me to consider the idea as one of my options; I still clung to the notion that Christians don't end marriages. Period.

Hannah's diagnosis of me, from the most current version of the Diagnostic and Statistical Manual, was Post Traumatic Stress Disorder, or PTSD, with Panic Attacks. PTSD had come about as a diagnosis following the Viet Nam "Conflict," and it described me to a T. She read me a definition: PTSD is described as "the psychological consequence of exposure to…stressful experiences, which involve actual or threatened death, serious physical injury or a threat to physical integrity and which the person found highly traumatic." The condition is, in itself, an anxiety disorder, so the panic attack I had was probably brewing for some time. Symptoms, Hannah said, include nightmares, flashbacks, avoidance of reminders, insomnia, and irritability. It didn't take much to convince me that I was experiencing all of them.

Hannah agreed to work with me, and she said the work would not be easy. I had to lie to Rex and my boss about where I was going when I saw Hannah. Her office was about ninety minutes from home or work, so I could not just see her on my lunch hour. I went once a week, for months. I spilled my guts about everything: the assault, my denial, my marriage, my lousy self-esteem, my upbringing. Everything. Hannah listened. She did all the "right" things, said all the "right" words. At one point, I stopped seeing her because she kept bringing up the option of divorce. I didn't want to consider it. I continued trying to make the marriage work, though on some level I knew it was a hopeless cause.

Around this time, I had a dream. Not a nice dream, like the ones I'd had when I first became a believer. This was a scary-bad dream. I was staring at a large glass shard, which was imbedded in my left forearm. There was lots of blood, and I remember thinking, *Where did this big piece of glass come from?* And then, in the dream, I heard a voice— a big, God-sounding voice, saying, *This glass shard is like your marriage*, Meg. *If you leave it where it is, you will surely bleed to death. If you take it out of your life, it will hurt—but it will heal.* The dream had been so real, I woke up panting to be rid of it. It was so real, and so true.

****

At Hannah's recommendation, and the insistence of friends, I stopped drinking and started attending Al-Anon. Perhaps I also needed to attend Alcoholics Anonymous (AA), but the important thing was to get into this wise Twelve Step program and practice it daily. In the Al-Anon publication, *One Day at a Time*, I learned the essence of the program: *mind your own business*. It was high time for me to begin "working my own program."

It would be impossible to write down everything I learned from Al-Anon. My *One Day at a Time* book was dog-eared on so many pages, it was falling apart. But if I had to sum up what I learned, I would say it like this: those who live with an alcoholic are one hundred per cent responsible for themselves, and are therefore responsible for the choices they make. When I quit drinking, I knew even one drink would send me back over to the other side where I would again be hypocritical in my judgments of others. I was in need of the One Day at a Time philosophy as much as any skid row bum. As one AA type put it, the highest rank in AA is "drunk." If I believed any differently about myself, I was dead wrong.

For years, I had been counseling other women to take care of themselves first, and I believed in the wisdom of that. When the flight attendants deliver their little "unlikely event" speech to all the passengers boarding a plane, they tell you to put the oxygen mask on *yourself* first, and then assist those who need help. I had a long history of trying to be all things to all people, but Al-Anon helped me realize that I really just needed to clean up my own backyard first.

****

Not all the "help" I got was useful. At some point during this time, I also sought counsel from a Baptist minister in Whitewater. I had occasionally attended the Baptist church in town because I had several co-workers who went there. I loved how much freer the worship services were, and the music was awesome, so unlike the tiny country church I had been attending. Once I even dragged Rex in to see this pastor for marriage counseling, but things did not go well. After the pastor was sufficiently shocked by all the junk Rex and I flung at each other in his presence, Rex left. I tried to talk to the pastor alone, telling him how schizophrenic I felt because Rex expected me to be involved in the music business, and I really didn't want to do that anymore because it compromised my Christian values and made my work with Al-Anon difficult. This Baptist minister said that he'd like to tell me I could play drums in "his" church, but he could not allow me to do that because I had "played in bars."

I was stunned. I thought Christians were supposed to build one another up, and here was a man of the cloth, tearing me down when I was already at rock bottom! Leaving his office, I wondered what to do (besides not seeing him again). I was still wondering the next day when the secretary at the church called and asked me if the church could borrow my drums that night for one of the youth bands to play. Coincidentally, this same woman had been to several events where our band had indeed played *in bars*, and she had indeed *danced* at those events. I told her maybe she had better check with the pastor on that, since the drums had, after all, been "played in bars." I wrote that pastor a letter telling him how much he had let me down. *Four months later*, I got a card containing a watered-down apology from him.

After the incident with the Baptist pastor, I resumed seeing Hannah, with a new goal of developing a plan to leave Rex. Rex was soon to be Ex Rex. In the end, however, it was not some loud and thundering screaming match that announced my departure, but a small, still feeling inside that it was just plain over.

Chapter 26
Over the River and Through the Casino

Addiction and Recovery: The Jellinek Curve

Chronic Phase: Indefinable fears…Obsession with drinking…Unable to initiate action…All alibis exhausted…Moral and physical deterioration…

Throughout the 1980s, news from my parents wasn't good either. I was busy seeking new heights through Christ and searching for my personal "bottom" through my pain, fatigue, and profound sadness. My parents were busy unraveling their own sanity while gambling away my inheritance. Following her downing champagne at my wedding, my mother fell off the wagon and soon returned to her old habits. It wasn't long until she was "on the sauce," as they say in the rural Midwest.

During the years I lived in Whitewater, I didn't see my parents very often. With a full-time job and band engagements several times a week, I was too busy to travel to Las Vegas. Besides, airfare seemed like a luxury at the time. My father was concerned about embarking on a trip of any kind with Mother, since she was so unpredictable. So they seldom visited us either. Once when I was in my late twenties, they visited us, but I ended up throwing them out of our house because of her drinking; and, more or less, shipping them off to see my sister. I am sure she found it hard to forgive me for that. After that, I didn't speak to my parents for a very long time.

****

I don't recall how long that silence between us lasted. At some point, though, I began to call them again. At least it was a start, towards what, I didn't know. The very thought of calling them would strike dread in my heart. What would I encounter on the other end of the phone? Would Mother be sober or drunk? Would Daddy be in his "poor-me" mode, or would he tell me everything was "just great."

The number of rings often determined whether or not I stayed on the line: too many meant Mother might be drunk and Daddy gone from the house. I would count to myself while my chest got tight and my blood pressure rose, *One ring... two... three...Come on!...Answer!* Sometimes I couldn't stand the suspense and would just hang up. They never had purchased an answering machine. I wouldn't have known what message to leave if they had. "Hi, it's me. Is anyone sane there?" or "Just checking in to see if you've done any serious bodily harm to each other lately."

It was clear Daddy was still trying to stay in control in an out-of-control life. When Rex and I were still on the road with the band, Daddy was admiring our thirty-three-foot Avion travel trailer, which was our only home for several years. He said he wanted to buy a motor home so he could travel around and see the sights, while leaving Mother "at home" in the motor home, drunk. It seemed perfectly logical to him; he had already taken over mixing Mother's cocktails. He stated quite matter-of-factly that, if he got the portions correct, she'd "be good" for several hours while he played tourist. Shocked and once again feeling more like parent than daughter, I pointed out to him that traveling only meant more chances for Mother to get in trouble, not less. I began to realize my father was in a downward mental spin just like my mother.

Years later I found a quote by Thomas A'Kempis in the Al-Anon *One Day at a Time* book that made me think of Daddy during those years:

> *Why art thou troubled because things do not succeed with thee according to thy desire: Who is there who hath all things according to his will? Neither I, not thou, nor any man upon earth.*

Around this time, I also noticed that my father had become completely unable to weather any changes or disappointments, even seemingly minor ones. While visiting Vegas, I rode with him once to Nellis Air Force Base and watched him have a meltdown when he discovered that there was road construction on base, with detours everywhere. He was unable to drive directly to the commissary and the base exchange, as he had done every week for years. All he had to do was follow the temporary signs and park in another lot a half block away. But he stopped the car in the middle of the street, and with a look of complete disgust on his face, began swearing. His mood could not be swayed. I wanted to take the wheel of the car myself, but instead, I sat quietly trying to console him while other motorists honked or just went around us.

And then there were the laxatives. Mother took them by the handful, a rainbow of colors. She established "laxative days," first twice a week, then every other day. She could not possibly go out of the house on a laxative day! She would consume mass quantities of them and then get into bed and lie perfectly still, with her hands folded on her chest like a corpse. Although I often suggested that her bowels might cooperate better if she would move around, she insisted that she must lie very still until she felt something happen. More often than not, nothing did happen. Her colon must have been in a constant state of compaction for decades. My father just stood by while all this happened, occasionally going to the pharmacy for more laxatives, but never suggesting any alternatives and certainly never speaking to Mother's doctor about her situation.

"Your mother refuses to participate in her own self care," he would often lament. But he was responsible, too, for not standing up to her and confronting her with the true nature of her problems. Unwittingly, he was furthering her descent into the hell of alcoholism by trying to force her to take care of herself when she had no desire to change. I, too, was a long, long way from understanding this, and so I just stood by and listened and tried to prop my father up in his impossible task of keeping Mother safe and happy.

"Your mother's been sober for years," he often said on the phone during those years. But when I would visit, he'd mix and serve her one or more highballs at night as I watched. It took me a while to realize that, when he described Mother as "sober," he meant she wasn't crawling down the hall to the bedroom. Translation: "I'm doling out the booze to her and that way I can keep her from getting totally sloshed."

In spite of protests from Rex, I resumed visiting them once or twice a year. Like a moth to a flame, I was drawn to my parents' home to check on them, even though I was powerless to be of any help to them.

Mother's fears, which had always been present in some form or other, seemed to be multiplying exponentially, especially her fear of death. I tried on several occasions to talk to her about my newfound Christian faith, to assure her that God would be with her now and always if she believed He would. I wrote several long, impassioned letters to her, quoting scripture and sharing insights that I had gained.

When I was there, I would visit with her about spiritual matters, but she always seemed so distant, like my words were more of distraction than a lifeline. I longed for her and my father to know God the way I had come to know Him. I no longer felt like that "imbedded reporter" of my childhood; now I felt like a missionary in a foreign land.

****

As the years went by, and my parents settled into retirement, my father assumed all of the household responsibilities. He did the cooking, the cleaning, the grocery shopping, and all the driving. The well-stocked pantry looked like a survivalist's bunker. Meanwhile, my mother became a recluse, her only outings being to the beauty shop (when she didn't cancel), the doctor (though not often enough), and to the Showboat Casino to gamble. She slept late every morning, took naps at least twice a day, and went to bed early every night. She always kept the blinds closed in the entire house. Though my father had bought them matching recliners, my mother preferred the couch, on which you could see a perfect indentation shaped like her backside. Next to her, she had a mini-pharmacy with her arsenal of prescription and over-the-counter drugs, chocolates, dental floss, needles and thread and thimble, Kleenex, crossword puzzle books, a deck of playing cards, magazines and catalogs. For lunch, my father brought her small sandwiches and Coca Cola and maybe a brownie or a cookie. She never had to leave her corner of the sofa, except to use the bathroom or go back to bed. Some days she didn't even get dressed. All the while, Daddy was whirling like a dervish in a flurry of activity, muttering and sputtering to himself while he took care of every tiny detail required to keep things running in his self-made nursing home/military base. Well into retirement, he was still functioning like he was in the military.

My mother never spent time with neighbors and soon had no social friends at all. Eventually, Mother just closed her little psychological circle closer and closer around herself, until she was just a little speck of protoplasm on Planet Earth.

My mother became, in a word, irrelevant.

****

In the 1980's, the doctors at Nellis Air Force Base seemed unaware of Mother's addictions (or didn't care). They prescribed huge amounts of medication at a time for her. Once on the phone, I mentioned I had a cold. Within a few days, Mother had sent me a hundred capsules of a prescription antihistamine. "I can get more where those came from," she cooed when I called her the next time. She was scoring drugs at the base hospital, with no apparent limits on the number or frequency of refills.

As a result of her drinking and falling, Mother had broken just about every bone in her body at least once, and only had medical attention for about half of them. My father would withhold information from the emergency room staff. He never told any of the doctors that Mother was an alcoholic. Perhaps some figured it out, but not all did. One time she had an emergency hemorrhoidectomy, after a particularly rough bout of abusing laxatives. Her blood pressure was dangerously low and they almost lost her on the operating table, but my father dutifully kept the family secret from the hospital staff.

Daddy once told me, "I watched all one night while your mother tried to hang herself on the patio. She put on quite a show, tying bed sheets together and trying to throw them over the railing, missing, and falling down." In horror, I asked, "How could you watch her do something like that?" "Oh, I wouldn't have let her go through with it," he said. "I just wanted to see how long she'd stay at it. She finally gave up and went to bed."

Perhaps the most amazing stunt my mother pulled during those years was the time she sent a telegram to the President of the United States (then Ronald Reagan) telling him that my father was a dirty, low down, rotten skunk and solely responsible for all of her (if not the entire nation's) woes. Though President Reagan was known to have a keen sense of humor, I doubt if he saw anything funny in the telegram. It probably never got past security.

My father found out about it when the bill came from Western Union, with the words of the telegram printed right on the invoice. I knew the two of them had reached an all-time low when my father sent *another* telegram to the White House asking the Chief of Staff to please disregard the first message as his wife was having a rough time in the mental health department.

Sometimes when my mother's narcissism got the best of him, Daddy would say to her, "Verel, you're nobody special! I'm nobody special either. We're just plain, ordinary people, and nobody owes us a living!" But his treatises fell on deaf ears; my mother simply would not accept anything less than total adoration and reverence from her husband. Her place in the world's hierarchy was secure, at least in her own mind.

It took me many years to realize the impact my mother's self-love had on me. I cannot recall my mother ever making any attempt to instill positive thoughts about ourselves in either my sister or me. We were simply left to decide for ourselves if we were worthy, and most times we believed we were not.

****

My sister eventually disowned both my parents. She and her family had moved to the East Coast, but she and I met in Vegas for my parents' 50th wedding anniversary in December of 1983. The visit started out pretty well. We went out to dinner and to a show. But after the little anniversary celebration, Mother just couldn't handle all of us around and retreated to the bedroom to drink in solitude. The next morning, we dragged her out of bed and had some maudlin conversation with her, trying unsuccessfully to get her to agree to get some help (again). My sister said if Mother didn't stop drinking, she wouldn't come to see her ever again—and she meant it.

Barbara never visited them again and even cut all phone contacts. The lives of both our parents were getting weirder and weirder.

Many years later, Mother asked me why Barbara got so angry that she wasn't speaking to them. I decided to explain.

"Mother," I began in my best little counselor voice, "Barbara and I were raised in the same household, and it wasn't a very good place to raise children." At this point, Mother began making her escape down the hall to her bedroom. I continued, in spite of her retreat. "Barbara and I have chosen to react differently to that fact..."

By now, Mother had her hands over her ears. "Okay, I won't ever ask again!" she shouted as she made her way down the hallway. And she closed her bedroom door along with any doors to the truth. She didn't come out until the next morning.

****

Although I struggled long and hard over my sister's decision to write my parents out of her life, I honestly couldn't blame her. Soon after her big decision, I read a book called *Toxic Parents* by Susan Forward. The author gave lots of great information on how people can overcome dysfunctional parents' hurtfulness and move on with their lives. One of the most shocking things Dr. Forward said was that *we don't need to forgive our parents!* Dr. Forward divided *forgiveness* into two parts: "giving up the need for revenge, and absolving the guilty party of responsibility." Though it seemed pretty straightforward, I really had to put a lot of thought into understanding the difference. *Of course* I didn't want revenge…*or did I?* And wasn't it absolutely futile to hold Mother responsible for her drinking and subsequent behavior?

Forgiveness for many years was a subject that just made me feel numb. Everything I had studied about the Christian way of life led me to believe I *had* to forgive my mother—*and even the rapist*—or I could not move on. Though it was difficult, I was able to forgive Mother. But what about the man who had assaulted me? Was I to feel what humanistic psychologist Carl Rodgers called "unconditional positive regard" in my heart for *him?* Dr. Forward's book helped me to see that we can let go of that *desire to inflict hurt when we have been hurt.* But even God would not expect us to say those hurtful things *simply never happened.*

Mother did go into treatment for her alcoholism a couple of times in Las Vegas, but nothing ever came of it—and each treatment cost my father several thousands dollars. In the end, she'd go home and celebrate her successful treatment by getting drunk.

****

In the late 1980s and early 1990s, I began to visit my parents more often. They were getting up in years, and I knew one or both of them might be gone soon. One night when Daddy and I were alone, my father asked me a question truly from his heart. "Margaret," he began, "how do you know you're going to Heaven?"

I was at a loss for words. For all the transforming that God had done in my life, when put to the test, I could not remember *one single* Bible passage to quote to him. I was instantly ashamed of myself. With a quick, silent prayer, I regained my composure and began to tell him, in my own words, why God's only Son came to walk among men on earth, why He had to die and be raised again, and why that ensured me, and others who believed, of eternal life in Heaven. To my immense surprise and relief, he accepted my explanation. Just accepted it. He didn't ask me to help him become a believer, he didn't say he wanted to make any drastic changes in his own life, but at least he didn't find my interpretation offensive. It was a start.

During those years, we had other discussions, about politics and world affairs, which I now believe were his way of "leveling the playing field" between us. He seemed to be acknowledging, finally, that I was an adult, free to make my own choices. Not only that, but that the choices I was making met with his approval. Me, the "baby" of the family, who never felt as if either of my parents thought I was worth the food they put in front of me, finally was able to hold my own in a high-level intellectual discussion with my father. But even more importantly, he was curious about the transformation that he could visibly see in my life since I had accepted Christ. That made me very happy.

Part V

Patrick and Me
On our Wedding Day, 1999

Chapter 27
Flowering From Within

Sometimes it is necessary to reteach a thing its loveliness...until it flowers again from within...

> Galway Kinnel
> Quoted in
> *One Day at a Time in Al-Anon*

The end of my nineteen-year marriage came not with a bang but a whimper. To be exact, it arrived quite unceremoniously, which hadn't surprised me. Rex was surprised, never believing that I would really go through with it until at last I did. I cried every day until one day I just stopped crying. That's when I knew it was time to go. This caused me to formulate the first of what I began calling "Meg's Counseling Precepts:" "It's not the lightening bolt but the quiet small thing in socks that changes people." I was also faithfully attending Al-Anon, and the wisdom of that program spoke to me every day— every *minute*. One of my favorite passages in the book *One Day at a Time in Al-Anon* was the entry for my birthday, January 13:

> *When will I learn that there is no compulsion in law or ethics that forces me to accept humiliation, uncertainty and despair?*

Preparing to "make my break," so to speak, I had been quietly saving money for years. I had to rent a motel room for a month before the apartment I wanted was available. The room was so small, it held only me, a few possessions, and a whole lot of feelings, both good and bad. Starting my new life alone in a cut-rate room decorated in Early Flea Market was not very exciting, but I remember thinking how blessed I was to have a good job and a reliable car. So many women I had counseled through the years had neither, and my first night alone I said a prayer of thanks. At age forty-five, I was now capitalizing on my own advice.

I recall sitting alone on the motel room bed and flipping through the channels on the television. After all, there was no one else to control the remote, and when I got to the local cable station, I found a rerun of our band playing at some town celebration. It was eerie and almost fitting to be watching my Former Life in Show Business in Living Technicolor. But it was most satisfying to realize I could end the images by simply clicking a button—which I did.

Shortly after I moved out, I planned a trip to Las Vegas. As I pondered the best way to break the news that I was getting a divorce, I suddenly realized that I hadn't seen my parents in almost three years. Where had the time gone? I hadn't intended to go so long without a visit, but my life had been crowded with other thoughts and plans, making it difficult to deal with what was going on with my parents. I was still calling once or twice a month, and I would get distinctly mixed messages from my father. Sometimes, he would be very sullen, speaking in a low voice and lamenting the fact that he couldn't do anything with Mother. Other times, he would answer the phone all bright and cheerful and tell me how wonderful things were before he handed the phone to my mother for me to have an equally meaningful conversation with her. It didn't take too much imagination to know that Mother was still drinking, and that the upbeat reports from him meant my father was covering for her.

Calling ahead with the short version of the divorce news, I wanted to give my parents time to let it sink in and to make sure Mother wasn't on a serious bender when I visited. She actually answered the phone and didn't sound half bad. I was apprehensive, but I decided my parents needed to know some of the details.

When I arrived and my father opened the door, I thought at first I had the wrong house. Yes, it was my 83-year-old father greeting me and giving me a hug. He was moving a little more slowly than I remembered, but I was pleased to see that he hadn't changed noticeably. But seated on the couch where my mother used to be was a woman I did not recognize. Her brown chin-length hair was gone, replaced by very long, pure gray locks pulled back tight from her face into a little bun. Her cheekbones were hollow sockets, her skin was ashen, and her eyes looked tired and watery. When I hugged her, my hands felt her spine protruding sharply beneath her clothing. My mother appeared to be wasting away to nothing.

After the typical pleasantries, but before I had even gotten my luggage through the door, my father started asking questions. Debriefing is a better word. I had been calling my father "General Halftrack" (though not to his face) for years. I secretly laughed about his similarities to the Beetle Bailey cartoon character, and surmised that Daddy would have a red phone to the White House if they would let him. Images of this came to me in what should have been a serious moment.

I tried to be matter-of-fact about what went wrong between Rex and me, but it still was awkward. My mother didn't utter a word but voiced a few disapproving clucks now and then. I felt myself holding my breath, hoping she wouldn't go on some tirade about Rex. I never thought she had liked him, but then she didn't like much of anybody. Finally, when my father felt he had obtained the necessary amount of initial briefing, he looked at me and with great compassion, said, "We'll get through this, Sweetie."

It was probably one of the most meaningful things my father had ever said to me, and I clung to his words like a log in a raging river.

****

Within a month after returning from Las Vegas, I had moved into a small apartment a few blocks away. I was now a grandmother, my younger daughter Shelly having had her first child the previous summer. I spent a good deal of time with her and little Austin once I settled in. I wouldn't say I took to single life like a duck to water, but I certainly had myself convinced that I would survive. Old friendships with women, particularly single ones, suddenly became more important. I closed ranks and prepared to go into survival mode.

Throwing myself into my job, I tried to focus on others rather than on myself. My faith inspired me to approach those I counseled with great compassion and understanding. And, surely by this time in my life, I recognized the value in having "walked the walk"–indeed, many different kinds of "walks." After my acceptance of Christ, it naturally followed that my career as a college counselor was a way to show God's love in action.

Henri Nouwen, Dutch psychologist and theologian, wrote about "the wounded healer." His philosophy is that one who is broken and seeks healing from God is in a position to empathize with others in similar circumstances. It was logical that the "brokenness" in me responded to the brokenness in many of the students I saw. I brought to the counseling experience the knowledge of survival, the confidence of perseverance. This concept is also the foundation of Alcoholics Anonymous and all of the Twelve Step programs—it takes one to know one.

A physical therapist I knew compared pain to a CD-ROM. Pain, she said, can be stored at many levels, in many different forms and intensities. The pain can be physical, emotional, or spiritual, and combinations of different types of pain can play off one another. Some of us find it easy to suppress at least some of the pain, while others seem to have every circuit blazing all of the time. So when someone goes to the doctor for physical pain, or goes to a counselor or a pastor for emotional or spiritual pain, the various practitioners are probably working with more than they bargained for. Although my own pain was with me constantly, in my work and in my life, I trusted in the words in I Peter 5:6 and 7:

Therefore, humble yourselves under the mighty hand of God, that He may exalt you in due time, casting all your care upon Him, for He cares for you.

****

After a year and a half living alone in Whitewater, it was time for me to move on. My chronic pain had gotten so pervasive that all my healthcare practitioners were advising me to get into an aquatics program. With no such program in Whitewater, I began to look at larger metropolitan areas. A counseling position became available at a small, two-year state-supported college on the outskirts of the Twin Cities of Minneapolis and St. Paul. After one interview, I was hired. I said good-bye to Whitewater and all the things that reminded me of Rex the Ex. The clean break was the best thing I ever did.

Though I was excited about my move, my fear level rose substantially when I got to the metropolitan area. In spite of the healing I had already experienced, those old ghosts would come around for a visit when I least expected them. I bought a small town home and a big security system. I felt safer because I was able to pull my locked car into my garage and close the overhead door from inside the vehicle, and then hightail it into the house where I quickly bolted the door and turned on the security system. I seldom went out at night in the beginning, but as I learned my way around the Twin Cities and made some friends, I got a little better about venturing beyond the fortified town home walls.

During the first couple of years of my new single status, I dated a few "Mr. Wrongs" and one "Mr. What-Was-I-Thinking?" In the relationship department, I felt like I was an overgrown toddler, trying to stuff round blocks into square holes. I was disappointed that I had not advanced a bit further in my emotional development by that time. After I relocated, I joined a large Lutheran church and played drums for some of their contemporary services and for a Christmas pageant. But I soon abandoned all hope of meeting a man there. I met several amazing *women*, some of whom became life-long friends, but alas, no eligible bachelors. In frustration, I decided to take about six months off from trying to date anybody. I concentrated on doing my best at work and staying as healthy as I could. I was forty-eight years old...and time was marching on. God was still my rock, a safe haven in times of distress. But I was the one who continued to wander away and try to do things on my own.

****

Around this time, I ran across a quote that really mystified me. It was from Elizabeth Barrett Browning, the great romantic poet of the Victorian era:

God answers sharp and sudden on some prayers,
And thrusts the thing we have prayed for in our face,
A gauntlet with a gift in it.

I pondered her words, and wondered if God would give me a "sharp and sudden" answer to my growing loneliness. It had been almost four years since I left Rex, and I was longing for a meaningful relationship in my life.

When I came to the end of myself (again), I sat praying at the edge of a lake (again) to try to discern God's will for my life (again), particularly in the area of romance. After some time reflecting and gazing purposefully at the majestic scenery, I got a rare, audible answer. As clearly as if He were sitting right beside me, I heard God's words in my heart.

"Marriage is a sacrament. It's not a contract."

That was all I heard. And then silence.

The depth of this statement, while somewhat puzzling and perhaps not the direct answer I had hoped for (like, "Go to the third picnic bench in such-and-such park, and there you will meet the man you are to marry"), was not entirely lost on me. God knew that one of the men I had dated was an agnostic, if not an out-and-out atheist and the same guy was more concerned about a prenuptial agreement than the actual nuptial itself. When my prayers by the lake revealed such a strong message, I believe God was making it clear to me that *this* time, I'd better keep my values up front and not compromise. No matter what.

So I decided to contact a dating agency. In spite of the fact that some of my friends thought I was nuts, and my Christians friends at least felt this action was not at all what God meant in our conversation by the lake, I concluded that a dating agency was the perfect way for me to "screen" potential male companions. I could agree to meet only those who professed to be Christians, who held acceptable, professional jobs, and who shared similar interests to mine, thereby avoiding the "dart board" method of meeting prospective life partners.

Fortunately, for once I was right.

I called up a dating service, which I'll name "Mate Matchers," and set up an appointment with a six-foot Swedish woman named Helena with big hair and four-inch-long fingernails. She wore a silk camouflage jumpsuit, size extra tall. Her eyelashes were longer than my arms. She explained the program to me while my head spun with visions of aging knights in shining armor. Then she asked me a most interesting question.

"How long do you expect it will take to meet your life mate?"

And then she stopped talking. A bad sign in high-pressure sales. She folded her arms and sat back in her chair, grinning at me like a Cheshire cat on funny mushrooms. Another bad sign. I knew I had to do some quick thinking.

Using a rating scale I had seen in a magazine that I'll call "Old Bride," I quickly calculated how long it would take me to meet the right man. I doubled my age, multiplied that by how many cups of coffee I drank a day, and divided by the number of pairs of pantyhose in my drawer (rough estimate). I knew my math was fuzzy, so I aired on the side of caution.

"Sign me up for life," I said brightly.

Helena eyed me suspiciously. "The longest contract we have is three years," she said without unfolding her arms or leaning forward.

"I'll take it!"

****

What happened after that must have been divine intervention, because the way things went, it is a wonder I ever met anybody. After

I wrote my check, Helena led me to stacks of "profile books," containing pages with an eligible male's first name and his member number, photographs and self-reported personal data. But when Helena was busy showing me what to look for, I was looking at one of the photographs, and missed her explanation of which number to use to request to meet a member.

Having already found the guy I wanted to meet first, I had missed completely the process to get him to contact me.

I filled out several of the little cards correctly (or so I thought), figuring I'd better complete more than one to increase my chances of getting my task completed in the three short years they were giving me. I turned them in and went home to wait. No calls. After a month or so, I went back to the Mate Matchers' office and asked what went wrong. When we finally pieced together what I had done, it was clear why I hadn't heard from anyone. I had put down the *page* number instead of the member number. A quick correction was made, and then my phone started ringing. Among those who called was the one I had spotted on the very first day.

****

When I met Patrick, he told me he was a recovering alcoholic with nine years of sobriety. I, on the other hand, had rediscovered the medicinal properties of alcohol, and I had a full bottle of wine in my refrigerator. We met for dinner on our first date, and it was true that we had many things in common. He was a Christian, and indeed, he said that it was only by God's unfailing grace that he was able to stay sober one day at a time. He was divorced, with two daughters, ages sixteen and twenty. He loved the outdoors, was an avid ("possessed" was a better term) bass fisherman, and he owned a four-year-old Basset Hound named Bayfield whom he rescued from "death row" at the St. Paul animal shelter. He was an orthopedic physician assistant who worked at a well-known neck-and-back clinic. At the end of our first date, which happened to be on my forty-ninth birthday, he *asked permission to give me a hug!*

When I got home, I took the wine out of the fridge and poured myself a glass.

I'll never give up my wine for a man! I said to myself out loud.

While I finished the bottle, I contemplated my next move.

Whether I had an alcohol problem myself may have been an important question once. I can only say that I believe it was God's will for me to meet Patrick. That wine bottle ended up in the recycle bin, and in the words of one AA member, "I never found it necessary to take a drink of alcohol after that."

****

As our relationship progressed, I was astounded by how different this was than any romance I had ever encountered before. Patrick was a man who had truly been broken and was being continually reconstructed in the eyes of God. And he wasn't afraid to check with God, or to lay himself bare so God could check on him, when things got sticky. The qualities I first recognized in Patrick were humility, vulnerability, and genuineness. Absent were pretentiousness, phoniness, and self-righteousness. When, inevitably, I saw any of those negative traits occasionally bubbling to the surface of his humanness, I knew he was struggling, and I trusted him to continue recovering from his own distress, one day—indeed sometimes one minute—at a time.

I knew that it was my own brokenness and my own quest for the Truth that allowed me to recognize the same images in his life. And, when Patrick told me the story of his time as an Army medic in Viet Nam, I realized that we shared the special bond of those who have known trauma and continue to work towards wholeness.

Chapter 28
Jungle Triage

There is nothing that war has ever achieved that we could not better achieve without it.

Havelock Ellis

It didn't occur to Patrick that the people of the small Southeast Asian country of Viet Nam had been fighting for their freedom almost since time began. Patrick didn't really care that its inhabitants can be traced as far back as 20,000 BC. Viet Nam had been occupied first by the Chinese, then the French, then the Japanese, then the French again. When President Kennedy sent thirteen hundred American "advisors" into Viet Nam to help "stabilize" the Vietnamese government in 1961, Patrick was in eighth grade at a Catholic high school in his hometown of Cedar Rapids, Iowa. He hadn't really thought about Viet Nam's story until his college grade point average dropped below 2.0, and the draft board caught up with him in 1969.

"I partied too hard and lost my deferment," Patrick said simply.

By his third year of college, he was already a heavy drinker and was familiar with many street drugs. Pot, psilocybin mushrooms, acid, mescalin–he had used them all. Though he was a smart student, in three years he still hadn't declared a major and was taking business classes that didn't really interest him. Now, in the Army, he was sent to Camp Dodge, Iowa for his physical, which he passed with only a minor hearing loss from having played drums in a rock band for several years.

Basic training took him to Ft. Polk, Louisiana in July. The heat and the humidity made the rigors all the more intolerable. But Patrick's antennae were already up, and he soon determined who were the "heads" (drug users) and who were the "juicers" (drinkers). He discovered that his own drill sergeant was among the "heads," and the two of them took to getting high after the sergeant played "hard ass" with everyone including Patrick during the daytime. Basic training was tough, but relief was just a joint away.

At the end of basic, Patrick was given his Military Occupational Status—a medic. "At least I wasn't going to have to shoot anyone," he said. His medical training at Ft. Sam Houston in San Antonio lasted about three and a half months, and consisted of learning to assess injuries and decide who needed help first, doing blood work, hanging IVs, and performing minor medical procedures. End of training.

While there, he again quickly identified more "heads." He and his latest group of buddies would get three-day passes and drive to Mexico. They would score kilos of pot and go back to the Army base with their stash safely stowed under the gas tank of a rented VW bug. They never got busted, but even if they had, the consequences wouldn't have been too dire. There was a war to fight and the Army needed all the men it could get.

After a brief trip home for Christmas, Patrick boarded a transport plane with his gear and his fear, and set off on his journey to Southeast Asia. A thousand thoughts ran through his head on that long plane ride. Would he ever see American soil again? Would he be able to get the drugs he needed now to make it through each day? And what would those days ahead hold for him, for anyone? What was the purpose of this stupid war, anyway?

His first assignment was with a ground crew that picked up injured personnel. Sometimes they went "up country" (north towards the 17th parallel, which was really just an imaginary line between North and South Viet Nam). There, the ambulance crew would retrieve soldiers brought to the "landing zones." Also called "fire bases," this was where the U.S. forces would take off and land, and where they would shoot artillery at the North Vietnamese Army and the Viet Cong guerilla fighters. The ambulance crew would take the wounded that usually had been brought in by the helicopters, and transport them to an evacuation hospital.

Patrick's first night in Nam was not a good experience.

"It was like a bad acid trip," he explained. "Here I was in a strange country, people speaking a foreign language, with strange noises and smells, and sounds of mortar fire and gunfire all around us. I was pretty freaked out."

Patrick took a stroll around the Army compound that was surrounded on all sides by a refugee camp. Refugee children were selling drugs through the fence—potent stuff, much stronger than anything he'd ever had before. He bought some of each, and thus joined the "heads" in Viet Nam. He decided the only thing to do was to stay high unless he was on duty.

Probably the best thing Patrick had going for him was that he believed he was invincible. Like many young American men, and especially those who had brains even if they are temporarily fried, it never occurred to him that he wouldn't know what to do to get himself out of any scrape, stateside or in Nam. In spite of his abbreviated medical training, he approached his new job as if he were a skilled surgeon. It was an unwritten rule that no one did drugs or drank while they were on duty—and a certain distrust grew up between the "heads" and the "juicers." When the "heads" weren't doing drugs, they believed they were operating at one hundred percent capacity (an arguable premise to be sure). But the same could *not* be said of the "juicers," who often came on duty with hangovers. Conversely, the "juicers" were leery of the "heads" *because* they were "heads." I'm not sure either of the two hopped-up groups would have won a vote of confidence from their patients, but that's how they saw themselves.

After a couple of months on the ground crew, Patrick was sent up to the central highlands, near the mountainous border of Cambodia, to become a "dust-off medic." His new job entailed flying in a helicopter ambulance. Each helicopter had a pilot, a copilot, a crew chief (mechanic) and one medic. The chopper ambulances were supporting infantry divisions, and were on duty around the clock until relieved by another crew.

"The most frightening thing in Viet Nam was that there was *no front*," he said. "People didn't realize that the war there was *everywhere*. You didn't know who the enemy was, which is why some civilians got blown up, because nobody could be trusted."

That's also why Patrick said he never had any close friends in Viet Nam. "You made friends fast, but there were *no* long-lasting friends. Individual soldiers were being shipped in and out every day, but there were never any battalions deployed at the same time. Consequently, most soldiers didn't know anyone else there when they arrived. Plus if you got to be friends with someone, he might not be alive tomorrow."

When Patrick's crew was out in the chopper, they knew the Viet Cong were listening to their radio communications. The ground forces would radio in that there were wounded personnel needing to be picked up. They would give their coordinates, or they would throw a smoke grenade so the medic crew could locate them. The helicopter crew was making second-by-second decisions all the time:

determining the type of injuries on the ground and deciding if the injured soldiers could wait awhile, or if the air ambulance needed to go in immediately, regardless of the weather and the enemy's position. The worst were the burn patients. They had to be rescued as soon as possible, but all that could be done for them was to give them morphine and get them shipped out to an Army hospital. And try not to listen to their screams.

The helicopters could realistically handle three hanging stretchers, and they could put one on the floor. They could still take three or four "walking wounded," sitting in the "hell holes," seats on each side of the motor with no protection from the wind. They flew with the doors open at all times in case they had trouble getting out over the trees or they got hit and had to start throwing heavy items out of the 'copter to give themselves more lift.

He remembered one mission in particular.

"We were totally terrified that time. It was pitch black, and we were in the mountains. We had no radar because there were no relay stations anywhere nearby. And it was foggy." It was very common in Viet Nam for aircraft to crash into mountains or trees. The pilots frequently developed vertigo so they didn't know which way was up or down. "This particular night," Patrick continued, "the ground troops were reporting that the injuries were very bad, and they were firing flares to show us the way. We were all afraid a flare would hit our chopper and ignite our fuel. We never got the rescue accomplished, and we even had trouble finding our own way back."

Patrick told me there was only one thing he actually looked forward to in Viet Nam: care packages and letters from his mother. Ellie Corrigan was a nurse by profession, and her care and regard for others showed in everything she did. She wrote to her oldest son almost every day, and she sent him homemade goodies and special treats the entire time he was away. Patrick wrote her too, and he knew that his mother's love and prayers were what got him through his two years in Viet Nam.

****

During the Viet Nam "conflict" (never declared a "real" war), each draftee's commitment was for twenty-four months. When at last he was home in Cedar Rapids, he stayed at his parents' home for about a month and then rented a house with a couple of high school buddies, who were also Viet Nam vets. He answered an ad in the paper for a new ambulance crew being put together at the local hospital, and was hired immediately. The group got some old hearses and converted them into ambulances. They wired the hearses with lights and sirens, built their own backboards and other equipment, and started the first emergency medical service at that hospital. The job was a piece of cake for Patrick, and he decided working in health care wasn't a bad idea. It wasn't long until he took advantage of the GI Bill and went back to school to become a physician assistant. He also met and married his first wife, and soon they had two daughters.

Patrick and his buddies tried to join the Veterans of Foreign Wars (VFW) club but they, like others returning from Southeast Asia, were turned away. Nam was not a real war, they were told—so they were not real heroes. Patrick was seething. How could they say it wasn't a war? Those who served were drafted just like others had been in World Wars I and II, and the Korean War, and they were sent on a mission not of their creation. Even Patrick's father, who served in the latter part of World War II, and never saw combat, was afforded the privilege of a hero's status—but Patrick was not. Had all that he had done in Viet Nam been a waste of time? Patrick found himself turning to drugs again, and, unlike in Viet Nam, he added alcohol.

"I would get high to do *this*, and I'd get high because I had to do *that*. I got high to go to work every day, and I got high when I came home again." Nightmares of Viet Nam plagued him. Eventually, he "hit bottom" and made the decision to enter outpatient treatment. After that came "ninety meetings in ninety days," and an aftercare program.

Patrick didn't know what his next move should be. His self-esteem was eroding away, he wasn't sure if he wanted to be a physician assistant, and his marriage was rapidly falling apart. When his wife filed for divorce, Patrick maintained his sobriety. But his anger still festered, and he became deeply depressed. He sought help from professionals and learned that he was suffering from Post Traumatic Stress Disorder—the exact diagnosis I was given when I "hit bottom" years after being sexually assaulted. Where the terror comes from is inconsequential; the demons must be dealt with, regardless.

"I heard in treatment to 'fake it 'till you make it,' and that's exactly what I did," he recalled. "I was in about my ninth month of sobriety, and I was studying the 'Twelve by Twelve' book when a light bulb went off and I got it."

It was the definition of the statement "our lives had become unmanageable," that was the turning point in Patrick's sobriety. Sometime later, I became curious and looked it up:

> *By going back to our own drinking histories, we could show that years before we realized we were out of control, our drinking even then was no mere habit, that it was indeed the beginning of a fatal progression. To the doubters, we could say, 'Perhaps you're not an alcoholic after all. Why don't you try some more controlled drinking, bearing in mind meanwhile what we have told you about alcoholism?' This attitude brought immediate and practical results...Following every spree, he would say to himself, 'Maybe those A.A.'s were right...' After a few such experiences...,he would return to us convinced. He had hit bottom as truly as any of us...*
>
> *Twelve Steps and Twelve Traditions*, pages 23 and 24

****

I took some time to process all that Patrick had told me. But at some point I began to realize that he and I were both survivors of different kinds of conflicts. Our common bond initially may have been the negative experiences in our lives, but it was clear that we were becoming soul mates in the lives we had left to live. I fell deeply and comfortably in love with him.

Some years later, Patrick and I happened to see a television program about military medics, going back as far as the Civil War. It was a well-done documentary, with a great deal of coverage of Viet Nam. It contained several interviews with veterans whose lives had been saved by medics, among them many who became prominent U.S. citizens. These survivors talked about how grateful they were to the medics who saved their life, allowing them to return to the United States, marry, have families, and live full lives in spite of many serious injuries. Patrick was mesmerized by the stories.

When it the program was over, I turned to him and said, "Did you ever stop to think about all the people walking around today, with wives and husbands and children and grandchildren, that wouldn't be here today if it wasn't for you?"

He paused for a moment and then said, "I never looked at it that way."

****

As those first months with Patrick went by, I felt as if I was finally at peace. Being with him was like wearing comfortable clothes. We moved effortlessly into a closer and closer relationship, sharing all that we each held dear and holding back nothing. I ran across a Scripture passage that said it all:

The boundary lines have fallen for me in pleasant places.

Psalm 16:6

Being with Patrick was, indeed, a "pleasant place." My life, up until now, had consisted of relationships full of loose ends and straggling expectations. I never felt I had found my perfect mate until Patrick. Being with him gave me a sense of earthly security that I had never experienced in any other relationship. But it wasn't a please-take-care-of-me security. It seemed Patrick brought out the best in me, giving me confidence in my *own* ability to take care of myself. He respected me as a woman, a professional, and a Christian. I had so often said to my students and clients through the years that a true caring relationship is when two people who are perfectly capable of taking care of themselves *choose* to care for one another. I had said that, but I had never found it myself, until I found Patrick

I thought back to all the times I had tried to "bring home a man" to gain my parents' approval. Either they had been unavailable for comment, or gave me the impression that, once again, I had made a poor choice. I had wanted some hint of approval, but now realized I had always been asking the wrong source. I prayed continually in the first few weeks of my relationship with Patrick, asking God to give me a sign that he was the one for me. It was God's approval I needed and no other. When I first realized that, I felt like my life had taken a huge sigh of relief. My heart had finally come home.

When I finally did call my parents, I did not try to convince them of anything, saying simply, "You'd better come and meet him because *this is the one…*"

****

Patrick and I were spending as much time together as possible, and I was getting to know his dog, Bayfield. This adorable Basset Hound, full of energy and mischief, seemed certain that it was his birthright to demand, and get my full and undivided attention. He was soft and cuddly like a big pile of leaves on a sunny fall day. His olfactory nerves, I would learn later, ran all the way from his cold black nose to the base of his long, gyrating tail, rendering it impossible for him not to investigate every new scent that crossed his path. I was no exception. He bathed me with wet canine kisses and wagged his tail until I was sure it would fall off. He followed me all over Patrick's house as I was given the grand tour. He would look up at me as we entered each new room, as if to say, "This is where I live with my Man-Dad. Would you like to live here too?" It was clear that Patrick loved animals at least as much as I did, another point in his favor.

****

We had a very *small* wedding ceremony, just us, a couple who stood up for us, and our pastor and his wife. The wedding was in March of 1999, on the edge of winter, but we held the reception on a glorious, sunny day in August, at our new home, in a yard that, by now, I had filled with flowers and shrubs and all the trappings. Our children, parents, and many friends and neighbors surrounded us. My parents attended and behaved pretty well—no liquor at *this* wedding! My father said he wanted to come to our wedding reception and see Mother through the turn of the new millennium, and then he was ready to go. After a whole week with them here, I was ready for both of them to go, too.

The cross into the year 2000 millennium came and left, and the world did not self-destruct. My father was pleased that he got to see the turn of the century; by that time he was almost ninety-two-years old. Daddy had developed congestive heart failure and diabetes, but he seemed to be managing both conditions well, with diet, exercise, and pacing himself. He was always good at putting himself on a "program," unlike Mother who refused to follow even the simplest of medical advice. Still, even Mother seemed to have sort of settled comfortably into old age. The visits that Patrick and I made to Las Vegas in the first few years of our marriage went as well as could be expected.

Life was *really* good.

Chapter 29
The World Held Its Breath

Those who are glad at calamity will not go unpunished.
Proverbs 17:5b

Your mind will muse on the terror,
Where is the one who counted?
Where is the one who weighed the tribute?
Where is the one who counted the towers?
No longer will you see the insolent people,
the people of an obscure speech that you cannot understand…
But there the Lord in majesty will be for us,
a place of broad rivers and streams…
For the Lord is our judge,
the Lord is our ruler, the Lord is our king;
He will save us.

Isaiah 33:18, 19a, 21, 22

I never thought I would see a hostile takeover in education, but that is exactly what happened at the small two-year college where I worked as a counselor when I met Patrick. Shortly after we were married, a series of events made my work life, as I had known it, a thing of the past. To put it bluntly, the good guys lost—and the bad guys won.

The issues at hand don't really matter; it was a drama that has been played out in many work settings. When it was all said and done, we had an entirely new administration with an equally new outlook on how a college should be run. Lines were quickly drawn between the "old guard" and the "new guard," and things were not going smoothly. One of my counseling colleagues had an old saying, "If you have relationships and no process, you can still get things done; if you have a process and no relationships, you can still get things done; if you have neither, nothing gets done."

We had neither.

Within this atmosphere, I found that my already precarious health was rapidly failing. Each day, from the moment I walked in the door, was tense. The old feelings were familiar to me; I felt like I was back in my dysfunctional marriage. Or my dysfunctional childhood. So many staff members had left and not been replaced adequately that now the students were being given bad information. We tried to help them get back on track. Misinformation, along with stress, became rampant.

We became absorbed in the situation, and tried to allow the grievance process to work, but it was a long and arduous battle. We had to juggle a myriad of student issues and our own work issues at the same time. I was exhausted, hurting, and couldn't sleep. Soon I began to recognize some serious signs of major depression in myself—and tension in my brand-new marriage. Many days I was shaking so hard, I could not hold my hand steadily enough to sign my name legibly.

I knew I needed to do something, and soon.

****

Like many people who have suffered from PTSD, I found my depression returning quickly as the work situation deteriorated. With the sleeplessness, my journal entries became darker and darker. One entry read: "I feel devalued, demoralized, dejected, disrespected, and just plain depressed."

Almost daily now I was crying, something I had not done for many years. So much energy was spent trying to stay in control at work that at night I felt like the dam was eventually going to burst. Many days, I cried all the way home from work, and could not turn off the tears all evening.

I had always told my students that two things cause anxiety; not knowing what's expected of you, and not feeling like you have any control over what's happening to you. Both things were very true at the college. I was involved in a delicate balancing act, like a tightrope walker with no balance bar. I had long believed that it was the intensity I felt all the time that caused me to go searching so diligently for myself, and finding myself to be a child of God. But where was my God now? Suddenly He seemed distant and remote.

One Saturday morning, I looked in the mirror and burst into tears. My image in the mirror has often made me want to cry, but generally a little make-up and a few minutes with a curling iron can improve my outlook immensely. But this wasn't about vanity; I simply did not want to "see" my image at all. I wanted to disappear altogether. I bounded down the stairs to where Patrick was cooking breakfast.

"I'm depressed," I announced.

"No kidding!" he said, without a moment's hesitation.

Hmmm, and I thought I was hiding it pretty well. We discussed my situation over breakfast. We both sensed that *he* would be on overload right along with me if I kept dumping on him. He suggested (strongly) that I contact the state's employee assistance program for an appointment to talk to a counselor there. At first I wanted nothing to do with this plan. After all, I *was* a counselor. (*Here we go again…*) Why did I *need* one, if I knew all about it already? But of course I was somewhat delusional by this time, and the more I thought about it I realized I did need some "professional help."

Though I was nervous at my first appointment, the very skilled and compassionate woman I saw did all the "right" things. She validated my feelings, helped me reframe some of my issues, and actively listened while I expounded on what I thought might improve things or provide me with some distance from things over which I had no control. All great steps to take, all things I'd done a million times with students and clients through the years. But not so obvious when I was feeling so overwhelmed. At least it was a start. Or so I thought.

****

The following Monday, I contemplated early retirement. I sat at my sad little desk in my sad little office and looked at my retirement status report, at the amount I would collect per month if I retired now, as opposed to an amount, say double, if I waited until I was sixty-two. I compared that amount to another amount, say triple, if I waited until my hair fell out and someone needed to mash all of my food in a blender. I concluded that financially I couldn't retire yet.

I tried to concentrate on the tasks I needed to perform, but it was all I could do to lift my arms off my lap. My head pounded and my hands were shaking. I could not imagine things getting much worse.

Then my co-counselor burst into my office. "I just heard on the radio that a plane crashed into the World Trade Center in New York City, and then another one crashed into it a few minutes later!"

September 11, 2001 was upon us.

****

In a break room full of people, most of whom did not even like each other anymore (or never had), we huddled around one of many television sets hastily hooked up by the college's audio-visual staff. We stared in disbelief as the events unfolded. We watched the aircraft hitting the Twin Towers and the Pentagon over and over and over, like a bad needle stuck on an old record. How many ways could the news staff say "shocking"? How many microphones were thrust in front of people who were already out of their minds with fear, just to force their response for the viewing interest of Americans, of the world?

When I finally shook myself out of the nightmare I had been watching for what seemed like forever, when it became evident that it was indeed the act of terrorists, but before we knew if there would be more, I dragged myself back to my office and called my parents. By the time the whole thing had unfolded, it was only about seven o'clock in Las Vegas. I heard my mother's sleepy voice at the other end of the receiver. *What do I say?* I thought to myself. *How can I break the news to them without them flying into a panic?* But I believed I must brace them for what they would see soon enough.

"Mother, it's me," I said. "I'm sorry to wake you up, but something's happened...Some people have destroyed some buildings...earlier in New York and now in Washington...Can you put Daddy on?"

"Mayhue, come to the phone, it's Margaret!"

"Margaret?" My father sounded terribly groggy. *Maybe I should have waited*, I thought.

"Oh, Daddy," I began, "I wanted to call you and tell you before you turned on the television..."

****

And so it began, those terrible days when the world held its breath, and we all mourned the loss of our illusion of security. Every good and decent citizen in the United States—no, in the world—had just been deputized in a crime fight that few of us understood and none of us wanted to be part of. This new war was with an undetectable foe; indeed, an *invisible* foe. Our vulnerability as a nation had just been fully exposed at the hands of nineteen maniacs who were willing to die in order to destroy us and our way of life. The most powerful nation in the world had been found sleeping at the wheel. Never again in my lifetime, and in the lifetime of so many others, would we ever take the word "freedom" for granted.

I was unable to reach Patrick because he was in surgery. When we both got home, we just held each other for a long, long time and said nothing. There wasn't much to say.

We dragged ourselves through that awful day and the next, with many students just leaving school, not knowing what to do. They left to be with family, or just to go home and be alone. Others stayed and held onto conversations about anything, just to feel the life breath of human contact. Inevitably, some learned of people they knew who had been killed or injured, or who were missing.

To my astonishment, the college leadership did nothing to acknowledge the event or offer any kind of collective solace to the members of the campus community. I asked permission to hold a memorial at noon on Friday of that week. We gathered in the cafeteria, and the campus day care children brought a flag they had made of tiny red, white and blue handprints to hold up while we sang "God Bless America" to a tape recording. At the last minute, an administrator arrived to deliver a short, obviously unprepared and disappointing speech. I could have done a better job myself.

I had bought a ticket to ride the train to see some friends in Milwaukee the week after the attack. People said, "Were you afraid to fly?" "No," I said, "I was afraid to drive." I knew I was too exhausted to make the six-hour car trip by myself, but I needed a break from work, and I had been looking forward to the trip.

On the train, I sat in the dome car, by chance, next to an American Airlines flight attendant who *was* afraid to fly, who said she probably would never fly again. She cried and told me her story, how she knew every single crew member on both the planes that hit the World Trade Center, and in fact, she had worked on both of those flights dozens of times herself except for now, while she was on vacation. She was stranded in Seattle when the planes were all grounded, and she refused to fly home. She was riding the Amtrak from coast to coast, preparing herself for the visits she would be making to the families of those she knew who were dead.

Although I had been looking forward to a quiet ride, if ever I felt I was put in a place by God to perform a duty, it was during the six hours on that train. I listened to, held her and cried with this woman, until then, a stranger to me. She was about my age, having lost her husband to cancer not too long before that, and she had no children. Now her life was in shambles. She told me things about the attacks that she had heard from fellow American Airlines employees, things the news media did not seem to know. Things that sickened me. Things I wished I had not heard.

When I got off the train, she gave me her address and phone number. I never tried to contact her again. Perhaps I should have accepted the fact that I was just there for her at that time.

****

After my visit to Milwaukee, I returned to my home and my work. The atmosphere there had deteriorated even in the few days I had been gone, and by November, I knew something had to change or I would collapse. I wanted to be free from the daily tension at that school.

Calling my doctor in mid-November, I asked for her help in getting some time off. Having used up all my sick leave, I was willing to take time off without pay. When the doctor said she would give me a medical excuse to take a month off, I jumped at the chance. I wrote a letter to my boss, saying something stupid about needing to take time off because of too much stress. He asked me to meet with him and explain. I took a union rep with me, but the conversation was a waste of time, and I left in a cloud of desolation.

For four days straight I slept. I barely got up to take a shower and make myself presentable before Patrick got home. The headaches subsided a bit, and I no longer felt like my body would disintegrate from the pain. Within a couple of days, I stopped shaking, which I took as a very good sign. Thanksgiving came and we spent it alone, just the two of us, resting and rejuvenating, enjoying each other's company by the fireplace.

Chapter 30
Honor Your Father and Mother

Honor your father and your mother,
that your days may be long upon the land
which the Lord your God is giving you.
Exodus 20:12

After Thanksgiving, I called my parents. My father had been sounding more tired than usual lately, but on this particular night, he sounded *beyond* exhaustion. Usually when I called, he would say, "I don't know how much longer I can hold this thing together," meaning that he was doing everything for himself and for Mother, and it was wearing him out.

This night, he said simply, "*I can't do this anymore.*"

Then he explained that Mother was having bowel trouble again, and her doctor had told him over the phone to go to the drugstore and buy a bottle of magnesium citrate. "Give her half a bottle," the doctor had instructed, "and wait. If nothing happens within four hours, give her the rest of the bottle."

"The rest of the bottle" caused my mother's bowels to blow a gasket, so to speak. According to my father's report, there was poop everywhere, on the bed, on the carpet, on the furniture. At age ninety-two, he had been on his hands and knees on her bedroom floor, scrubbing the stains with a steel brush. He had done four loads of laundry, insisting that everything be hung outside rather than using the dryer. Once my mother had gotten some relief, she passed out on the filthy sheets, so he was working around her to get everything cleaned up.

He refused to listen to any reasonable ideas from me. I begged him to call their housecleaner and tell her he would pay her double to come out and help. He would have no part of it. Eventually, he agreed to put the wash in the electric dryer. We talked for a half hour or more, and I told him I would call him the next day.

****

Saturday I was cleaning up the breakfast dishes when the phone rang. It was a female voice I didn't recognize, calling me "Margaret."

Not a good sign. She was a nurse in the critical care unit of a Las Vegas hospital. My father had been admitted sometime after midnight, picked up by the paramedics after he called 911. He was unconscious and on a ventilator, his heart functioning at about twenty per cent. The nurse asked how fast I could get there.

Mother was home alone.

The next time the phone rang, it was my parents' next-door neighbors, calling to report the same thing I had just learned from the nurse. Yes, Mother was at home alone, and she wasn't in very good shape. The neighbors had gone over to my parents' house the previous night, when the ambulance came, and again that morning. (Years earlier, my father had the good sense to give the neighbors a house key.) Both times the neighbors had checked, Mother was in bed breathing and fairly coherent.

I made arrangements to fly out that night. What would I find? It was probably better that I did not realize how bad things would be. My father had made more comebacks than an aging rock star. Emergency room doctors had told me in the past that my father had recited from memory all of his medications: names, dosages, last time taken, in alphabetical order. It would be just like before. He'd be home in a couple of days.

When Patrick dropped me off at the airport, I was not sure I could stay awake to hear my flight announced. Still, I stretched out across three connecting seats in the waiting area, and in spite of the metal chair frames poking into my back, I fell asleep.

I was awakened by a National Guardsman who had sat down at the end of the row of seats. It was hard not to notice the post-911increased security, and like most people, I was grateful that they were there.

"Is this your flight?" he asked pleasantly.

I sat up and heard the last announcement to board.

"Yes," I answered. "I guess I'd better get going."

He smiled and began to eat a fast-food sandwich. He was spending at least part of his Thanksgiving weekend protecting me and other travelers. I turned back to him as I walked toward the boarding gate. "Thanks for being out here," I said with a lump in my throat.

"You're welcome, Ma'am."

Fighting back the tears, I boarded the plane. Tears for the victims of 911. Tears for myself because I was so exhausted. Tears that I was terrified to fly and never wanted to do so again in my natural lifetime. Tears for what I imagined I'd find when I got to Las Vegas.

The flight left Minneapolis at 11:30 p.m., full of starry-eyed, prospective jackpot winners having cocktails and swapping stories about previous wins or techniques to "break the house." *How could these people all be so happy and excited? Don't they know about the terrorist attacks? Don't they know there are addicted and crazy people in Las Vegas—and that's just my family?*

Wide awake, I suddenly sat upright and remembered "the black book." I had stuck it in my carry-on bag because I knew my father would quiz me about it. I took it out and began reading.

My father had been working on "the black book" since I was born, maybe since he was born. It was *the official Blaine family logistical manual*, updated at least annually, about what to do in the event of an emergency, real or imagined. It contained my parents' vital statistics including little-known information such as their birth weight, first words and the date they cut their first teeth. It had the names and addresses of all the relatives, living and dead, in case we wished to contact any or all of them. That's one reason it had to be updated so often, because the older ones kept dying.

In the back a special section marked *Critical Information* contained both of my parents' advance medical directives (most "recently signed" thirty years ago), burial arrangements, and each of their wills. The middle section was what I liked to call *Everything You Always Wanted to Know About Your Parents Dying But Were Afraid to Ask*. Here were the names, addresses and phone numbers of every possible government and private agency and organization to be contacted in the event of "said emergency," from the chaplain at Nellis Air Force Base to the current President.

Lofty reading on your way to a crisis.

I glanced through the book for a good three minutes, not allowing my eyes to rest on the section marked Wills—off limits until absolutely necessary. I skimmed the section on my father's advance directive, but I assumed (correctly as it turned out) that the hospital had already blown right past the words contained therein, since it clearly said he didn't want to be intubated. Though they said he had called 911 himself, I doubted if he took a copy of "the black book" with him in the ambulance.

I wasn't ready for all that awaited me, so I closed the book and visited with the lady sitting next to me for the rest of the trip.

With the time change, when I arrived in Vegas it was almost two in the morning for me. Grabbing my carry-on luggage, I went directly outside and grabbed a cab. In a half hour, I was standing on the doorstep of my parents' town home. In the front flap of "the black book" I found the extra house key (since I had long since misplaced mine). My father, ever the highly organized military officer, was always ready for anything.

I inserted that key and opened the front door. The familiar smells infused my brain: stale air since my mother never allowed the windows or even the curtains to be opened, faint cooking smells probably from my dad fixing dinner the night before, and Lysol from him cleaning up the mess last evening—the strong smell still pungent in my nostrils. I turned on the nearest light switch and tiptoed down the hall to my mother's bedroom, opening the door to memories that were palpable.

"I'm the one who's supposed to be sick," her voice came at me from out of the dark.

"Hello, Mother. Nice to see you too."

"You must be tired," she managed.

"I am. Did you talk to anyone from the hospital?"

"No, Daddy didn't call." She obviously didn't know how bad things were.

"Well, why don't we try to get some sleep, and I'll go over there in the morning."

"Okay," she murmured. I heard her snoring softly before I even got down the hall.

****

At six-thirty that morning, I called the hospital. I hadn't been able to sleep, and my throat was getting raspy. Was I was coming down with something–a cold or the flu or a panic attack–or all three?

The nurse assigned to my father explained once more that he was in rough shape, still on a respirator, unable to breath on his own. "To put it bluntly," she said, "a CAT scan showed that heart is worn out."

No kidding.

After I showered and dressed as fast as I could, I looked in on Mother. She was awake but lying in her corpse pose. I told her I was going to the hospital, and I'd be back later. Did she want anything to eat? No, she'd just lie there awhile—hours, weeks, years? My mother must have missed a good half of her life, "just lying there a while."

I entered the hospital with "the black book" under my arm, and consulted a directory with a little X saying "You Are Here." I found where they were keeping my father. The double doors to the intensive care unit were closed, with a huge sign in big black letters:

NO ADMITTANCE

IMMEDIATE FAMILY ONLY

FIFTEEN MINUTE VISITS ON THE HOUR

It was ten till eight. I paced the floor, seeing no one who looked like they might give me special dispensation to enter. Another visitor indicated that the nurse would inflict bodily harm to anyone who disobeyed the rule. Sit tight, he said.

At eight o'clock on the nose, the big double doors opened and Nurse Godzilla came out. I told her who I was and after a brief lecture about "why did it take me so long to get there—doesn't anybody care," she led me down the hall to my father's private room.

Now, I'm not particularly good in a medical emergency. In fact, I suck. Give me a good old psychological crisis with people hearing things and seeing things and wanting to kill things, maybe including themselves, and I do fine. But when I saw my father—my smart, capable, ready-for-anything, in-charge-of-everything, father–lying there unconscious with at least a thousand tubes running in and out of him, I just about lost it. Sensing this, Nurse Godzilla softened and approached me gently.

"You can touch him," she said. I didn't want to touch him. "You can hold his hand." I was scared to hold his hand. "He can probably hear you. Say something to him."

I watched his chest pumping up and down, propelled not by his own effort or will, but by the machine attached to him. I touched his arm. "Daddy," I managed, "it's Margaret. I'm here now."

Nothing.

After a moment, the nurse motioned me outside and started asking questions. Did my father have an advanced directive? Yes. Did I understand what was wrong with him? Not exactly. She started telling me again about his heart only working at fractional capacity because of his congestive heart failure. I explained about the home situation and how he was scrubbing floors when he collapsed. We discussed how my father would not be able to return home, if and when he was able to breathe on his own. At a minimum, he would need to go to a long-term care facility and have extensive rehab services. She was very clear that my father would *need* a caretaker now, and that he could no longer *be* the caretaker. I explained that my mother needed fairly constant care as well. When she asked me if I wanted to talk to a hospital social worker, I said sure.

The social worker's name was Mike. I reviewed the situation again with him, and told him I would need to take over my father's affairs as soon as possible. He said there wasn't much I could do in the finance department. I heard all about Nevada law, and learned that it would be next to impossible to get power of attorney over my father, even to pay his bills.

"Nevada is the fleece capital of the world," he said. "As long as your mother is still breathing and can sign checks, you will not be able to convince a judge to let you be power of attorney."

I remembered that my father had set up a family trust. Did this make any difference?

"Are you a full trustee?"

I got the papers out and we looked. I was only a successor trustee, but my mother was a full trustee, which meant exactly what the social worker had just said. If Mother was breathing and could sign checks...

"She can't pay the bills!" I cried. "She doesn't know anything about their finances!" *Neither do I*, I thought dismally.

The social worker agreed to begin looking for a long-term care placement for when (if) my father got off the ventilator. I drove directly to my parents' bank, turned on the tears, and got a young bank officer to agree to give me some sort of limited signing power to write checks, *if* I got a note from my father's doctor, *and* got a signature from my mother.

****

Back at the house, Mother was busy indenting her sofa pillow on the living room sofa. I absently studied the wall behind her. The entire house was painted harvest gold and avocado green, a veritable fading monument stuck in the '70s.

"How's your daddy?" she asked brightly.

I sat down beside her. "Not good, Mother."

She frowned.

"Mother, he is very, very ill this time. I think you need to go with me later today and see him."

"Oh, I'll just wait 'till he's home," she answered.

"Mother," I said, trying to keep my voice as calm as possible, "Daddy is very ill, and he may not be coming home."

I could clearly see this did not register with her at all.

"Okay," she said, smiling a little bit, "well, you tell him I hope he'll be better soon!"

I was getting no place.

The next several days were a blur. How did they go by so fast? Each day I woke up earlier than was necessary because of the time change. I went to the hospital at least twice a day, sometimes three times, coming home in between to check on Mother. She slept a lot, her way of escaping from reality, as she had done all of her life. I didn't know if she was drinking, but I knew she was abusing medication. The first full night I was there, I was awakened around midnight by what I thought was a knock on the front door. In Las Vegas, you do not open your door in the middle of the night for any reason, so I tried to peek out between the tightly drawn curtains. Seeing no one, I went back to bed. Just as I dozed off, I heard another knock. On the way to the front door again, I then realized the knocking was coming from Mother's bedroom.

Walking down the hall, I stood at her partially open doorway. "Mother, is that you knocking?"

"Oh, yes!" she said. "That's my little signal for your daddy to come and get me another sleeping pill."

I paused to compose my thoughts and take a deep breath.

"Mother, I am not Daddy, you do not need another sleeping pill, and if you need anything else, you can walk. I'm going back to bed."

As I climbed back into the guest room bed, my face was hot with anger. I tossed and turned, trying to fend off the rush of resentment that was rapidly closing in on me. It wasn't that she was a helpless eighty-seven-year-old woman; I could have dealt with that. It was the fact that she had always been helpless and selfish and child-like, for as long as I had remembered. Someone, almost always my father, had *always* bailed her out of every jam.

Now it looked like it was my turn at a game I didn't want to play.

****

By day three, I had called all of the relatives and explained that my father was gravely ill. I reluctantly called my sister, knowing that I could not count on her to come out to help me. I was right. I was on my own. I called my niece several times and she was more than willing to listen. I didn't expect her to fly out to help me, but at least she was someone who knew the situation and could appreciate what I was dealing with. She finally called her mother and encouraged her to lend her support as well—over the phone, at least. I called Patrick several times a day, just to hear his voice.

My father's doctor gave me a letter stating that Daddy could not manage his own finances. I dragged Mother to the bank, presumably in a state of full orientation to time, place and person, to sign papers so I could write checks. Though I had explained to her several times what I was doing and why, when the papers were placed in front of her, she looked at me with her rheumy eyes and said, "Now, what am I signing?" The bank officer looked at us suspiciously, but once Mother signed, I was in business.

The next day I visited a few long-term care facilities, and decided on one that had several levels of care, including senior apartments and assisted living, just in case my father made a semi-complete recovery. I continued to visit the hospital at least twice a day, but I knew that such a recovery didn't appear likely. I had to have a neighbor come to "watch" Mother when I was away from the house too long. Mother was up and around, but she was very weak, refused to eat, and continued to operate under the delusion that my father would be calling a cab at any minute to come home and resume his care taking duties.

Still, Daddy lay motionless, drifting in and out of consciousness, with only the artificial, rhythmic up-and-down action of the ventilator filling the silence with its *suck-hiss-suck-hiss* sound.

By day five, I was going down for the count myself. My throat was on fire, and now I ached in places that I didn't know existed. I had developed a "nonproductive" cough, as they say in medical circles. I was afraid to breathe on either of my parents lest I speed up their mutual demise. The neighbors took me to an urgent care where we waited, along with what seemed like the majority of Las Vegas' "finest citizens," for almost two hours. Eventually, I got to see a frazzled doctor who gave me a prescription for an antibiotic and some cough medicine with codeine. Now my entire family was on drugs.

I also began communicating with Mother's doctor, an evasive young woman who spoke only through her nurse. Apparently she didn't really like seeing patients, which was why she had prescribed the magnesium citrate over the phone. I needed medical orders to get Mother admitted to the long-term care facility. The phantom doctor signed them without even talking to me—or Mother, and I picked them up at her office. Mother needed a chest x-ray; the doctor arranged for this over the phone as well. So much for responsible elder care.

Mother still refused to go visit Dad with me. The neighbor graciously offered to go, to sort of "pave the way" for Mother. My father was sitting up, with the vent tube still in his mouth. We had a rousing conversation with him during which he tried to write (and draw) his thoughts on paper. He was so weak, he would get a couple of scribbles down and then we would try to decipher what he was trying to say. Daddy would get angry, scribble some more, we would fail to figure out what he meant, and so it went. It was like playing charades without the party atmosphere. I don't know which one of us was more exhausted by the end of the visit.

****

Day nine. My father pulled the ventilator tube out by himself. Then the real fun began. He came up swinging. He was angry and scared and he very much wanted somebody–anybody–to give him back control of his life, if not the universe.

He was also delusional. The first day breathing on his own, he asked me about Mother. Which hospital room was she in? Puzzled, I said she was at home, and he said no, that he specifically told the paramedics to load her in the ambulance with him because she couldn't be left alone. Hell hath no wrath compared to my father when his perception is challenged. After a couple of minutes of an escalating argument, I said I'd go check with the hospital staff. They indulged me, checked the records. No sign of Mother in any ambulance.

I started crying. The nurse explained that it was typical for people to hallucinate for some time after their oxygen supply is cut off. She accompanied me back to my father's bedside to tell him the truth. He didn't say anything. He just looked perplexed, distrustful, and very, very anxious.

The next day he told me about the fully costumed geisha girls who came into his room every night and made his supper on a small hibachi. At least Mother being in the ambulance could be passed off as an unconscious, unspoken wish; geisha girls were pure fantasy. I didn't try to get to the bottom of that one.

****

Day eleven. He was moved from ICU to a medical-surgical unit. It was here that my father rediscovered the telephone. Having nothing to do except sit and worry day and night, time meant nothing to him. He started calling the house non-stop.

"Margaret," he would begin, "I think I've got this thing figured out. If you will just come and get me and take me home, I can go to the commissary and get supplies for your Mother and me and then you can go back to Minnesota."

"Daddy, you can't come home right now."

"Whadyamean, I can't come home!" he would explode.

And I would explain for the umpeenth time, just as we had done several times by now with the doctor and the hospital staff in his room, that he wasn't strong enough to leave the hospital yet, and when he was ready, he'd have to go to the Pleasant Valley Senior Care Center for a while. Maybe indefinitely. We conducted variations of the same conversation every few hours or minutes, depending on his ability to retain what he'd been told before.

Then he began calling in the middle of the night. "Margaret, I lie here and look at this goddamn clock and the hands *never move!*" he would say. "Do you have any idea what that's like?"

When I thought he was well enough, I decided to try to discuss his financial situation. "Do you realize that you have the Blaine Family Trust set up so all the responsibility goes to Mother if you are incapacitated?" I challenged him, treading on decidedly shaky ground. "My hands were tied when I got here. I couldn't even write checks to pay your bills."

His right eyebrow shot up towards the ceiling. "*HA*, ha!" he exclaimed with a sinister look.

"Did you do that on purpose?" I inquired, not appreciating his brand of humor.

"Damn right I did!" he howled. "I don't want you paying my bills! Bring them to me and I'll pay them!"

"Too late," I said. "I've already gotten a letter from your doctor."

"He's not my goddamn doctor!" he shouted. "I *fired* him!"

It was true, he had gotten in the middle of a really frustrating power struggle between his own doctor and the hospital staff. The ambulance had taken him to the closest, but wrong, hospital, where his own cardiologist did not have privileges. Professional courtesy should have allowed for the medical staff to work out the plan for his care, but the hospital cardiologist apparently took my father's case as his own private challenge. Twenty per cent or no twenty per cent, he was convinced he could bring Daddy's heart back from the dead. He began treating my father with an entirely different protocol than his previous doctor had, and he wasn't interested in any other medical opinions.

My father was also furious about his current diagnosis. He'd known about the congestive heart failure for several years, but he was angry because he was now being told it was too late to do much of anything. His first cardiologist had been more proactive a few years ago, but that physician had retired and referred my father to another colleague whom Daddy didn't like as well. He was incensed that procedures might have been done earlier to prolong his life, but the second cardiologist chose not to "treat him aggressively," probably because of his age. Now it was too late. His anger at the physicians was understandable, but it didn't change the fact that he was gravely ill.

Still, I couldn't understand why my father was so angry at me. In spite of his advance medical directive *not* to do CPR or to intubate him, he seemed relieved that the emergency room staff had preserved his life. But he wanted it back on his terms only, and somehow this was all my fault. And when I reminded him that his "black book" really only addressed what should be done if he and Mother died instantly together in a screaming car wreck, *not* what to do in the event of incapacitation, he just got angrier. Nothing I could do or say could solicit his help or support in what action to take next. Like he always said about Mother, now he was the one refusing to participate in his own self-care, and I was being hung out to dry in the process.

I started taking the phone off the hook when I went to bed. One morning, I had no sooner cradled the receiver when it rang again. I picked it up to hear another "Margaret?"

"I've asked you not to call this early!" I yelled into the phone.

Silence.

Then, slowly, my father's brother, who sounds exactly like my dad, said, "Oh, I'm sorry if I woke you..."

Instantly ashamed, I apologized, explaining how Daddy would call all night if I didn't take the phone off the hook. My uncle listened to my complaints and offered moral and spiritual support to me more than once during that time. He is a bit younger than my dad, but was not in the best of health himself. Otherwise, I know he would have flown out to help me. I will always be grateful for his patience and wise counsel during my father's illness.

****

The weekend after Thanksgiving, I got my mother installed in the Pleasant Valley Senior Care Center, in a double room in anticipation of my father joining her. She was a model new resident. For starters, she loved the attention, and when they got her medications untangled and began dispensing them regularly, she felt better, was less disoriented and had more energy. I dined with her at least once a day, to the sound of live music, a battered but in-tune piano with an equally battered "mature" pianist. The food was actually pretty good and each table had a cloth cover set with beautiful dishes and flatware almost reminiscent of Mother's "gracious lady" period. I suggested she regard the senior center as a five-star hotel, and she bought it.

Back at the hospital, Daddy kept having setbacks, and I was getting really anxious to get him to the care center so I could go home for some much-needed rest myself. One of the last days I was there, I went to the hospital and was standing at the desk hearing the latest update from his charge nurse, waiting for Mike the social worker. I heard some sort of crash down the hall, but figured, like everyone else, that someone dropped a bedpan.

"Can somebody please help me!" came a muffled voice. Everyone turned and there, lying in a heap outside the door to his room, was my father. I took off running, but was soon passed up by hospital staff. Realizing that they were going to be better at handling this than I, I stopped in my tracks. Then the tears came. Mike materialized out of nowhere, spirited me off to a conference room, and listened to me sob and wail about how my dad was acting. Why was he being so stubborn? Why couldn't he just accept the fact that he needed help? Someone came in and said he was okay. He had been sitting up in the chair in his room and had decided to "go AWOL," dragging his IV cart with him. He made it as far as the door and then collapsed. The only damage was a few bruises, mostly to his ego.

I had spent more than half of my own medical leave from work in Las Vegas, and I certainly did not feel like returning to *that* madhouse back home without first getting a little rest. The hospital promised me that he would be transferred to the care center the following day, unless there was a setback. I bought a return ticket home for the next day. The neighbors took me to say good-bye to Mother, and then to the hospital one last time.

Daddy was still angry. He stayed angry. He said he'd never forgive me for "making" him go to the care center. He didn't want to hear that it was *not* my doing—it was doctor's orders. He didn't want to hear that Mother was doing well there. When I kissed him good-bye, he hardly looked at me. The neighbors took me to the airport, and I flew home. The worst twelve days of my life were over. Or so I thought.

****

By now it was mid December, and I had about two weeks left until my medical leave would end. I still wasn't getting the rest I needed because I was either on the phone with someone in Vegas (doctors, care center staff, Daddy, the neighbors), or I was worrying about what was going on. Daddy had been transferred to the care center where he had managed to intimidate Mother right back into her dependency shell. She wouldn't come to the phone. He wouldn't go to meals so she ate in the room with him instead of socializing in the dining room like she had the first few days. He hated the food, the layout, the staff, the care he was getting. He was kicked out of both physical and occupational therapy for non-cooperation. And he was still angry.

At my request, his regular cardiologist got involved in the case again. He knew my dad was angry, but it didn't change his diagnosis. To put it simply, my father was dying.

Then a turn of events gave me new hope. On the phone one night, my father said he was ready to go to the assisted living facility. I was elated. He could have twenty-four-hour monitoring, with a little buzzer to press whenever he needed help. And he could go back and forth to the skilled care area when he needed it. He could even get hospice care at the assisted living facility at such time as it was needed.

But he was only manipulating all of us. While we were busy trying to set up an assisted living placement for the two of them, he was trying to bribe the handicapped van driver at the care center to sneak him and Mother out and take them home in the middle of the night. Exasperated, I called the cardiologist with a new idea. If he wanted to go home so badly, could we just send him there with twenty-four-hour, non-medical care and hospice services? The doctor said sure. Christmas and New Year's Eve passed while I was making the arrangements. I sent huge boxes and baskets of goodies, Daddy's favorite cheese, Mother's favorite chocolates. I called every night and wrote Daddy's creditors and paid his bills. Some nights I was so tired, I couldn't even think clearly enough to subtract an entry in his checkbook. Luckily, Patrick took over this duty for me. It didn't help that I felt unreasonably guilty every time I even looked at his affairs.

"Meg, put the checkbook down," Patrick would say. "You are too tired and stressed out to be doing this now. It'll wait until tomorrow."

New Year's Day, we planned to sleep in a bit. The phone rang about four that morning. Showtime.

"Margaret!" Guess who. "I want you to get a pencil and write this name down!" He sounded energetic but not the kind of energy that denoted health improvements.

"Daddy, it's the middle of the *night!*" (Two hours earlier their time.)

"I don't give a goddamn what time it is! Take down this name! It's a lawyer, you see him all the time on the television out here. He gets people out of all kinds of scrapes, and I want him to take this goddamn nursing home to court for holding us hostage!"

Like a robot, I got a pad and paper and wrote down the lawyer's name—an ambulance chaser that I'd been seeing on television ads at my parents' home for years. I had no intention of calling him. Ever.

Later New Year's Day, I wrote my father a nasty letter. I blasted him about not appreciating the help he was getting, and I said he was wrong to make Mother go along with his every whim, when it wasn't in either of their best interests. I sent back his checkbook and all the unpaid bills, and I told him that he could just handle it all himself. I said I was adopting a new policy of hands off when it came to his finances. And then I cried until I didn't think I had any tears left.

Less than a week later, I lost my job.

Chapter 31
Agony in My Bones

O Lord, do not rebuke me in your anger,
Or discipline me in your wrath.
Be merciful to me, Lord, for I am faint.
O Lord, heal me, for my bones are in agony.
My soul is in anguish.
How long, O Lord, how long?
Turn, O lord and deliver me,
Save me because of your unfailing love.
Psalm 6:1-4

Thank God for teachers' unions. In the world of education in Minnesota, school districts and state-supported colleges are required by contract to give a six-month layoff notice to faculty (of which counselors are a part). When I opened my layoff letter on January 7, I felt the bile rise in my throat and the muscles in my neck twist into knots. The letter was telling me that my job would be done at the end of the school year, just six short months away. My co-counselor had also been laid off, along with several classroom faculty members. Other staff and even administrators would get the axe later; their contracts did not call for such long notice.

The days at work were agonizing. At night I worried about my parents. I was called in to an administrative conference, in case I had any questions about the impending layoff. Of course I had questions but I wasn't about to ask them without union representation present. I took my cell phone into the meeting, explaining that my father was dying. Phony condolences came from around the table. Though the words were not being spoken, I knew beyond a shadow of a doubt that these people would be thrilled if I left work to go see my father. I had no sick leave or personal leave left, and leaving now would be grounds for firing me on the spot. No unemployment, no claiming rights to other positions, no retirement. Clearly, the ball was in their court. (Later I learned that I could have filed Family Medical Leave Act papers to allow me to be with my father without losing my job, but no one at the college advised me of this at the time.)

It would make their jobs so much easier if I was to break the rules—but I wasn't about to give them that satisfaction.

Not long after I returned to work, there were several confrontations between members of the "new order" and me. After a great deal of teeth gnashing and soul-searching, I decided to file a human rights complaint. It was a battle I did not expect to win, but I felt it was necessary at the time. I was scheduled to meet with a state investigator the second week in February.

****

We had been able to have Mother and Daddy transported home by the care center staff, who by this time were probably glad they were leaving. I had made all the arrangements over the phone. I hired a non-medical caregiver company called "Home Again," which I later dubbed "Home Alone" when I learned the type of employees they were sending to the house. Mother went home first, and the caregiver did fine with just her. The woman's name was Nellie, and Mother had her completely conned. Nellie thought Mother was the sweetest, kindest little old lady she had ever taken care of. But when my dad arrived, Nellie concluded that he needed way more care than she could provide, and she asked to be replaced. From there, it went downhill, until finally they sent a woman who could not even take care of herself, much less my parents.

Eunice had several strikes against her from the beginning. The Home Again care coordinator assured me that they wouldn't send anyone who didn't have a car, since it would be necessary for someone to go to the pharmacy and the grocery store a couple of times a week. Eunice arrived on a city bus, and not a very convenient one. She came through the door dragging her suitcase and complaining bitterly that she hadn't gotten very good directions and had walked around the neighborhood for the better part of an hour before she found my parents' home.

In fact, Eunice never stopped complaining the entire time she was there. Though it seemed my mother was willing to give her a chance, my father took an instant disliking to her. Eventually, the two of them got into a violent verbal argument, my father gasping for air from the oxygen tube that was now part of his daily routine. I happened to call when things had reached the boiling point. Mother answered the phone.

"Things are not good here," she said. At least her perception of reality had improved. I asked what was wrong; I could hear Daddy shouting at the top of his lungs, which was really more of a hoarse whisper. "Daddy fired Eunice," Mother said.

"*Fired her!*" I said. "He can't fire her! You have to have someone there to take care of you!"

Once again, I felt like my father was sabotaging my efforts to make sure he was being cared for. I continued babbling to my mother, saying this just wouldn't do, that if she could just get him to calm down, I could try to get a flight out over the weekend...

"You don't need to come out here!" It was my father. Mother had handed the phone to him. "I can take care of this by myself!" he roared. "This woman is stealing us blind! She's taking groceries out of the pantry and putting them in her suitcase!" Then he started gasping for air. I took the opportunity to try to talk some sense into him.

"I doubt that's happening, Daddy. If you're so sure, why don't you have Mother take a paper and pencil and go in the pantry and inventory your food?"

"Your mother couldn't inventory her goddamn *toenails!*" he croaked. I was appalled at his rage, but he sounded more alive than he had in weeks. I wondered how much damage this was doing to his heart.

"Daddy, you can't be left alone there! Please let Eunice stay until Home Again can find someone else."

"I fired the whole stinking lot of them! Found a new company, had the owner out this afternoon."

It was true, he had found another caregiver service, and they sent someone out to complete the paperwork. Eunice was still waiting for *her* manager to come pick her up. The neighbor, who had been summoned from next door as a character witness, told me later that Eunice sat in my parents' living room and contradicted everything they said to the new company representative. Once she was gone and the new people came in, my father calmed down considerably. Actually, it was amazing that he was able to make the switch in caretakers in his condition. The new company sent three women, each taking an eight-hour shift. Daddy especially liked one woman named Colleen. He called her his "little red-headed Irish girl." Hospice was coming on a regular basis too, and after a few days with the new company, I almost felt I could breathe a sigh of relief. Silly me.

****

I feel my job performance is suffering because I am spending so much time and energy dealing with my feelings about being harassed.

Those were the words in my journal in early February of 2002. The working conditions were unbearable. I dragged myself to the college each morning and wondered if I would make it through the first hour, much less the whole day. Intellectually, I knew that people suffering from depression display certain signs, like inability to focus, memory impairment, and lack of interest in formerly favorite activities. And, as I had said to so many students and clients, it is natural to grieve a job loss: it is truly the loss of your productive self. But I was blind to the danger signs in myself.

I also thought I was prepared for my father's impending death. I knew all about Elizabeth Kubler-Ross's work with the grief process. I could recite the stages by heart: shock, denial, anger, acceptance. I believed I would readily recognize each stage and embrace them one by one, dealing with them in an orderly fashion. I had also heard about a special kind of strength people of faith draw upon called "dying grace," by Chuck Swindoll. I was certain that God would help me come through all of this with flying colors—the loss of my father, the loss of my job, relocating my mother, the huge life changes that were approaching so fast. It never once occurred to me that I would be completely blindsided by all of it. Like our nation on September 11, I was caught completely off guard.

I thought I knew what depression looked like, felt like, but I was so wrong. What I had experienced in my life before this time was nothing like what I was going through now. I felt like I was standing on the seashore, watching the sand swirl around my feet. I could feel it melting under my weight, dissolving away until I had nothing to stand on. And I was absolutely powerless to do anything about it. Until that time, I thought I had all the tools to live a comfortable life: faith in God, optimism, and common sense. I was completely shocked by this persistent low mood.

I would sludge through the workday fighting the tears, then drive home at night anticipating the newest disaster that had, no doubt, befallen my parents. I was obsessed with death, not just the likelihood of my father's certain demise, but with the way it might feel to actually be dead. I don't think I wanted to die; I just wanted to feel some assurance that death was not the end. I had believed that, all these years. I had trusted God that eternal life was assured for those who believe. I wondered if I had indeed made certain that my father knew that God loved him. Did he believe? Would he go to Heaven? Was it up to me to determine that? Confusing questions set me on edge and kept me from the sleep I so desperately needed.

My physician called it "anxious depression." I went to him on the insistence of friends and my husband. I wanted the doctor to tell me he was putting me in the hospital, that I had no choice. I used to read about famous people being hospitalized "for exhaustion." Couldn't I do that too? Like my mother before me, they would come and take me away, ha ha, and strap me down like a corpse and I'd be screaming just like her.

The doctor gave me medication to help me sleep. *Oh, good, more drugs*, I thought. *I'm just a hopeless druggie.* In my journal, I wrote:

I am internalizing these feelings to the point of making myself sick(er). I cannot even experience the "normal" emotions I should be able to feel over my father dying because my emotions are already "overcharged" because of the atmosphere at work. Why is this happening to me? Why am I the target for this victimization? Do I have a red "V" on my forehead that is only visible to those who perceive themselves to be more powerful or smarter or better or anything even remotely resembling competent? So why do I feel like I'm the crazy one?

I could not seem to let the worry go and trust God. Where was all the faith I thought I had? Why did I feel God was abandoning me in my hour of need? Why could I not define for myself that which I had become so adept at defining in others?

****

The second Friday of February, I called my parents after our evening meal. I talked to Mother for a few minutes and then I asked her to put Daddy on. For once, he didn't yell at me or complain about anything. He was, in a word, somber.

"I don't know how much time I have left," he said.

Fighting the tears, I replied, "I know, Daddy. I know."

"I know you did what you had to, Margaret." It wasn't an apology, but it sounded good enough to me. He continued. "I just want to know that your mother…will be taken care of." This last caused his voice to break, and I could tell he was sobbing on the other end of the line.

"You know I will see to it that she has good care, Daddy," I said, choking out the words that were so very hard to say to him.

We visited a few more minutes and then we hung up. It was the last conversation I had with my father before he died.

Chapter 32
We Loved Not Enough

When we lose one we love, our bitterest tears are called forth by the memory of hours when we loved not enough.
Maurice Maeterlinck
Wisdom and Destiny, 1901

Other families I knew had used hospice services, so I had believed things would go a certain way. I would receive a call, and some individual who specialized in death would tell me that my father's toes were turning blue, and it was time for me to come to be by his side as he parted this world. And I would catch the first flight to Nevada, and I would get to say all the things I wanted to say to him on the phone but couldn't. If I was brave enough, I would certainly assure him one more time that his soul would enter heaven and that he would receive eternal life. What better wish could I have for him than to assure him of this "good news?" My father and I would say our good-byes, and he would hold my hand and drift off to be with Jesus. It wouldn't even matter what Mother did or didn't do, or if she was even there. I had it all rehearsed in my head.

"You can't play God, Meg," Patrick would say. "You might fly out there and then you'd have to come back and that might be worse."

He was right.

In the end, the phone just rang unceremoniously on Sunday morning, February 10th, and I heard the voice of the home-care company's manager.

"Your father died sometime during the night. The caretaker discovered him about five o'clock this morning. Your mother is doing all right, and I told her I would call you."

I hung up the phone and tried to collect my thoughts. Patrick put his arm around me and held me for a long time. "I'm sorry, Honey," he said. It was all he needed to say.

After the logistics were dealt with; calling Mother to tell her I'd be there soon, making plane reservations, calling my sister and my niece Virginia, the folks in Missouri, my coworkers and so on, Patrick and I decided to go to church. Where else should we be? It would be a few hours before I could get on a plane, and church was preferable to sitting around the house. Besides, church was full of people who had been praying for my dad anyway. We were actually a little late getting there, and we slipped into a back pew just as the fire alarm went off.

Our church had never had a fire *or* a fire drill, and after some confusion, a female church staff member stood up and directed everyone to leave the building. Who says women are the weaker sex? We might still be there today, crispy critters in our pews, if she hadn't taken some reasonable action.

Patrick had already called the church that morning to report my father's passing, and ask the pastors to pray for our family. I spoke with the senior pastor in the parking lot during what ended being a false alarm (the fire, not my father's death). And we said all the things that are supposed to be said. I managed to be lighthearted enough to remark that I expected my father had arranged the fire drill from wherever he was, since he would probably think I should have been home going through his "black book."

****

I was the first of the family to arrive in Vegas, with the others coming in two days later. The cab delivered me from the airport mid afternoon. Colleen, my father's "little Irish girl," greeted me on the front lawn. She was smoking a cigarette in spite of the fact that she had a terrible cough and cold. I wondered absently if she had smoked around my father with his oxygen. I expressed my gratitude that she had stayed until I got there. I thanked her profusely, and she wasted no time saying her good-byes. I asked her if it was possible for her to come the morning of the funeral and help give Mother a bath. She agreed, said a quick good-bye to Mother and left.

Mother was seated on the couch, right where she had been when I arrived the last time. She wept a bit as I came up to her and, not surprisingly, she seemed a little disoriented.

"He was so cold," she said at last.

"I know, Mother. But he's finally at rest," I responded.

"He was lying on his side...He looked like he might have been trying to get out of bed..."

And where might he have been going? I thought to myself. *Did he hear Mother rapping on the wall? Did they need supplies from the commissary? Was he "ground flying all over the United States?"*

"He asked me to lie down with him last night!" she blurted out. "I said, 'I can't lie down beside you! I won't get any sleep!' And then he said, 'Get a chair from the dining room and sit with me,' and I said, 'I can't sit in a hard-backed chair all night long! I've got to get some sleep!'"

She looked me full in the face with a glint of what looked like defiance in her eyes. I let her words sink in and then I tried unsuccessfully to force them out of my consciousness again. I fought my thoughts. *How could she deny him her company for the last precious hours of his life when he gave her so many hours of his? How could this be? His last illness was not of his own doing, but so many times her calamities were brought on totally by her own refusal to take better care of herself.*

Instantly I was ashamed of my selfish thoughts, but in the next second I was angry again that it was *her* selfishness that was evident here, not mine. *How could she not have been here for him when no one else was?*

My thoughts throughout the week of the funeral, and in the coming days, would keep returning to her statements the day he died. The most painful emotion I dealt with during that time was not the loss of my father. It was the profound sadness I felt that my father had loved my mother so completely, but so strangely, that *his* last request seemed so selfish to *her*.

****

In the first few hours after my arrival, I busied myself with tasks that needed to be done, feeling reluctant to spend my energies comforting my mother. The dining room table was completely covered with paperwork: cancelled checks, bills paid and unpaid, envelopes, stamps, tablets with notes and figures all over them. It looked as if my father had been trying to go through an entire lifetime of personal affairs. The caregivers told me he had actually gotten his taxes done and signed just a couple of days before he died. He had used an accountant, but the preliminary work had been his own. I was amazed at his tenacity, but frustrated by his inability to allow anyone to help.

By the time my sister, my niece and Patrick had arrived, I had a good bit of the funeral plans taken care of. I had avoided sitting down in Daddy's chair, but once everyone was there, no other spots were available. Seeing no other qualified candidates, I had put myself in charge. Without realizing it, I claimed his chair and his position as head of the household, and began assigning jobs, giving orders. I was so effective in my new role that my niece Virginia dubbed me "the little colonel." All I needed was that red phone to the White House…

Since the plan had always been to take Mother directly to Minnesota with us, Patrick offered to cancel all services such as telephone, daily paper, and garbage collection. He also agreed to go through my father's personal items in his bedroom, a great relief to the rest of us. He came out of the bedroom the first night, brandishing a half-full bottle of whiskey he had found in my father's bottom dresser drawer (where he kept it in order to dole it out to Mother). Patrick held the bottle so Mother couldn't see it. He pantomimed pouring it out, and we all nodded our heads in approval.

Next we needed to plan a luncheon for after the funeral. Since my parents had no church affiliation in recent history, I knew it would have to be at the house. I brought it up at supper the night before the funeral.

Mother, always the recluse said, "No luncheon."

I said, "Mother we *have* to have a luncheon. Most of the people coming to the funeral will be neighbors and those that don't come to the funeral can at least come pay their respects to the family." Then I added with my newfound authority, "We *are* having a luncheon."

She reluctantly conceded.

****

The funeral was dismally small. Those in attendance included Mother, my sister, my niece, my husband and less than a half-dozen neighbors. It was a stark reminder of the solitary life my parents had led. After the hospice chaplain made a gallant effort to dignify the occasion, I gave a eulogy, which had actually been in my head for several weeks. I said, in part:

When Patrick and I visited Las Vegas a year ago, my father asked me to find the passage in the Bible about "my Father's house." The only Bible my parents had was a *Reader's Digest* condensed version with no chapters or verses. Not being a theologian, but knowing the words he spoke of were Jesus' words, I began searching the Gospels. I searched through Matthew, Mark and Luke, stopping at the end of John 13. It was getting late and we needed to get back to our hotel room. The next morning, by chance, the devotional that Patrick and I read was John 14:2, "In my Father's house are many mansions; if it were not so, I would have told you. I am going there to prepare a place for you...I will come back and take you to be with me that you also may be where I am."

I then spoke of my father's love of aviation, how his life had spanned the first flights of crude biplanes all the way to the space age.

"My father watched with great interest as aviation 'grew up,' all the way to men and women in outer space. Like those astronauts who wear a 'space suit' so they can survive in an unfamiliar environment, we wear 'earth suits' while we are in this world. We are seeing my father in his 'earth suit' for the last time today, but he has actually gotten a new 'suit,' a new body because he is with our God in Heaven."

We followed the Honor Guard out to the gravesite, where someone played taps and others folded the flag that was draping the casket and gave it to my mother. I thought back to the day my dad and I watched the Kennedy funeral without Mother and how sad he was that she wasn't there. I hoped he'd known I'd make sure she was here this time.

And that was it. A few words, a few tears, and the celebration of the life of my father came to an end. Later, my mother said she was glad we had the luncheon after all. Several people who were unable to make the funeral came to the house, and they all had good things to say about my father. Mother was astonished that he was so well known within the neighborhood. She barely knew the ones who came to pay their last respects.

After everyone had left the house, I remembered that I had brought home several small pamphlets I picked up at the mortuary. They were brief and to the point, and they talked about things like getting through the first weeks after the funeral, and understanding the grief process. I brought them to mother.

"Would you like to read these, Mother?" I said. "They might be helpful."

"Oh, that's lovely, thank you, Margaret," she cooed.

Patrick was sitting across the living room reading the *Las Vegas Sentinel.* Later, he told me that Mother had read for a couple of minutes, and then she had thrown down the pamphlets. "That's the biggest bunch of crap I've ever heard," she exclaimed.

****

After supper that night, Patrick and I went to the computer room in the basement of the public library to run off his e-ticket for the return flight home. My father had once accompanied me there for the same purpose, and I had demonstrated my computer skills to his amazement. It was a touching few moments, me with this man who flew airplanes before there was even reliable radar, showing him my very limited but still respectable knowledge of the tools of the "information age." As I thought back to that day with him, I was suddenly aware of a low moaning sound. It seemed at first to be some sort of mechanical equipment in the library, but soon I was eerily aware that this sound seemed not to be of this world. It rumbled up and around me, from within me but still somehow separate, literally shaking my rib cage and choking off my breath.

"I've got to get out of here!" I said suddenly to Patrick.

"What's the matter?" he asked, startled.

"I don't know. This room is just creeping me out!"

I pushed back my chair and stumbled to the door, up the stairs and out to the parking lot. The feeling had subsided, but my memory of it had not. *What was that?* I whispered to myself. I fumbled for the keys to my father's car and sat down in the passenger seat. That's when the tears came.

It seemed like eons until Patrick came back to the car. I was certain the feeling had been my father's spirit, a disquieting enough thought. I am not one to believe in ghosts, but what I felt simply could not be denied. I was grateful that Patrick listened to me talk about it without saying, *Oh, it was nothing.*

That wasn't the only time we "heard from" my father. That night, my sister Barbara, was sleeping on an air mattress in the open-air courtyard of my parents' home. She heard a stamping noise coming from the window of my father's dark and silent bedroom. She remembered the caretaker Colleen telling us that Daddy would stamp his walker up and down in frustration when he got so weak he couldn't walk alone. The next morning, we found Barbara sleeping inside on the floor in the living room.

The days went by like lightning, and soon everyone had left for home except Mother and me. Patrick got us tickets to Minneapolis for a week after Daddy's death. I tried to enlist Mother's help in packing, but she was in a fog. I finally made a great many decisions on my own, dreading the thought that I would have to come back to that house and those memories again in the near future. Mother slept much of that week.

****

As the plane began its descent to the Minneapolis/St. Paul airport, I could feel myself relaxing a bit. It had been a long day, a long week, and a long, long time since I began preparing myself for these days.

I glanced over at my mother. She was sleeping peacefully, just as she always had whenever someone provided her with motion and background noise. I felt no particular tenderness for her, this recent widow. When I asked, she said she thought the funeral went so well she did not wish to visit my father's grave site again before we left Las Vegas. I knew in my heart it would be the only chance she would ever have to see the grave again, and I seriously doubted that I would visit Las Vegas ever again. (My mother had always wanted to be cremated, but my father had talked her into buying these plots together in Las Vegas. I could not have known then that she would have the last word. Within a year after my father's funeral, my mother prevailed upon me to have his body exhumed and cremated, and to have his ashes sent to Minnesota.)

Patrick met us at the airport, and we took Mother directly to a care facility where she would stay until her assisted living room was available.

"I can't stay here," she exclaimed when she realized she would have a semi-private room. "Just let me come live with you and Patrick!"

It took all of my intestinal fortitude—and one serious look from Patrick—to say no to her. She stayed at the care facility for about two weeks, complaining daily, until I moved her to her new home.

****

One of the lowest points during the days after my father died was a brief period when I thought even my husband had turned against me. I know now that it was my own low mood that made me feel this way. But when it happened, I could not see the truth for what it was. I called my sister and tried to talk to her about it. She did her best to convince me that I was doing everything I could do for our mother, and that Patrick was probably just distancing himself from the *situation* and not from me, as it seemed.

Satan was messing with me big time, making me doubt myself, and even Patrick. My sister sent me a card in which she had copied the exact words from a greeting card that I had sent her once when she was particularly down:

> *You've overcome too many things, and every time, you've grown through sheer determination and the wisdom that you've shown. So as you face this journey, from the moment you begin, know that God will guide you, and you'll have the strength to win. I believe in you.*

In time, I knew that Patrick had not abandoned me. He was just "working his own program" just as he always had.

****

Everything came to a head in late April. I was alone in the counseling office, attempting to handle the onslaught of students, double what should have been scheduled. Minnesota was experiencing a rare, early spring hot spell, with temperatures rising into the high eighties all week. To top things off, the air conditioning in our part of the building had been permanently disconnected, since the entire section was to be demolished, hopefully not with two condemned counselors still inside.

I was seeing students as fast as was humanly possible, trying not to make them feel rushed. My head had been pounding all day. The chest pains had started about noon. I tried to take deep breaths and appear calm. Dismissing my last student for the day, I called the hospital where Patrick was just leaving surgery.

"I'm having severe chest pains," I said into the phone when he picked up.

"Call 911," he said, always the pragmatist.

"I'm *not* going to call 911!" I shrieked. I feared that the administrators would think I couldn't handle my job, and they would fire me on the spot. I still had about eight weeks left in my contract, plus the bidding rights to other positions in the state.

Patrick finally agreed to meet at a hospital halfway between where he worked and the college. I should not have been driving. In fact, I don't even *remember* driving. I only slightly remember pulling into the parking lot next to the emergency entrance and hyperventilating all the way into the building.

As a counselor, I have always been the caretaker, the one in charge. I was used to helping others, not myself. It was my crisis and I didn't know how to act. I arrived before my husband, and it was painfully obvious I didn't have my act together

I approached the desk, starting out in a rather professional tone. "Hello there! I'm having chest pains and can't breathe."

Just then, the entire room seemed to come to life, sort of like a Broadway musical where one minute the lead singer is doing a slow ballad and then huge sets come down out of the ceiling and stagehands come in carrying big theater props and fifty dancers come leaping in from all sides. A pudgy tenor arrived, booming loudly, "She's having CHEST pains!" He was immediately followed by a perfectly choreographed group of little nurses echoing an octave above, "She's having CHEST pains!' I was being pushed into a wheelchair and asked a lot of extremely personal questions like: What is your name? and How long have you been having chest pains? My first thought was: *This sort of thing must not happen around here very often because everyone is acting like it's a big deal.*

Suddenly, I was on a gurney in a cubicle with curtains all around. Several long-faced hospital staff in a stunning array of fashion scrubs came in. We went from Gilbert and Sullivan to Alfred Hitchcock in thirty seconds. They had me put on the little designer hospital gown with the strings to the front, leaving me more vulnerable than I cared to feel at that particular moment. One woman put a blood pressure cuff on me and another started gluing electrodes to my chest.

My husband arrived. "You look awful," he said.

I didn't ask if that was his considered medical opinion. "I *feel* awful," I answered.

We waited for what seemed like forever, listening to the people on the other side of the little curtains. We could hear *everything*. Next to me were a man and his elderly mother, who apparently had a small stroke. The son was sobbing and a nurse was trying to calm *him* down. The mother was quiet and cooperative, clearly a champion caretaker herself. I expected any minute that the curtain would open between us and she'd offer me a homemade chocolate chip cookie and a glass of milk.

Across the way, the nurses were inserting a urinary catheter into another female patient. We heard the blow-by-blow description of how *that* was progressing, including comments from the patient when the catheter finally started to *work*. Nearby, they were questioning a *third* woman. She had suspicious bruises and said she fell, but then changed her story and insisted a doorknob jumped up and bit her. Everyone including me knew perfectly well she didn't fall, that her boyfriend beat her up, but nobody could get her to say so. I contemplated going over to help in the questioning, but by now I hurt so bad all over that I didn't think I could move. I was extremely light-headed from not breathing well.

Next, a six-foot-tall nurse in teddy-bear print scrubs came to put in an IV. She grabbed my right wrist and held it aloft while she began using what I *swear* was a Swiss army knife to insert the IV, into a vein right over my sore thumb joint that needed reconstructive surgery. Had someone/anyone told her about my thumb? Was she just going to take care of it right here, right now, without benefit of anesthetic?

"What are you *doing*?" I shouted at her. My husband had by now adopted his medical-staff-on-call persona, and his face showed no alarm. "That joint is very painful," I managed. "I'm supposed to be having surgery on it soon…"

"It's the *best* vein for inserting an IV," she said emphatically, dismissing my increased pain. She continued stabbing away at my angry little vein. I gritted my teeth, and looked at my husband, who had an angelic look on his face like staff in the psych ward who are trying to maintain normalcy in the height of someone's psychotic breakdown.

After what seemed like hours, with continuing protest from me, the IV was in. It still hurt, but at least I could relax a bit. Now hooked up with all the wires and tubes, I had to use the toilet in the worst way. My husband got me a rolling commode and helped me onto it. Because I was so nervous, I used that commode about fifteen times, expecting any second to accidentally disconnect myself from all the hospital apparatus–if not from reality itself.

Finally, an actual physician came in and examined me and asked me the same questions all over again. He was the only person in the entire place not dressed in Winnie the Pooh hospital wear, having chosen a conservative ensemble of pure white, with a silver-toned stethoscope draped fashionably around his neck. He was a slim man, with a kind face that belied the type of work he did in this place. He had the ability to make me feel like I was his only patient, that I had always been his only patient, and that he was there to help me. Plus he offered drugs.

He ordered the Swiss army knife nurse to put morphine into the throbbing IV. The warmth of the drug coursed through my body up to the blood-brain barrier that I learned about in my pharmacology class in grad school, except that the morphine abruptly stopped at said blood-brain barrier. No admittance. I could feel it knocking but it couldn't get in. After a few minutes, the doctor asked me if my pain was gone.

"No," I said.

"What do you mean, 'no'?" he asked, the Mister Rogers look on his face now fading.

"It helped some, but the pain isn't *gone.*"

The doctor looked dumfounded. I explained to him that I have *chronic* pain, and that means that something hurts *all the time.* I conceded that I felt a lot better, but *my pain wasn't gone.*

This puzzled the doctor, who appeared to be mentally cycling through his recently read medical articles for some study that would dispute my empirical report. Reviewing my test results, he eventually informed me that I would probably live. He said I had not had a heart attack, but rather a severe anxiety attack. Dr. Mr. Rogers wrote something in my little chart when I explained about my dad dying, and my mother needing care, and my job going down the drain. He dispatched my husband to make a drug run to the hospital pharmacy for an anxiety medication. He told me to lie still for a while, and then he'd release me to go home. He insisted that I stay home from work the following day. I held my breath, hoping he would suggest I never go back to my job at all, which, unfortunately, he never said.

I had no sick leave left, but had no choice but to call in sick the next day. Later I learned my supervisor suggested that I had been faking it. More fuel for my human rights complaint?

****

After the emergency room incident and my assurance that life would go on, I returned to my life and my job. If there was ever a time in my life where I felt I was in that "valley of the shadow of death," it was during the last two miserable months I spent at that college. I knew God was with me, but He, like the morphine drip in that hospital, appeared to be just outside my consciousness. Though I was praying hard all day long, I could not imagine what part of God's plan for my life was unfolding.

Chapter 33
Potential Catastrophes

As children, Adult Children of Alcoholics became anxious and hypervigilant. They remain so in their adult lives, constantly scanning the environment for potential catastrophes.
Substance Abuse and Mental Health Services
U.S. Department of Health and
Human Services

On the advice of a good friend, I purchased a book called *Helping Parents Who Were No Help To You*. What a crock. The author told me to suck it up, set aside my differences with Mother and display compassion and unconditional positive regard for my aging parent. That book tried to lay a serious guilt trip on me for feeling the way I did and for sometimes acting the way I did. No matter how pitiful Mother appeared, I knew I needed to detach and set boundaries or I would never survive.

Nevertheless, I did consider the ideas in that book and others, thinking—hoping—there might be something of some use, something that would pull my mother out of her bombed-out shell of an existence.

I knew my mother was a high-maintenance woman. It was agonizing now to be the person she looked to for everything. How was it fair that she was never really there for my sister and me, not once in my memory, and now she thought she would get to have me there for her *always*? Without fail, on call, twenty-four/seven. And she was completely clueless about what it was taking out of me (or was she?). Was the notion that I might harbor some unkind flashback thoughts about my own needs not being met at age three or fifteen or forty completely foreign to her? And the "peace" I made with both my parents was really after I had figured out how to survive on my own anyway. I envied my older sister, who had her reasons to exclude our parents from her life, shutting and tightly locking the door. But here I was, always "the good daughter," trying to meet Mother's impossible needs. I recalled the ironic wisdom of a co-worker years before: "No good deed goes unpunished."

****

The first few months Mother lived in the care center in a suburb of St. Paul, we had some pretty rocky times. Her assisted living unit wasn't available for about a month, and although I had explained that this first room was temporary, she was not happy. She also needed to be "evaluated" to see if she was even appropriate for assisted living. At the first facility, the rooms didn't have doors for privacy, and she had to share a bathroom with another woman, something my mother had not done since childhood and wanted no part of. She begged me to let her come and live with us. I remember being so worn out and anxious that I was afraid I would relent and change the plan. But I knew she and I would never survive under the same roof. And it would have been totally unfair to Patrick who would never have allowed it, for himself, or me. So I was resolute with Mother and told her it would be much better when she moved into her own room.

She loved to go out to dinner. The first time we bundled her up and took her to a nice restaurant, she promptly ordered a glass of wine. I froze.

After I regained my composure a bit—and saw the look on Patrick's face—I said, "Mother, you may have a glass of wine tonight, but after that, there will be no more alcohol."

And there wasn't. It must have been divine intervention, because she never asked again. Miracles do happen.

****

One frigid night in late February, I went out after work to look for furniture for her. Her furniture from Las Vegas would not fit the room, so I was searching for some smaller pieces. I was exhausted, as usual, and the bone-chilling cold drove through my aching joints like shards of ice. I could not find what I was looking for and finally decided to order a bedroom set that would be delivered in several weeks. Mother would have to make do until then with odd pieces the care center had left over from other residents. When I got home, the care facility had called, saying that Mother had suffered a small stroke and had been transported to a critical care hospital in downtown St. Paul. It had begun to snow quite hard, and I knew I was too tired to drive. Patrick talked me into calling the hospital before racing down there. The nurse I spoke with said the stroke was very mild, and that Mother was sleeping peacefully.

Of course she was. I wished I could sleep as well as she did.

The next day I worked all day, checking in with the hospital every couple of hours. I visited her that night, and she went home the next day. Within a matter of days, Mother had regained most of her motor control, with just a tiny bit of residual numbness in her left hand. But the worst was yet to come.

Not surprisingly, her bowels locked up again. Since she now had 'round the clock nursing care, including medication dispensing, she no longer had the option of downing laxatives by the case. Though having her meds controlled was a positive step, it took a while for her body to understand that. She landed in the hospital again, twice in the next few weeks, both times with an impacted bowel.

The doctors tried everything short of dynamite, and in the end, it was a very gracious and dedicated nurse who took care of the problem manually. This was a bad thing because it hurt a whole lot, but it was a good thing because now I could threaten Mother that she'd have to have it done again if she didn't eat properly, get a little exercise and *take her prescribed laxatives*, which she had been refusing because they were different colors than the ones she used to abuse.

Her old prejudices resurfaced. Many of the nurse's aides at the care center where she lived were black immigrants from Africa. At first, she called them "the boy" and "the girl" and asked them to take out her trash and clean up her spilled food. I explained, patiently at first, that they had names (though many were hard to pronounce) and that their jobs entailed minimal nursing duties, not housekeeping or laundry. She had other people to do that.

She had people to do everything, since she refused to do anything for herself. A charge could be added for just about anything she desired, and those first months we chalked up a whole list of extras on her bill. Besides "complex medication administration," we added escort services to get her to and from meals and activities (both of which she refused on a regular basis), laundry services, bathing "assistance" (which meant an aide gave her a bath twice a week whether she wanted it or not), and my all-time favorite, the "unscheduled nurse visit." Sometimes the nurses were summoned for something important, but usually for what the care center called "redirecting," to try to get Mother to do something or to *stop* doing something.

She refused to do things all the time. The aides wouldn't force meds on her; they simply documented that she refused and reported it to the nurses, creating the need for another "unscheduled nurse visit" and more "redirection" (and more charges). She had escort service to the dining room (another charge), but she would pick at the food and eventually cover the plate with a napkin to hide what she had not eaten (she apparently thought she was fooling the kitchen staff). She lost about ten pounds the first month after my father died. "They put all that food on my plate, and I can't stand to look at it, much less eat it!" she would complain.

She refused to allow the lab techs to draw her blood. "I'm calling my daughter, and we'll see what *my* doctor has to say about that!" she said to them. I would remind her that "her" doctor was the doctor who came to the care center, and that the blood draws were to monitor the blood thinners she was on so she wouldn't have another stroke. She refused her bath for several weeks straight. During a huge fight on the phone, I told her she was beginning to smell, and she slammed the phone down in my ear.

People would say, "Give her a break. She's ninety years old!" But they didn't understand that she had *always* been this way, as long as I could remember. Her bad habits were just multiplying exponentially.

All of this, of course, was simply her attention-getting behavior, and I wasn't about to play into it. But her nurse practitioner got sucked in and did us all a wonderful favor by *prescribing* a sandwich for her at night. The care center would not do this for her automatically; there would be another charge for making the sandwich and a charge for delivering it. I decided we didn't need any more charges, and I tried to come up with another solution. Of course, Mother couldn't be trusted to make the sandwich herself. There was bread there in the common shared kitchen, and peanut butter and jelly. Maybe the aides could make her a PB and J every night.

"I don't like peanut butter," she announced.

Trying to appease her once again, I started buying sandwich meat (roast beef or corned beef, the only two kinds she would eat) and mayonnaise. I put the meat in little bags and froze small amounts with a date on them so they wouldn't spoil. And the aides were instructed to go into her room and ask her if she would eat a sandwich. If she said yes, they brought her one; if she said no, they sometimes brought her one anyway.

"How are the sandwiches, Mother?" I asked after the first week, after reminding her that she needed to eat to keep up her strength.

"Great!" she answered brightly.

Maybe we were on to something.

One day, I came to pick her up and take her out for some reason, and she couldn't find her gloves. Remembering our childhood rule and first asking her permission to open things, I began looking in her dresser. I opened one drawer, and there under her pajamas, in living color, were five untouched sandwiches on five paper plates.

****

I was mortified at how rude she was, and amazed at how gracious the aides were with her. More than once, I scolded her for her comments to them. It took awhile, but soon she had her favorites among the aides, and she mellowed some with those she did not care about as much. Her prejudices were diminishing but they certainly hadn't expired completely.

I tried very hard to bring some degree of normalcy to her life, a sort of ironic penance for thinking I had my own act together. She had been a large part of why it took me so long to figure life out, but here I was imparting my own grace and serenity to the one who robbed me of it to start with. I theorized that if I could expose Mother to happy, healthy individuals and uplifting, meaningful activities, she would see how enjoyable life could be—and her personality would do an about-face.

Dream on.

Patrick and I took her to church. The first time we went, it was the Sunday school year-end program, with all the children's choirs singing. I had explained this to her beforehand. We picked her up in plenty of time, making sure to take along all the items she believed she needed for an extended stay of, say, two hours away from her room. She had several tissues folded into fourths and stuffed individually into her pockets. She had her medicated lip ointment, a bottle of Coke and a Styrofoam cup so she could pour just a little out at a time. She had her wrap around sunglasses, all tucked into the cloth bag on her shiny new walker. We got her into the church and into a pew. The concert began with a flourish.

She took out her tissues and formed them into little balls, which she stuffed into her ears. "It's too loud," she shouted over the music, pouring herself a kiddie kocktail from her bottle of Coke (spilling droplets on the pew cushion).

After two choirs of various ages of cherubic children sang their introductory numbers, I was gritting my teeth and wondering if bringing her was such a good idea. Patrick appeared to have checked out mentally, and was probably happily reliving his latest bass fishing excursion far, far away.

A third choir got up to perform. "They're not going to have another group of children sing, are they?" she exclaimed, loudly enough for all those children's parents and grandparents (indeed, the entire *congregation*) to hear.

A week or so later, I asked her if she wanted to go to a grief group led by a delightful woman named Edith, the wife of a retired minister. To my surprise and disappointment, she said okay. She could have won the Oscar for her performance in those meetings. Everyone thought she was this sweet, kind little old lady. Edith offered to come visit her at the care center, and when she said yes, Edith encouraged her to have our outreach pastor, Roy, visit her too. I knew we were headed for trouble before the first visit.

"Margaret," she said into our voice mail one day while I was at work (she had long, meaningful conversations with the voicemail, as if someone were really listening on the other end). "This *woman* came to see me today from your church. I don't recall inviting her. *What does she want?"*

I would go to see her, knowing where the conversation would take us. She went on and on about Edith and Pastor Roy visiting her, saying she didn't know what they were supposed to talk about and why were they coming, and could I please make them stop. At first I said no. I had spoken to both of them at church, and they both said how *interesting* my mother was, and how much they enjoyed visiting with her.

"That woman——what's her name?"

"Edith," I repeated for the hundredth time.

"Edith," she repeated. "She seems to think we have so much in common because her husband traveled as an Army chaplain and my husband traveled with the Air Force, but we really have *nothing* in common. I don't want her to come any more. And that minister, what's his name?"

"Roy."

"Yes, Roy. Well, does he think I'm going to hell or something?"

"I don't know, Mother. *Are* you going to hell?"

She glared at me.

In the end, Mother told Edith she couldn't see her because she was too busy (hiding sandwiches, I suppose). I finally called Edith. She already knew what was up before she talked to me. She assured me that she didn't take it personally. We talked briefly about my mother's situation. I expressed my concern that Mother didn't seem to want to interact with anybody at the care center, especially when I was with her.

"Maybe she's jealous," Edith pointed out. Good point. I recalled how Mother acted when I tried to be pleasant with other residents there, learning their names, asking them how long they had lived there and where they came from. If we were on our way somewhere, Mother would just walk off, saying, "Let's go!" Or she would say *directly to the person*, "I've already heard all about it, and I don't want to hear it again!" She took advantage of the fact that most of the residents were hard of hearing, though her hearing was super sensitive (thus the need for stuffing tissue in her ears). She knew she could speak loudly enough for me to hear, but not her neighbors.

One day, I couldn't stand it anymore. A woman who was nearing a hundred years old wanted to show us something she had received as a gift, and Mother refused to go into the woman's room with me. I graciously accepted, had a brief conversation with the woman, and returned to escort Mother to my car. I was seething.

"What does it *profit* you to deny that woman a few minutes of your time to see her little treasures?" I hissed at her. "I never knew anybody like you, in all my life!"

She gave me her best naughty-turned-nice look. "I *must* try to be more kind," she answered dramatically.

I learned *very* quickly that when Mother said I *must* do something, what she really meant was, "I have absolutely *no* intention of doing that, *ever!*"

She did continue to allow Pastor Roy to come see her for a while, although he told me he knew he was "skating on thin ice." She always took communion and allowed him to pray for her, which surprised me since I wasn't sure she even *knew* about the sacraments, much less understood them or wanted to partake of them. Eventually, though, she began to make excuses when Pastor Roy would call, and soon he too discontinued his visits.

Chapter 34
Fuel For The Journey

We must embrace pain and burn it as fuel for our journey.
Kenji Miyazawa

Adult Children of Alcoholics are hypersensitive to the needs of others…They have a compulsive need to be perfect.
Substance Abuse and Mental Health Services
U.S. Department of Health and
Human Services

While Mother was busy closing her social circle in around herself, my anxiety and depression were escalating rapidly. One of my pressing tasks was to sell the house in Las Vegas without going there. Mentally walking through that house constantly, I would try over and over to remember what we might want out of it and what could simply be sold or given to charity. I was scared I would do the wrong thing and then have my mother *and* my sister angry with me. Once again my parents' former neighbors came to the rescue. They found a good realtor who lived down the block. This woman was heaven-sent. She found people to go through everything in the house, using a list I mailed to her. They boxed up and shipped everything we wanted to keep and arranged to have the rest hauled off to a thrift shop. A buyer with squeaky-clean credit soon surfaced and we transferred ownership very quickly. I sent both the realtor and the neighbors a dozen roses.

Meanwhile, my situation at work grew more intolerable by the day. Still scared I would somehow lose my job before the formal layoff, I tried to tough it out until the end. My journal entries got scarier and scarier as the weeks wore on. I wrote:

What do we have left when our lives cease to be productive? All that is left many times is our God, our family and our thoughts.

Was I describing Mother or myself? And another entry:

We took Mother out to dinner last night. Even the most casual observer could see that she was not enjoying herself at all. Somewhere along the journey, she has lost the capacity to find joy, experience humor, and look on the bright side. How much did my father have to do with this??? I want her life to count for something. Is the something me?

That last statement haunted me. My prayers to God all began with, "What is the purpose of all of this?" Like Jeremiah, some days I could have cursed the day I had been born. *Do you know what happens when you lose a baby?* My mother's ugly words rattled around in my brain. *Well, you begin to bleed...* I was bleeding now, bleeding from the heart. Mortally wounded from care-taking what seemed like half the people in the universe, sickened and devalued in my chosen pursuits.

What's the use? I would say to myself. *I'm going to die anyway. My father proved that.* I had never been this low before. I almost marveled at how bizarre my thoughts were, like I was in some study of psychopathic behavior, and it was important I record every little nuance of thought. Always the counselor—even with myself. Like my sister before me, who was convinced she had every symptom she learned about when in nursing school, I was sure I was losing my mind. Research has shown that the earlier schizophrenia appears, the harder it is for a person to respond to treatment because they don't have a fully developed personality to which to return. Did that mean I had a good chance of recovering if I was indeed going crazy? Or was I only fooling myself into believing I wasn't already crazy?

Once I had to take some supplies to Mother on my way home from the college, and try as I might, I couldn't stop crying. I arrived at her room, blubbering away, unable even to carry on a simple conversation. It must have shook her up pretty badly too, because she actually wrote me a nice note the next day.

"I wish I could kiss it where it hurts," she said. "Since I can't do that, it's best to say, 'To thine own self be true.'" She was referring to the passage from Shakespeare's *Hamlet*, which continues: "And it must follow, as the night the day, thou canst not then be false to any man." Mother had quoted that to me my whole life, and I was touched that she could remember it and send it to me again. I was genuinely grateful that she had at least some words of encouragement in her. She also added, "You are a perfectionist (like your dad was)."

And I knew it was true. It was such a difficult time for me; the wheels of change were already spinning out of control and I was powerless to stop them—or even roll *with* them, if I wanted to.

Somehow, suddenly, our house seemed so dark and foreboding, though nothing physical had changed. How did it get that way? The nights were the worst, but they came anyway. I would descend into my nocturnal version of hell, *into* the pain, seldom if ever *through* it or *around* it, under it or over it. It became my constant companion, from bedtime until the alarm went off in the morning. It shaped my dreams, drove me to switch positions relentlessly, roused me to get up and wander the house aimlessly, never successfully avoiding the fridge or the pantry. (*Chocolate, after all, is a great stress reliever and stimulates the production of endorphins*, I told myself. Besides, I was *losing* weight, not gaining…).

My "mean sleep"——that nocturnal adventure which neither refreshed nor energized, was back with a vengeance. I tried all my old remedies, got new drugs from my doctor, none of which seemed right. I was either too groggy in the morning or the drug wore off in the middle of the night. I collected pajamas—dozens of pairs of soft, comfortable ones, in the hope that they would add their magical powers to the other remedies I had accumulated over the years. I had one pair I called my "lucky pajamas." I believed I could get a better night's sleep when I wore them.

I also believed I was losing touch with reality.

And then there were the dreams.

The first and most profound one happened a couple of weeks after my father's funeral. I dreamed I was in my kitchen cooking dinner when I heard laughter upstairs. I followed the sound, and found it was coming from behind the closed door of our bedroom where my father had slept on their first visit to our new home. In the dream, I opened the door, and there on the bed, as clearly as if it were actually happening, sat my father, very much alive, and well and vibrant. He had an arm around each of my two oldest grandchildren, and they were reading a book. He was smiling broadly, delighting in those children like he always had when he had been alive. He looked up and spoke to me. "Close the door, Margaret, or I'll have to go."

Other dreams followed, mostly of him alive, some of us talking quietly as though old disagreements didn't matter any more. In all of the dreams, he had a peace about him that I had not felt when he was alive. I prayed desperately that this was some sort of sign from God that my father was all right, that he approved of the way Mother was being cared for. A pervasive sense of role reversal—of me needing to be the good parent who did everything right—was being played out over and over in my thoughts, both day and night.

In the years we had lived in the house, I had taken up gardening with a passion. In the springtime, our backyard was a veritable explosion of flowers. Each year, I put in more and more perennials and I spent every waking hour of every summer day that I could, tending those blossoms. I worked out my frustrations by digging in the dirt. It gave me a sense of accomplishment to see what I planted with my own hands, coming up in a riot of colors. We had two massive crab apple trees, one white and one pink, that for two glorious weeks around Mother's Day, displayed the most perfect, delicate blossoms I have ever had the privilege to admire.

In the spring of the year my father died, even the apple blossoms and the spring flowers appeared gray against the void of my emotions.

****

The battle with the New Guard at the college raged on until the bitter end. If an opening at another state two-year college became available, even a temporary one, I would have the right to claim it since I was the most senior counselor on the layoff list. But most colleges in the state system were not replacing counselors if they retired or left, and it looked unlikely that a position would open up. Then, literally at the eleventh hour, a permanent opening at another college became available. The school had a great reputation and an administration that clearly supported the counseling role. Plus it was much closer to where we lived. I was ecstatic to claim the position.

I had been experiencing more joint problems. My right thumb had come out of joint, and the pain was excruciating. Surgery was imminent. This was not something I felt I could do immediately before starting a new position. I wanted at least two weeks between jobs to recuperate. The union tried to negotiate the days I had left so that I could work them off as fast as possible. The administration expected me to spread them out and work on certain important dates. The irony was amazing: they wanted me gone but not until they had used me for their purposes right to the bitter end.

The grievances and complaints ground on, bogged down in red tape and miscommunication. My office was moved once again, this time to a tiny room with no phone and no computer. I was using my personal cell phone to communicate with people down the hall from me. I felt gone. I wished I *were* gone.

Somewhere during these last few days, I realized it was completely futile to try to help students navigate their way through the intricacies of the less-than-perfect campus atmosphere. I started just giving them the basics and not going the extra mile. It felt awful. It was not the way I worked.

****

With a week between those "important" dates I had to work, Patrick and I went to fish in a bass tournament at Old Hickory Lake in Hendersonville, Tennessee. Though I was not very confident as an competitive angler, I was looking forward to getting away and spending some time with my husband. That is, until he told me I would have to back the boat into the water.

He had gotten a letter from the tournament directors, explaining the need for one of each pair of contestants (me) to back the boat down the ramp and then pull the trailer out of the water and park it, while the other contestant (Patrick) drove the boat away from the landing. The second boater was to pick the first one up at the dock. With a hundred and fifty boats in the tournament, each team had to get their boat into and out of the water as fast as possible.

Now, under normal conditions, with my brain intact, I would not have been happy about this, but I would have at least tried to rally and do what needed to be done. But this request, which seemed so innocuous to my husband, just about completely sent me over the edge. I probably should not have been operating a motor vehicle *at all*, much less trying to jockey a thirty thousand dollar bass boat down the ramp and into the lake. I tried practicing with my own vehicle while Patrick was at work, succeeding in getting pretty close to the boat trailer, but taking out one of my tail lights in the process.

I told him I couldn't do it.

We discussed it from St. Paul all the way to Paduca, Kentucky, where we spent the night on the way to the tournament. We had some ridiculous argument in Paduca at a Red Lobster restaurant, and I started crying. I cried myself to sleep, and the next day in the truck, I cried for four hours straight, all the way to Hendersonville. Patrick tried everything to get me to stop crying, everything except letting me off the hook about backing the boat down the ramp and into the lake.

As we pulled into town, he asked me quietly, in his best Health Professional voice, "Do you want to go to the hotel, or the hospital?"

"Neither," I said tearfully. "I want to go to Walmart. I forgot my new skinny jeans, and I want to get another pair." *I'm such a mess I can't even pack right!* I thought.

"Will that make you feel better?"

"No, but at least I will look good."

But I didn't look good. I looked horrible. When I took my sunglasses off, anyone could see I was in distress. Even the clerk at Walmart eyed me suspiciously, and then she looked at Patrick, like maybe she should check the age-progression pictures they put up in the store entry of people who have been kidnapped. Was my tear-swollen face on a milk carton forty years earlier? Even with new skinny jeans, I could not be swayed to back the boat.

"I can't do it!" I lamented over and over. "Not now, not while I'm this far down emotionally!"

"I believe you *can* do it," he said emphatically. "I have faith in you and I believe you are capable of this."

By the time we arrived at the tournament headquarters the afternoon before the event, I had convinced him at least to talk to the directors about having someone help me, if not do it for me. We had no need to worry because I wasn't the only one who had a problem with the rule. The directors had so many complaints that they designated several experienced boaters to help back boats in on the day of the tournament. My meltdown had been for nothing.

****

Even though we didn't catch any keepers, we actually had fun during the tournament. It was the beginning of June and the weather had been weird for days. That must have been why the fish weren't biting, we told ourselves. When the day ended, we made our way back to the check-in point. Dozens of boats were milling around the water away from the docks, waiting their turn to pull their boats out, swapping stories and trying to find out who had the biggest catch. Patrick drove at top speed all the way back. I wondered if we had broken the sound barrier. I had been in the boat with him zillions of times, but I could never get used to him driving at full throttle. I was hanging on for dear life, trying to ride the waves like I used to ride a horse. A huge cabin cruiser was coming right at us, its pilot probably curious about why all the boats were there. Patrick slowed to cross the cruiser's wake, but it was too late. The waves came up fast and high. We made it over the first one, both bouncing out of our seats and back down again. The second wave caught me off guard. I lost my balance and lurched forward, hitting the passenger side windshield with the left side of my forehead.

"Am I bleeding?" I asked Patrick, once he had slowed the boat to a crawl.

"Just a little," he said. I wasn't sure I believed him, since he seemed to be into minimizing my distress of late. When I wiped my forehead with my hand, no blood came off, although I could already feel it starting to swell.

By that night at the farewell dinner, I had one heck of a shiner. Jokes about the other guy abounded. I was not amused.

****

When I returned to work for my last two days, I heard more jokes about the eye. I tried to be good-natured about the ribbing, even when it came from those who were getting rid of me. Using my cell phone to make the last few calls to assist the students, I sat in my soon-to-be ex-office with no computer. Mother was back in the hospital with more bowel trouble, and the doctor called me in the middle of one of my appointments. I managed to excuse myself and take the call in the hallway, since I didn't think the student wanted to hear my conversation. At the end of the day, I slipped out the back door without a word to anyone; the ones I cared about had already said their good-byes. Driving home, I could already feel myself relax. In our mailbox was the response to the final appeal of my complaint. The letter read, in part:

"After review of the investigation report...no violation of board policy is substantiated...We encourage you to continue to work with your colleagues and supervisors to resolve workplace concerns in an appropriate manner."

****

Arriving at my new office at my new job at the good college, I tried to make light of the still prominent shiner and the huge bandage on my right hand. I hung up my little Mary Engelbreit poster of the girl with her hands on her hips, saying "Snap Out of It!" This is not my counseling philosophy; it is a joke that I play on myself every morning when I come to work. It helps me take myself less seriously. I do not believe or expect those I counsel to "snap out of it" with a depression as severe as the one I went through the year my father died. I take seriously every concern that is brought to me by someone who displays the signs of depression.

But for me, relief from my downward spiral came in a most unexpected way.

The week after I started my new job, I discovered that my depression was lifting. I stopped writing in my journal altogether. The troubled dreams and sleepless nights vanished, as did my feeling that I was going insane. My mother was still driving me crazy, but I reminded myself that perhaps only God knew how she got the way she was. He knew my mother was His child, and He loved her immeasurably. I was beginning to learn how to "detach with love," and to set boundaries with my mother. I was even beginning to feel some compassion for her. I had allowed my mother's alcoholism to block my own healing for most of my life. It was time I got back to working my own program. My depression had indeed been situational, brought on by my father's death, how I was treated at work, and the subsequent loss of my job. It was not, as I had feared, true clinical depression, the kind that persists regardless of positive changes or events. With the passage of time and a new, positive work environment, I was in recovery once again.

Although I didn't realize it at the time, a small, quiet presence within me was making changes for the better. I know now that it was the Holy Spirit.

Chapter 35
Christmas Grace

Christmas Eve 2005.

It was going to be a quiet Christmas. Just Patrick and me. And Mother.

At first, I didn't notice when we picked her up. She seemed the same and even carried on the same small talk, repeating herself every three minutes and talking about inconsequential things. After I helped her on with her winter coat and pulled the hood up over her head, she peered out at me with the same chiseled features I had seen the day before: the same watery eyes and the same pointed nose and the same tight little frown. But over the course of the evening, it seemed that Mother grew brighter, happier, almost radiant.

Radiant? My mother?

Well, perhaps *radiant* was a bit of a stretch, but there seemed to be a certain glow about her that hadn't been there before. At first, I tossed it off as my own wonder at the miracle of Christmas, just my perception of the world on the night my Lord and Savior was born that made everything and everyone look special. But as we visited over dinner, Mother did not display one shred of cynicism or pessimism. She was articulate and enthusiastic and seemed genuinely *interested* in everything Patrick and I had to say. I knew my mother could be an actress, but this time, it seemed she was really sincere.

Patrick and I had moved across town, to a house more centrally located to work for both of us. Having not found a new church home, we had been sporadically attending our old church, now about twenty miles away but very near where Mother lived. Though there were many services being held near our home, Patrick and I both seemed to be leaning towards going to our old church. I asked Mother if she'd like to go with us. Much to my surprise, I got a resounding "yes." She even said we'd be close to her care center and we could take her home after the service.

I bundled her up again, like a child going out to play in the snow. We left early and we were the first people there. I kept waiting for Mother to throw a tantrum or at least express her displeasure that we had to wait so long until the service began. Patrick let us out under the front portico, where a church staff member was just unlocking the door. He went to park the car. I was already nervous about how Mother was going to behave.

"Mother, let's just get you through the door and over to the first bench…"

"Merry Christmas!" she exclaimed to the custodian.

"Merry Christmas!" he replied heartily.

"Merry Christmas," I said sort of as an afterthought. Then I turned my attention to her again. "They've moved the bench, so I see some chairs…"

"I'm all right, Honey! Let's just keep walking!"

She clung to my arm as I propelled her slowly down the long hall to the coat rack. To my amazement, she greeted each staff member as they scurried past to get ready for the service. We got our coats off and proceeded to the sanctuary. Patrick joined us just as we were sitting down.

The musicians were warming up. We made polite conversation among ourselves until others began to arrive. Soon the church was full. Full of noise, I thought. I expected Mother to express herself out loud about anything she saw wrong: babies crying, people blocking her view, music too loud, sermon too long…

Nothing. She just sat there, taking it all in, like she did this every day.

Who is this woman and what has she done with my mother? I thought to myself. This can't be happening!

But it did happen. Mother maintained rapt attention throughout the entire service, from the opening Christmas carol to the benediction. Though all the songs that night were old standards, she didn't sing along. I don't believe she knew the words, and she never prided herself as a singer. But she listened attentively and actually *smiled* at me when I looked over at her. As unbelievable as it seemed, my Mother was actually *enjoying* herself!

And then it hit me: how could I believe so strongly that the Holy Spirit is in us and around us constantly, and yet I had not been able to stretch that same belief to cover my own mother as well as all the rest of us? And on this, the Holiest of Holy Nights! Didn't God say that *nothing* is impossible with Him?

I recalled the words of an old friend who once said to me, "Your parents probably did the best they could with what they had to work with at the time." I had politely agreed with the friend, but I remember thinking, *How could I say that my parents, especially my mother, did the best they could? If that was the best, what on earth would have been the worst?* The old wounds of distrust and contempt for everything my parents ever did and ever stood for had hounded me for years.

But on this night of wonder, there in the sanctuary of The Great I Am, when we lit our little candles and sang *Silent Night* as the lights were dimmed, it wasn't just the miracle of Christ's birth that touched my heart. For one perfect moment, I saw my mother as Christ sees her: holy and blameless, forgiven and redeemed. God bids us, no, he *commands* us to seek the highest good in another, and He is there, just as He promised, to help us do just that.

Suddenly, I recalled the entry I had made in my journal when I was struggling with my grief and depression:

"I want her life to count for something. Is the something me?"

Now, as we sang the last verse of that old familiar song, I understood. With God's help, I *had* counted for something: I had given my mother a chance to be her best, even now, even at her advanced age. Surely she could feel it too, that night. I reached over and held her hand, and we both had tears in our eyes.

As the saying goes, it isn't over until it's over. *Mother could live to be a hundred*, I thought, *and she could outlive me!* I knew that she and I would probably never be the best of friends. She was still deeply troubled, and it seemed unlikely from a human perspective that she would become (to quote Alfred Maslow) "fully self-actualized" before she died. She might never get her Adlerian Parent, Child and Adult in perfect balance. But if for one brief moment in that church service, she could experience God's love, poured out, pressed down, running over—if she could truly know the transforming power of the love of God—then I believe her life *has* counted for something.

Her life produced life in me, and *my* life, in turn, had surely touched hers again.

Thanks be to God for His indescribable gift!

Epilogue
Saying Goodbye

For we are what God has made us, created in Christ Jesus for good works, which God prepared beforehand to be our way of life.

Ephesians 2:10

The funeral director was stereotypical, with a serious but gentle face, combed-over hair, three-piece black pinstriped suit, white starched shirt, and ultra-conservative tie. He leaned forward across the massive mahogany desk with his elbows propped up and his fingers forming a little steeple, like children making a "church" in Sunday school. His work was not so hard this day. There was little to plan since they (the parents) had taken care of it all years ago, to keep us (the children) from needing to make decisions "at a time like this." The funeral itself was even prepaid. I made a mental note to do all of this soon for ourselves, so our children would have a similar experience when the time came.

And the time was here. Time to say that final good-bye, time to choose the casket spray with the ribbons that proclaimed her duties in this life: wife, mother, grandmother, great-grandmother... Add a cymbidium orchid (her favorite flower) for each of those great grandchildren. Choose scripture—will you read, Meg? *Of course I would.* It was the least I could do for this woman that I loved so dearly.

Except it wasn't my mother.

It was Patrick's mother, Ellie, fifteen years younger than my mother and different in infinite ways. As she lay dying, I told her, "You are the mother I never had, and I love you so very much." She hugged me so tightly with one of her last bursts of strength and said, "I love you too, Meg."

Patrick had some continuing medical education in Hawaii, and we were packing for our trip when his sister Linda called from Iowa to say Mom was in ICU with pneumonia. She's strong, we thought. She'll pull out of it. We talked about not taking the trip or coming back early, not taking the extra days after his meetings. While we were in Hawaii, we called every day, and we were so pleased when she began to improve. She sat up, she was alert. We relaxed.

But we missed his sister's call while we were flying home. She took a turn for the worse. Please come. They've taken her off of all life support... We drove to Cedar Rapids in an ice storm, fearful that we wouldn't make it in time. We gathered with the rest of the family, and we watched as this woman we all loved passed from life into death, from pain into peace, calling to her parents, repeating the prayers of her childhood. And then she was gone.

Nearly six hundred people came to her wake. It was a bitter cold February night and the funeral home opened two extra staterooms to wind the people through so they didn't have to stand outside. Some waited two hours to pay their respects. We heard that they began exchanging stories down the line of how they knew her, honoring her even before they came to our little group of family members..

Although I had known this woman for only a little more than a decade, I felt honored and privileged to stand in that line and shake every hand, hug almost everyone, and hear the stories of how she touched each of their lives. Some said they worked with her at the hospital where she was a nurse. Others volunteered with the chapter of the Alzheimer's Association that Ellie had founded many years earlier, after her own mother succumbed to the disease. Still others knew her from other types of volunteer work, from the Red Hat Club, from being a good and thoughtful neighbor, or from just crossing her path by some chance and admiring all that she said and did and believed and stood for.

"She prayed for every single person in this room," the priest said that night, and it was true. Ellie Corrigan was everything I had always longed for in a mother, in a mentor, in a friend. And she was all of these to me.

Throughout those sad and sorrowful days, I kept coming back to thoughts of my own mother. Why, I thought, does God use one woman so greatly while another is left to exist as a person no one knows very well, no one remembers, no one admires, no one really enjoys. *Can I really say those things,* I wondered? They were all true to me, and so I was led back to my same old question: What was my mother's purpose in life? What is the purpose of any person so beaten down, so defeated, so emotionless as she had become and had always seemed to be in my mind?

****

When we came home from Ellie's funeral, I cried after seeing my mother the first time. I had lunch with her at the senior home, and she didn't mention Ellie's passing during our entire visit. I was sick with grief, exhausted with that raw kind of fatigue we experience when life hits us between the eyes, and we cannot believe for the moment that there will be any relief, that anything will ever be "normal" again. And yet, my mother sat across the table, unflinching, talking about the same old things over and over again, neither noticing the pain that must have shown on my face nor offering one word of condolence to me—her only daughter who even speaks to her.

I had to leave the room.

I found the nurses' office at the care center and spent fifteen minutes sobbing and pouring my heart out to these nurses who hardly knew me. I expect they already knew my mother was a hopeless case. Perhaps she has some dementia, one said, and she really can't recall that your mother-in-law just died. Yes, yes, I said, perhaps that's it. We'll send the psychiatric nurse, they said. She'll test your mother and let us know…

Was I wrong to be relieved when the nurse called and said Mother was in a not-so-early stage of dementia? At least it gave me something to hang my hat on, something to help me excuse her apathy, her complete and total lack of emotion and caring.

I began to look at her slightly differently. Instead of harping on her to clean up after herself, I simply began to take her half-empty glasses to the sink and wash them out. I listened slightly more patiently to her attempts at conversation, even if the same conversation had just taken place three minutes before. I began to realize that she really could not remember what day it was, or whether she needed to put on her "good shoes" so we could go out. If she refused her bath or her medication or her hair appointment, I just let it be. I didn't try to "fix" it. It only made my own blood pressure rise, and it certainly wouldn't change her.

"Remember, she *is* 95 years old." With a jolt, I recalled those very words, spoken to me by Ellie Corrigan, less than two months before she died.

Could my mother-in-law's spirit be with me now? Could having known Ellie Corrigan and her compassion for others around her now be translated into my own dealings with my mother? In the days following Ellie's death, I had jokingly said to my husband that we should all get bumper stickers that said WWED? (What Would Ellie Do?) because she had been such a great example to us all. Again I was struck with the idea that perhaps my mother's entire existence on this earth has been for the purpose of my own spiritual development. Could God be testing me to see how I handle this adversity? Am I up to the challenge? Can I "do Him proud?" Can I follow the example set by my dear mother-in-law?

In humility and gratitude, I bowed my head and asked God to help me.

****

On New Year's Eve 2009, the day before we left for a much-needed Caribbean cruise, I brought my mother all her favorite foods: shrimp cocktail on a bed of shredded lettuce, cream cheese and crackers, lemonade, chocolate truffles. She had been sleeping, like she did most of the time by then. The "gracious lady," so feisty, so quick to judge and blame to see all the bad in life, now had become completely docile. Her dementia had led her down a path of quiet confusion, a withdrawing into herself. She seemed to have no fight left, no desire to be contrary, a blessing in many ways. She spent her days sitting or sleeping, submitting to the dozens of caring services provided by "someone else."

"She has 'internal work' to do," the hospice nurse told me. "At the end, they don't have much energy so they turn inward. It's hard to say what she's thinking of."

And what was she thinking of? An earlier time when she entertained heads of state with china and silver and crystal? A cold martini? Where she might go when it was over? It was hard to know.

She took a bite out of the first shrimp, spat it back into her hand and threw the whole plate into the trash. I felt no surprise.

"Are you tired of all of this, Mother? I asked.

She looked at me with distance in her eyes and, almost imperceptibly, nodded.

I cleaned up the rest of the food I had brought, said my good-byes and went home to pack. Another little vacation, another chance to take a break from it all. She would be well cared for, I told myself.

It was the last time I saw her alive.

****

It had been eleven months to the day since Ellie died. Patrick and I were screaming along a beach road on a rattletrap Harley Davidson in Cancun, the tropical sun beating hot on our "skid-lid" helmets. Our cruise ship had docked that morning and by nine, we were on a cycle tour of Mayan ruins, picturesque villages, and spectacular ocean views. No snow, no cell phones, no newscasts. We didn't have a care in the world.

The next day we learned that my mother had passed from this life while we were joyfully riding those Harleys.

What a contrast Mother's funeral was to Ellie's! There were five family members: Patrick, me, my daughter, my granddaughter, and my niece, my sister Barbara's only daughter. Other mourners included two co-workers and five friends. No long lines of mourners; just a small table with her ashes and a few photos. And a display of the pillows a friend made from her favorite dress, one for me, one for my niece.

And a silver fork.

My mother's favorite story, before her mind went, was about a lady who called the pastor and said she wanted to plan her funeral. She gave him all the details, and then she said, "I want to be buried with a fork."

"A fork?" the pastor asked. "Whatever for?"

"Well," the old lady said, "when you go someplace and you have a meal, and they say, 'keep your fork,' you know there is something better coming. So I want to be buried with a fork so I'll be ready for the good things that come next!"

We laid her ashes next to my father's and it was over.

****

Sometime before my mother's death, as I read through a Scripture passage and my daily devotion, I saw the point of this entire book—indeed, my life. *Our Daily Bread* writer, David Roper, began with a quote from F.B. Meyer: "The main end of life is not to do but to become." Roper went on to say, "As silver is refined by fire, the heart is often refined in the furnace of sadness…The refining process may be very painful, but it will not destroy us, for the Refiner sits by the furnace tending the flame…monitoring the process, waiting patiently until His face is mirrored in the surface."

In my lifetime, I have felt the flames of anguish and despair, of fear and anxiety. I have survived living and dealing with one alcoholic parent who was not there for me, and another parent who could not reach his own potential because of the craziness of his partner's addictions. As a child, I found myself trying to parent my parents. When I became a seemingly sensible, well-educated young adult, I found my world hurtling down around my ears again when I was sexually assaulted. I married the wrong man and stuck with him far too long, for all the wrong reasons. I nearly became an addict myself, escaping that tragedy only by the grace of God. Eventually, I had the good sense to find a qualified therapist and to surround myself with healthy people, one of whom turned out to be the love of my life, Patrick.

My approach to life changed drastically when Jesus Christ became my Lord and Savior. But even before I allowed Christ into my life, He was there all the time, at each twist and turn, each trial and triumph. I know in my heart of hearts that God has saved me more than once from worse perils than He allowed me to endure. As I have looked back over my life, I realize that I have never once lost my faith in God. In all of my trials, even those which could be directly attributed to other people in my life, I have never once doubted that He was beside me each moment, each hour, each minute and second. And His purposes have been revealed over and over in the patience, understanding, and success I have enjoyed.

And what can I make of my relationship with my mother in her last years? It was excruciatingly difficult to have her re-enter my life after I had so painstakingly worked to determine who I was, away from my family of origin. But I can honestly say that there were lessons to be learned in caring for her at the end of her life. I know now that in my Christian walk one piece missing for me until recently was that of true forgiveness. It says in Romans 3:23 that we have all sinned and fall short of the glory of God: me, my mother, each of us. And God does not distinguish between sins; sin is sin is sin in His eyes. But God's mercies are new every day, and He forgives each of our sins if we only ask Him to do so. I have always been determined to be a survivor in this life; what higher form of survival is there than for me also to finally forgive all? For then surviving becomes thriving, and life becomes victorious.

Because of my relationship with Christ, I can now be counted as one who has moved from a great darkness into the Light. If I truly am to "live in Christ," the Bible says this must come to me through the transforming of my mind. When I am able to view my weaknesses as opportunities for God to show His strength in me, I have truly reached that transformation. As the Apostle Paul states in II Corinthians 12:10, "My contentment comes from knowing that when God is with me in my weakness, then I am strong."

MENTAL HEALTH RESOURCES

Then I Am Strong: Moving From My Mother's Daughter to God's Child by Meg Blaine Corrigan is a story of how the author moved past the pain and confusion of a mentally unstable lifestyle into one of growth, serenity and purpose. The resources below are recommended by the author to assist the reader seeking a healthy, balanced approach to her/his life. These are national websites and hotlines; many also have links for local services. Another good place to start is with your family physician.

Chemical Dependency
http://www.aa.org
http://www.al-anon.alateen.org/
http://www.adultchildren.org/
http://www.alcoholaddiction.org
http://www.nicd.us/
Addiction Treatment Hotline 1-800-993-3869

Chronic Pain
http://www.webmd.com/pain-management/guide/understanding-pain-management-chronic-pain
http://www.arthritis.org/

Depression and Suicide
http://www.nimh.nih.gov/health/topics/depression/index.shtml
http://www.save.org/
http://www.depressionscreening.org/depression_screen.cfm
http://www.suicidepreventionlifeline.org/
National Suicide Prevention Lifeline 1-800-273-TALK (8255)

Domestic Violence

http://www.ndvh.org/
http://www.theduluthmodel.org/wheelgallery.php
National Domestic Abuse Hotline 1-800-799-SAFE (7233)

Sexual Assault

http://apps.rainn.org/ohl-bridge/
http://www.womenshealth.gov/faq/sexual-assault.cfm
National Sexual Assault Hotline 1-800-656-HOPE   (4673)

Veterans' Services

http://www.militaryonesource.com/skins/MOS/home.aspx
http://www.nimh.nih.gov/health/topics/post-traumatic-
stress-disorder-ptsd/index.shtml
Military OneSource 1-800-342-9647

DISCLAIMER

The resource information contained in this book is being made available as a public service. No information, quotes, or materials provided are intended to constitute psychological or counseling advice. This book makes no representations or warranties, either express or implied, as to the accuracy of any listed information and assumes no responsibility for any organizations listed herein. Furthermore, no warranty, express or implied, is created by providing information in this book, and the presence of an individual licensee on the web site does not in any way constitute an endorsement of that licensee by this author. The author of this book is not a licensed counselor or therapist, and cannot provide such services to the reader.

In addition, the author assumes all responsibility for any liabilities resulting from the use of names in this book, real or otherwise, and holds Cloud 9 Publishing and its employees harmless in this regard as agreed upon between the parties.

PERMISSIONS

Page 13. Quote by Eleanor Roosevelt, public domain.

Page 17. Quote by Charles Swindoll, www.quotegarden.com

Page 21. Quote from the Online Dictionary of Military Terms, www.milterms.com

Pages 24, 28, 29, 30, 47, 210. Quotes from *Toxic Parents* by Susan Forward , used by permission.

Page 39. Quote by Martin Luther, public domain.

Page 61. Quote by Edward Roland Sill, public domain.

Page 83. Quote from *Time and Eternity* by Emily Dickinson, public domain.

Page 93. Quote from *Locksley Hall*, Alfred, Lord Tennyson, public domain.

Page 99. Quote from *The Neurotic's Notebook* by Mignon McLaughlin, public domain.

Page 105. Quote from *The Death of Flowers* by William Cullen Bryant, public domain.

Page 111. Quote from Henry Ward Beecher, public domain.

Page 117. Quote from Jose Narosky, public domain.

Page 121. Quote from Agatha Christie, public domain.

Pages 127, 137, 207. Quotes from The Jellinek Curve, E. Morton Jellinek, public domain.

Page 167. Quote from George McDonald, *Our Daily Bread*, Copyright RBC Ministries, Grand Rapids, Michigan, used by permission.

Page 185. Quote from *Look Me In the Heart* by Wayne Watson, used by permission.

Page 185. Quote from *Teaching A Stone to Talk* by Annie Dillard, used by permission.

Page 197. Quote from *O Love That Will Not Let Me Go*, Lutheran Book of Worship #324, public domain.

Page 221. Quote from Elizabeth Barrett Browning, public domain.

Page 225. Quote from Havelock Ellis, public domain.

Page 261. Quote from *Wisdom and Destiny* by Maurice Maeterlinck, public domain.

Pages 273 and 281. Quote from Substance Abuse and Mental Health Services, U.S Department of Health and Human Services website, http://www.samhsa.gov.

Page 281. Quote from Kenji Miyazawa, public domain.

Page 290. Quote from *Our Daily Bread* Devotional Series, used by permission.

Alcoholics Anonymous and Al-Anon Materials, including The Big Book, public domain.
Bible Quotations from the New Revised Standard Version, unless otherwise noted.

Appendix: Family Photos

Above: my maternal grandparents, Birdie May (Day)
and Walter Rollins

Above: my paternal grandparents,
"Altie" and William Blaine

Right: my father, Mayhue Blaine,
About 12 years old (1921)

Below: the Blaine home place (my Father's birthplace),
Bible Grove, Missouri,
painted by me as a gift to my father

Below: my father, Mayhue Blaine about 19 years old (left), and my
mother, Verel Blaine, about 20 (right)

Above Left: my parents, Mayhue Blaine and Verel Rollins,
visiting the Blaine farm, about 1930

Above Right: my father, Mayhue Blaine, in flight school at Kelly
Field, San Antonio, Texas, 1931

Right: 27th Pursuit
Squadron, Selfridge
Field, Michigan, about
1932 (my father's
plane #39, third from
front)

Above: my father's plane before it crashed at
Pana, Illinois, April, 1932

Below Left: my father (left) and his flying buddy, Willy Taylor,
about 1932.

Below Right: my father in the cockpit of a TWA passenger plane,
about 1938

Below: my father in front of a TWA "Mainliner", about 1938

Right: my aunt, Ethel (Sally) Blaine, about 1941

Above: my parents on the USS
American Legion, December
1940

Above Left: my sister, Barbara, about one year old

Above Left: me at about five months old.
Above Right: me with Mother and Lois, our first nanny

Below: our family at Maxwell Air Force Base,
Alabama, 1947

Below Left: me, feeding my stick horse
Below Right: Mother, Barbara and me, Easter, 1951

Above Left: Barbara, me and a friend in Ottawa, Canada, 1955.
Above Right: Barbara and me in our "gracious lady" outfits in
Canada about 1954

Me on yet another horse, Arlington, Virginia, about 1956

Left: our daschund,
Nicky and me, about 1960

Below:
my parents and me at
my college graduation,
June, 1968

Above Left: my parents' 50th wedding anniversary, December, 1983
Above Right: my father's 90th birthday, June 1999

Below: my husband, Patrick with Bayfield I, 1997

Above: Patrick and me on our wedding day, 1999

Below Left: Mother on her 96th birthday, August, 2008
Below Right: Patrick and me in Cancun, Mexico,
the day Mother died

6978260R0

Made in the USA
Charleston, SC
05 January 2011